THE DANCE OF 17 LIVES

THE DANCE OF
17 LIVES

THE INCREDIBLE TRUE STORY OF
TIBET'S 17th KARMAPA

Mick Brown

BLOOMSBURY

To Patricia, Celeste, Dominic and Clementine

'. . . We are such stuff
As dreams are made on, and our little life
Is rounded with a sleep . . .'

Shakespeare's *The Tempest*

CONTENTS

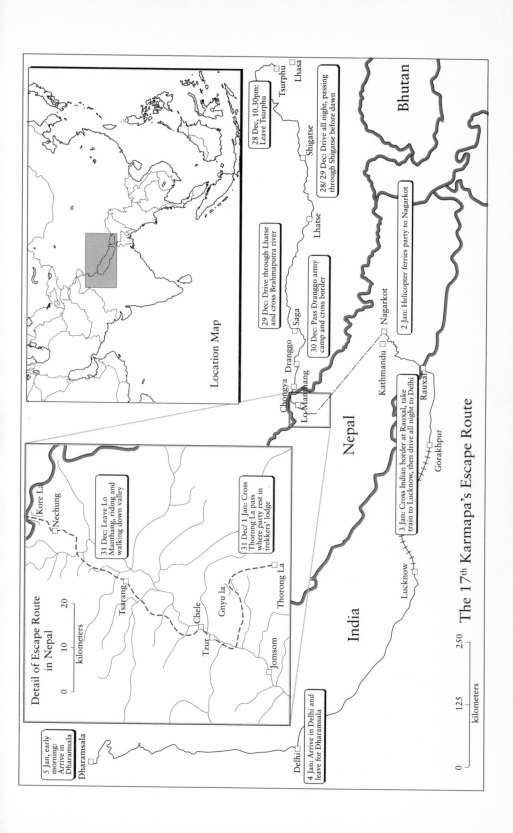

Location Map

Detail of Escape Route in Nepal

0   10   20
kilometers

31 Dec: Leave Lo Manthang, riding and walking down valley

31 Dec/ 1 Jan: Cross Thorong La pass where party rest in trekkers' lodge

Kore La
Nechung
Tsarang
Tzur
Chele
Gnyu la
Jomsom
Thorong La

28 Dec, 10.30pm: Leave Tsurphu

Tsurphu
Lhasa

28/ 29 Dec: Drive all night, passing through Shigatse before dawn

Shigatse

29 Dec: Drive through Lhatse and cross Brahmaputra river

Saga
Lhatse

30 Dec: Pass Dranggo army camp and cross border

Chongya   Dranggo
Lo Manthang

Bhutan

Nepal

2 Jan: Helicopter ferries party to Nagarkot

Kathmandu   Nagarkot

Rauxal

3 Jan: Cross Indian border at Rauxal, take train to Lucknow, then drive all night to Delhi

Lucknow

Gorakhpur

India

Delhi

4 Jan: Arrive in Delhi and leave for Dharamsala

5 Jan, early morning: Arrive in Dharamsala

Dharamsala

250

125

0

kilometers

The 17th Karmapa's Escape Route

CAST OF PRINCIPAL CHARACTERS

His Holiness the 16th Gyalwa Karmapa, Rangjung Rigpe Dorje (1923–1981)

The spiritual leader of the Karma Kagyu school of Tibetan Buddhism from his enthronement in 1931 until his death.

His Holiness the 17th Gyalwa Karmapa, Ogyen Trinley Dorje (1985–)

The present spiritual leader of the Karma Kagyu school, who was enthroned in 1992 and escaped from Tibet into India in January 2000.

The Four Heart Sons

The principal disciples and students of the 16th Karmapa, and the main lineage holders of the Mahamudra teachings of the Karma Kagyu school. Following the death of the 16th in 1981, the four heart sons took responsibility for finding his successor. They are:

The 14th Kunzig Shamar Rinpoche, also known as the Shamarpa (1952–)
The 12th Tai Situ Rinpoche, also known as the Tai Situpa (1953–)
The 12th Goshir Gyaltsab Rinpoche (1954–)
The 3rd Jamgon Kongtrul Rinpoche (1954–1992)

His Holiness the 14th Dalai Lama (1935–)

The spiritual and temporal leader of Tibet until his flight into exile in India in 1959, following a popular uprising against the occupying Chinese army. He is now the leader of Tibetans in exile.

Damchoe Yongdu

The general secretary of the 16th Karmapa's administration, or *labrang*, at both Tsurphu monastery in Tibet and Rumtek monastery in Sikkim, until his death in 1982.

Topga Yulgal

A nephew of the 16th Karmapa and a cousin of Shamar Rinpoche, who was general secretary of the Karmapa's *labrang* at Rumtek from 1983 until 1992.

Tenzin Namgyal

Since 1992, the general secretary of the 17th Karmapa's *labrang* at Rumtek.

Thinlay Thaye Dorje

Shamar Rinpoche's contestant to the Karmapa's throne.

Akong Rinpoche

Co-founder of Samye Ling monastery in Scotland.

Drupön Dechen Rinpoche

Abbot of Tsurphu monastery in Tibet from 1984 until his death in 1997.

Ole and Hannah Nydahl

Danish devotees of the 16th Karmapa, who went on to found a number of centres around the world under the name of their own organization, The Diamond Way.

CHAPTER ONE

Be Sure Your Motivation Is Correct

His first memory is of horses. They are galloping across the plain, the sound of their hooves, he says, 'like thunder', their breath like plumes of smoke in the cold air. They are caparisoned in scarves and silks, their riders clad in finery. They are a wedding party, coming to celebrate the marriage of his elder sister.

Apo Gaga watches them from the opening to the tent where he lives with his parents and his eight brothers and sisters. He is three years old. By the standards of nomads in this part of eastern Tibet, the family are relatively wealthy. Apo Gaga's father, Döndrub, owns eight horses, some 200 sheep and goats and between fifty and sixty yaks, enough for the family's own needs, and to trade for barley and other goods in the lowlands. The yak is the source of all that is bountiful and sustaining in the family's life. The tent in which they live in the summer months, when they drive their animals to the good pastures for grazing, is made of yak hide; the fur of the animal is used to line jackets and for blankets. Its thick, sweet, often rancid, butter is used for cooking, to flavour tea and to burn in the small lamps that surround the shrine which stands in one corner of the tent; its dung is the primary fuel for cooking, on a grate made up of piled stones, and for heating. In winter, when the snows lay thick on the ground, their animals are unable to graze and movement is difficult, the family retreat to a sturdy wooden house, built by Apo Gaga's father.

Even before his birth, Apo Gaga was considered special. For years his parents had yearned for a son, but without success. And then his mother, Loga, became pregnant. During the pregnancy,

Loga experienced a series of unusual indications that the child she carried was in some way extraordinary. She dreamed of three white cranes offering her a bowl of yoghurt. Resting on the bowl was a brilliant golden letter, indicating that she was expecting a boy. The cranes told her that they had been sent by Guru Rinpoche, the founder of Tibetan Buddhism, and that the boy would be a great reincarnation, but that she should keep this a secret until the right moment was revealed to her. In another dream, she saw eight auspicious symbols wreathed in rainbow light streaming out from her heart. The night before the birth, Döndrub was astonished to see rainbows over the tent, although the sun had already disappeared behind the mountains.

Shortly before sunrise the next morning, on 26 June 1985, the child was born. At that moment, a cuckoo was seen to land on the tent and burst into song, and Loga felt no pain.

Three days later, the sound of a conch shell – an omen of a great birth – resonated across the valley, astonishing all who heard it, for no one could be found blowing such a shell, and no conch shell could sound as loudly as this one. In the years to come, these legends will spread like ripples in a lake around his name. But for the moment Apo Gaga is treated no differently from the other children. His parents, knowing that their child is special, have not yet given him a proper name; that will be for a lama to decide. For the moment he is known as Apo Gaga – 'happy brother' – the name that his sister heard a magpie call him one day as they played by the river. He follows behind his elder sisters as they look after the animals, and plays the games that all nomad children play, a gentle, sweet-natured child.

His family, like every family they know, are devout Buddhists. Thirty years of Chinese occupation and 're-education' in Tibet have done nothing to quash their faith. On holy days they travel to the nearest monastery, to make offerings; and sometimes a lama comes to their village, to officiate at a wedding or a festival. The children imitate lamas in play, making pujas, or prayers, building makeshift thrones from stones and taking it in turns to sit there, saying, 'I am a lama.' And, 'Now it's my turn.' In the corner of the family home is a shrine. There is a small statue of the Buddha Shakyamuni, seven offering bowls, butter lamps, and a *serchem* – a long-stemmed container, which sits on a copper plate, and into which black tea is poured each day as an offering to the protector deity Mahakala. Also on the shrine is a photograph of a venerable lama, a jovial, full-faced man resplendent in gold robes. This is the 16th Karmapa, one of Tibetan Buddhism's most venerated enlightened beings, who died in America – a country of which Apo Gaga's family have barely heard, far less visited – four years before Apo Gaga's birth. Döndrub has a particular connection to the 16th Karmapa. When Döndrub was a baby, his parents had taken him to see the Karmapa, who was visiting Kham, where Döndrub lived, at that time; and it was the Karmapa who had formally named him Karma Döndrub Tashi.

The seed of this link between the great lama and the nomad family has already come to fruition in a way which Döndrub and Loga could hardly dare to imagine, but if Apo Gaga is aware of this he says nothing. How could he possibly know that even as he is growing up, the followers of the Karmapa are searching for their teacher's reincarnation, and that far from his home the wheels of religion and politics are turning in a way that will draw him, little Apo Gaga, inexorably into their orbit.

But by the age of seven it seems he does know. One cold, bright morning he runs to tell his parents that soon more horses will be coming, to take him away. And three days later, they come, and from that moment Apo Gaga's life will never be the same again.

I ask, does he remember that too?

'To be honest, not so much,' he says. 'Maybe because I was so young at that time . . .'

And was he happy as a child?

'Yes, very happy . . .' His voice is little more than a whisper, rising and falling, almost musical in its cadences, so quiet that the monk who stands beside him, translating, has to bend forward to catch his words. He answers these questions politely, but perfunctorily. The small detail of his childhood, his personal feelings, these are not things that seem to concern him much. It is as if he has more important matters on his mind. He is sixteen now: tall and big-boned; his skin the colour of caramel; his almond-shaped eyes widely set in his broad face; his mouth sensual. He is seated on a raised dais, dressed in a gold-coloured shirt of the finest silk, intricately brocaded, a red cotton robe thrown over one shoulder.

He is utterly poised, still – a legacy, perhaps, of his years of training for just such audiences, the endless round of obligations to be fulfilled. His long, tapered fingers folded in his lap betray no sign of agitation or unease.

Earlier, a Western devotee, a woman, leaving his presence, seemingly dazed, whispered to me, 'He is the most beautiful person alive.' Certainly, there is something dazzling about him, a regal quality, an air of self-assurance and authority uncommon in anyone, and all the more extraordinary in one so young. Occasionally, he glances towards the corner of the room, where two plain-clothed Indian security officers stand, monitoring our conversation. If their presence bothers him, he does not let it show. His glance, momentarily imperious, seems simply to cancel them out. Downstairs, there are more security officers, to frisk and question visitors. And outside, on the steps of the monastery, soldiers with carbines slung over their shoulders.

It is nine months since he arrived here, nine months that he has been kept here, unable even to walk in the monastery grounds without permission – a prisoner in all but name. Now another monk appears and whispers into the translator's ear. It is lunch time. The audience is over. The translator produces a silk protection cord, which he hands to the young boy. He rises from his seat, blows on it gently, passes it to me without a word, then walks towards the door behind him, leading to his private apartment. The monk ushers me out of the audience room, back on to the veranda. Outside the door, a magnificent white cockatoo sits on a perch. A gift from a devotee in Singapore, the bird is tethered by a chain attached to one claw, unable to do more than inch impatiently back and forth, contemplating the mountains which rise up behind the monastery, tantalizingly beyond its reach.

On the morning of 5 January 2000, two Ambassador taxis crawled up the narrow, twisting road towards the town of Dharamsala, in the Himalayan foothills of northern India. For almost forty years, since his flight into exile from Tibet, Dharamsala has been the home of the Dalai Lama, the spiritual leader of Tibetan Buddhism and the Tibetan people. His residence, in the tiny hamlet of McLeod Ganj, in the hills above Dharamsala, has made the region the centre for Tibetans in exile – 'little Tibet' – a magnet for pilgrims and tourists. The road up from Dharamsala leads past small hotels and guesthouses, with commanding views over the valley below. It winds through an Indian army camp, and past a Victorian English church, nestling among the pines. At the top of the hill, the road runs into the town square, crowded on this – as every other – morning with a motley mixture of local villagers and tradesmen, Tibetan monks, and dawdling tourists and back-packers, their numbers swollen by the new arrivals disgorging from the buses that turn in the square.

Horns blaring in characteristic Indian fashion, the two taxis nosed their way through the square and on to the narrow, rutted lane which passes as McLeod Ganj's main thoroughfare, edging their way between pedestrians, past the small shrine where pil-grims turn large metal prayer wheels endlessly and then past the shops and stalls selling clothes, jewellery and tourist trinkets. They turned on to an unmade track, lined with tourist hotels, finally coming to a stop outside the Bhagsu Hotel. Set slightly apart from its neighbours in its own gardens, the Bhagsu is an Indian-run establishment, more usually frequented by Indian or Western tourists than by Tibetans. It is a place where an important new arrival in town is more likely to pass unnoticed. A short, stocky man in his early forties named Lama Tenam, dressed in the maroon robe of a monk, led the party of six people inside. The rooms had been booked the previous evening by telephone. In the hotel register, under 'purpose of visit' Lama Tenam wrote 'H.H.D.L' – the customary shorthand for 'visiting His Holiness the Dalai Lama'.

For the group, this was the end of a journey that had begun eight days earlier in Tsurphu monastery, some fifty miles from the Tibetan capital of Lhasa, and which had brought them 900 miles across the desolate, mountainous regions of western Tibet, into Nepal, and thus to northern India, risking death and capture by Chinese forces. Among the group was a tall boy, looking older than his fourteen years, dressed in a windbreaker and heavy walking boots, wrapped in a scarf, a woollen hat pulled down over his ears. His face was chapped and wind-burned. He looked haggard and tired, and he was walking with some difficulty. While Tenam busied himself with registration, the boy was ushered quickly upstairs. Tea was sent up. From his room, Tenam telephoned

Khedup, a secretary in the office of religious affairs of the Tibetan government-in-exile, and an old friend.

'You must come quickly,' Tenam told him. When Khedup asked why, Tenam simply replied, 'Come now.'

Half an hour later Khedup was knocking on the door of Tenam's room.

Tenam came straight to the point. 'Karmapa is here!' he told his friend. 'You must go in and greet him.'

Khedup sat down on the bed, shock registering on his face. 'Karmapa?' For seven years, since his discovery and enthronement, the 17th Gyalwa Karmapa had been the most important Buddhist figure in Tibet, prohibited from travelling to India. Now he had escaped into exile, and it had fallen to Khedup, a mere secretary in the religious department, to officially greet him. He couldn't possibly do it, he told Tenam. He was improperly dressed, in his Western work clothes rather than his traditional Tibetan robes; nor did he have a *khata* – the ceremonial scarf that it is customary to present to high lamas as a mark of respect. But Tenam brushed his objections aside. 'Don't worry about that. It's your duty to greet him.' He led Khedup into the next room where the young boy was waiting. The civilian clothes he was wearing on his arrival had gone. He was now dressed in the yellow silk shirt and maroon robes of a high lama.

Khedup prostrated himself three times in front of the boy, stammered a greeting and his respects, then left, to hurry back to his office as quickly as he could to notify the Dalai Lama of the young boy's surprising arrival. Within an hour, a car had arrived from the Dalai Lama's office to collect the young boy. At the Dalai Lama's residence, the Karmapa was ushered into a drawing room, where the Dalai Lama was waiting to greet him. Bowing deeply, the young boy presented the Dalai Lama with a *khata*. The Dalai Lama accepted the offering and draped it back around the young boy's neck as tradition demands, then, putting formality aside, clasped the Karmapa firmly by the hand, his face wreathed in a smile. Forty years after his own flight from Tibet, the young Karmapa had followed him into freedom.

Dharamsala is a small town where word travels fast. Within a matter of hours the escape of the 17th Gyalwa Karmapa would be on the front pages of newspapers around the world. It was a story with the epic qualities of a thriller. He had travelled 900 miles from his monastery in Tibet, across some of the most hostile, mountainous terrain in the world, evading Chinese troops, risking death by exposure.

The weary and footsore fourteen-year-old who arrived in Dharamsala carried an enormous weight on his shoulders. The head of the Karma Kagyu, one of the four great schools in Tibetan Buddhism, prior to his escape the Karmapa had been the only high lama to have been both recognized by the Dalai Lama, the supreme spiritual authority in Tibetan Buddhism, and endorsed by the Chinese government, who saw the 17th Karmapa as a valuable pawn in their attempts to impose their control on the people of Tibet, and, at the same time, to demonstrate their religious 'tolerance' to the world at large.

The young boy represented an unbroken line of succession reaching back to the twelfth century. The great wisdom teachers of Tibetan Buddhism, the Karmapas were the first lamas to establish the practice of identifiable reincarnation – some 400 years before the advent of the Dalai Lamas. They were spiritual teachers to the khans of Mongolia and the emperors of China, renowned as miracle workers, reputed through their spiritual development to have mastered a range of talents including divination, prophecy, the ability to appear simultaneously in different places and the power to control weather. Their spiritual authority was enshrined in the form of the Vajra Crown, or 'Black Hat' – a magnificent crown dating from the fifteenth century, and said to represent the 'ethereal' crown, woven from the hair of *dakinis*, or angelic spirits, which had been presented to the first Karmapa to mark his attaining enlightenment. (Accounts vary as to whether the hair of 100,000, 300,000, or one million *dakinis* was employed in weaving this fabulous object.) Woven in black cloth and studded with rubies, sapphires and other precious stones, the Black Hat became the symbol of the Karmapa's spiritual authority, and the centre-piece of the most important of all Karma Kagyu rituals – the Vajra Crown ceremony, in which the Karmapa dons the Crown and, it is believed, becomes the living embodiment of Avaloki-teshvara (the Tibetan name is Chenresig), the bodhisattva of compassion.

The Vajra Crown was among the treasures which the 16th
Karmapa, Rigpe Dorje, brought with him when, in 1959, he fled
from Tibet, joining the Dalai Lama and more than 100,000 Tibetan
refugees in exile. The Karmapa settled in the tiny Himalayan
kingdom of Sikkim, a mountainous wedge between the neighbouring powers of China and India. There he established a new
monastery, Rumtek. The Tibetan diaspora brought to the rest of
the world for the first time the profound Buddhist teachings that
had shaped Tibetan life and culture for more than 1,000 years. Like
other exiled Buddhist masters, the 16th Karmapa travelled the
world, establishing monasteries and teaching centres in Europe,
America and the Far East. In time, the Karma Kagyu became the
most ubiquitous of the four Buddhist schools outside Tibet.

In 1981 Rigpe Dorje died from cancer in an Illinois hospital. He
was fifty-eight. Historically, it is believed that the Karmapas have
foretold the circumstances of their own reincarnation by way of a
letter or instructions given to a close disciple before their death.
But it was to be a further eleven years before the boy known as Apo
Gaga was recognized as the 16th Karmapa's successor. He was
born in 1985, the son of a nomadic family, in the remote and
mountainous region of Kham in eastern Tibet. His early years
were spent herding yak with his family and as a novice monk until,
in 1992, at the age of just seven he was recognized and enthroned
as the 17th Karmapa. He was given the monastic name Ogyen
Trinley Dorje. For the next seven years, the Karmapa lived in
Tsurphu monastery, being carefully nurtured by the Chinese to
fulfil his role as a 'patriotic' lama. And then, on the eve of the
millennium, he fled.

His astonishing escape, risking not only capture but death in the
harsh, midwinter elements in the Himalayas, might have been the
end of his ordeal; in fact, it was to be only the beginning. A cause for
celebration to the Tibetans, and to hundreds of thousands of Kagyu
followers around the world, his arrival presented a difficult problem for India. For more than forty years the hospitality of the
Indian government to the Dalai Lama, and to his Tibetan government-in-exile, had been a cause of friction with their powerful
Chinese neighbour. The sudden appearance of such a high-profile
refugee as the Karmapa presented a difficult political dilemma. For
the Karmapa, the immediate objective of his escape was to travel to

Rumtek in Sikkim, to assume the throne of his predecessor and to once more don the legendary Black Hat that is the crowning symbol of his lineage. But the formerly autonomous kingdom of Sikkim was now an area of extreme political sensitivity. Sikkim was forcibly annexed by India in 1973 and declared as the country's twenty-second state two years later. However, China has never recognized India's claim over the territory. Within hours of the Karmapa's arrival in Dharamsala, rumours began to spread that rather than being a daring bid for freedom, his escape was actually a carefully engineered Chinese plot to foment trouble in the disputed territory. India's caution over the situation in Sikkim – and the Karmapa's future plans – was further complicated by an even more delicate problem: a schism within the ranks of the Karmapa's own school, the Karma Kagyu, which over the previous ten years had ripped apart the veneer of Buddhist peace and harmony to reveal a vicious internecine war.

The death of the 16th Karmapa in 1981 had driven a deep rift into the Kagyu hierarchy. For ten years the four regents who had been charged to look after Kagyu affairs until the Karmapa's rebirth had been unable to locate his prediction letter, or any sign of where his next incarnation might be found. Finally, in 1992, one of the regents, the Tai Situpa, announced that he had discovered the document, which led to the recognition of Ogyen Trinley Dorje as the 17th Karmapa. But his claim was disputed by a rival regent, the Shamarpa, who in 1994 brought forward his own candidate, a boy named Thaye Dorje. The dispute brought to a head a feud of Byzantine complexity, replete with stories of miracles and allegations of murder – a saga of a political intrigue and the settling of scores going back more than 200 years.

I first heard of the Karmapa in 1990. Travelling in America, I found myself one evening in a Tibetan-Buddhist retreat in Woodstock, New York, where a young lama, Dzogchen Ponlop Rinpoche, visiting from Sikkim, was giving a talk. He was one of the coming generation of Tibetan teachers, I was told, the generation who had benefited from years of exposure and travel to the West. I settled myself on a cushion in the shrine room among a couple of dozen people. Ponlop Rinpoche was in his mid-twenties, a slight, smiling figure wearing steel-rimmed glasses and an outsize digital wrist-watch. His talk was on 'Contemplation and Meditation'. He spoke quickly and methodically, peppering his address with Americanisms; he spoke of 'spiritual cash or credit', 'audio dharma' and 'visual dharma', and 'using a route map to enlightenment', playing with the terms as if they were children's toys, beaming with undisguised pleasure whenever a particularly felicitous phrase tripped off his tongue. Emptiness, he said, was the first step to gaining enlightenment. 'The question is, how do you attain enlightenment without spacing out!'

His audience listened attentively, earnest people wrestling with the subtle complexities of Buddhist philosophy. Afterwards, they gathered in twos and threes to discuss their own progress along the spiritual path. 'I get that we have to move from emptiness to enlightenment,' said one woman to her friend. 'But what I want to know is, how do you manage to give up cigarettes and coffee?'

The next day I returned to explore the retreat more closely. The secretary – a tall, thin bespectacled man in his early forties named Miles, with the slightly dreamy air common among Western Buddhists – walked me around. The retreat was a handsome wood-frame building which had once been a lodging house for summer visitors to Woodstock. It had been the American seat of the Karmapa since 1978. A handful of Tibetans and Westerners lived there permanently, with a constant procession of visitors passing through for courses and talks. A temple in the traditional Tibetan style was under construction, and outbuildings had been added, along with a number of cabins scattered around the neighbouring woods, where monks and practitioners conducted their private retreats. In one of these, Miles explained, an American Buddhist nun from Phoenix named Ani Wangmo (Ani means 'sister') had spent twelve years in solitary and silent contemplation. Miles led the way down an overgrown footpath to the cabin where she had lived. It was a small, ramshackle structure. Downstairs was a washroom and a wood-burning stove. A rickety stepladder led to an upstairs room, no more than ten feet square and furnished with only a chair, a table and a Tibetan box – a cross between a chair and a shortened bed – for sleep and meditation. Throughout her time here, Ani Wangmo would meditate for up to sixteen hours a day. Her presence seemed as palpable a thing in the room as these few sticks of rudimentary furniture, and I was struck by the depth of devotion which would lead an all-American girl from Phoenix to spend twelve years of her life in such austere and demanding solitude, in pursuit of a vision of enlightenment.

But that, said Miles, was the sort of devotion that the Karmapa inspired. The 16th Karmapa, he explained, had died in 1981, and his reincarnation had yet to be recognized. 'We're waiting hopefully.'

And when, I asked – for at that time I had scant understanding of the complexities of identifiable reincarnation, and no idea whatsoever of the particularly vexed circumstances surrounding the recognition of the Karmapa – might that recognition be?

Miles indulged me with a wan smile. 'These things don't work on a timetable.'

After my visit to Woodstock I thought no more of the Karmapa, and then, eight years later, I found myself in another Tibetan Buddhist monastery. I was writing a book about the subject of spiritual search, and in search of somewhere myself to write in peace. A friend suggested Samye Ling in Scotland.

Samye Ling was founded in 1968 by two exiled Karma Kagyu lamas, Chögyam Trungpa and Akong Rinpoche, and was the first Tibetan Buddhist centre in the West. Over the years it had grown into a flourishing monastic community of some sixty monks and nuns, most of them Westerners, and an equal number of lay-people. The 16th Karmapa had visited Samye Ling on two occasions, in 1974 and 1976. The monastery's retreat centre, a complex of small bungalows a mile from the main building, was then at the planning stage, and the Karmapa offered his blessing, placing his foot on a huge granite boulder about to be laid in the garden. It was only later that it was noticed that where he had placed his foot a footprint had appeared, as if scorched into the stone, clear and unmistakeable.

By the time of my visit to Samye Ling, the 17th Karmapa had been recognized and was installed in Tsurphu monastery in Tibet. His photograph was everywhere in Samye Ling – always the same image, showing the young lama staring straight into the camera, youthful, fresh-faced with the vivid rosy cheeks common among nomadic people in Tibet; he was seven or eight years old in the picture – but with eyes that seemed curiously, unsettlingly ageless.

It was this photograph that had changed the life of Ani Chudrun – one of the nuns at Samye Ling. We struck up conversation one morning in the dining room, waiting while the antique toaster went through its interminable motions. In an early life, Chudrun had been Becky Shaw, a television journalist who presented a motoring programme called *Top Gear*. Feeling there was more to life than glorifying fast and expensive motor cars, she resigned from her job and travelled to Nepal. Becky knew nothing about Tibetan Buddhism, but on a visit to a monastery a monk had given her a photograph of the Karmapa – the same image that decorated the shrines and notice boards in Samye Ling. Something about the young boy had struck some deep inner chord. She returned to Britain, unable to get the image out of her mind. At length, she had learned that there was a centre in Britain associated with the Karmapa – Samye Ling. She had come to visit, and never left. A year after arriving at Samye Ling she had relinquished her old life and taken vows as a Buddhist nun.

This story, strange and powerful, steeped in the intimation of fate was not so unusual among the monks and nuns of Samye Ling. Many had similar tales of chance encounters, meetings, a casual conversation with a stranger, a missed train – small flips of chance and fate which had proved to change the course of their lives. In Buddhism, I was told, there are no coincidences. I was intrigued and amused by their stories, and then came a coincidence of my own.

In January 2000, the Karmapa drove into Dharamsala, for a moment the most famous refugee in the world. A month later I arrived in Dharamsala to write a magazine story about his escape. His stay in the Bhagsu Hotel had been short-lived. Within a matter of hours the Karmapa and his party had been moved to another hotel, the Chonor House, owned and run by the Norbulingka Institute, a branch of the Tibetan government-in-exile. He had remained there for three days, secreted behind a protective cordon of Indian soldiers and Tibetan and Indian security men, while the media clamoured at the door and the Indian government and the Dalai Lama's secretariat deliberated on what to do next. He had then been moved again, this time to a small monastery, Gyuto, in the village of Sidbhari, ten kilometres from Dharamsala. The monastery belonged to the Gelug, another school of Tibetan Buddhism. It was still under construction. Its main building, a three-storey temple with a small warren of rooms, had been completed. But what would be monks' quarters and outbuildings were little more than piles of bricks and sand. It was no place for the most eminent lama in the Karma Kagyu, but it was supposed to be only a temporary arrangement. Few would have imagined that three years later he would still be there.

Dharamsala is a hotbed of gossip and rumour. Its small cafes, tea houses and restaurants throng with monks, officials of the Tibetan government-in-exile, refugees newly arrived from Tibet; young, fiery Tibetans who have grown up in exile but who are ready, it seems, to storm across the border and reclaim their country from the Chinese tomorrow; Western aid workers, NGOs, teachers, dharma bums and backpackers. The grapevine was working overtime. The Karmapa had fled from Tibet, it was said, because he feared arrest or assassination by the Chinese. He was a good Tibetan patriot who could no longer bear to be parted from Tibetan Buddhism's supreme spiritual authority, the Dalai Lama. The CIA had planned it all. No, he was a Chinese spy who had been spirited across the border in a phoney 'escape' to sow discord among the Tibetan community and undermine the Dalai Lama's authority. But that couldn't be right because the Chinese, furious at the defection of their most important Buddhist pawn and the loss of face his escape had brought them, had requested Interpol to track down the Karmapa and hand him back. Rumours and more rumours . . .

I took tea with the Dalai Lama's younger brother Tenzin Choegyal, or 'TC' as everybody in Dharamsala knows him, a man of delightful informality and friendliness, and a reliable source of gossip and speculation, particularly beloved by journalists. The Karmapa's arrival, he told me, had taken everybody completely by surprise. He had heard the news on the afternoon of the Karmapa's arrival from the medium of the Gadong oracle – one of the clairvoyant oracles that the Dalai Lama, the government and senior clergy consult on matters of state and church. 'He went and had his blessing, and then telephoned me,' said TC, smiling at the recollection. 'Normally he's a bit of a depressed case, but he was very happy.'

In his office in the secretariat of the government-in-exile, Tashi
Wangdi, the Minister of Religion and Culture, greeted me with a
smile, offered tea, and asked how he could help. On the day after
the Karmapa's arrival in Dharamsala, Xinhua, the official Chinese
State News Agency, had issued a terse bulletin, quoting a spokes-
man for the Information Office of the Chinese State Council. The
Karmapa, the bulletin read, had left a note in Tsurphu stating that
he had left Tibet 'to get the musical instruments of the Buddhist
mass and the black hats that had been used by the previous living
Buddhas of Karmapa'. The boy had reportedly added that he did
not mean to 'betray the State, the nation, the monastery or the
leadership', Xinhua said. The implication was that they expected
him to return.

Tashi Wangdi struggled to disguise his merriment. 'Well, they
have to say something, don't they?' Pinned to the wall behind him
was a cartoon depicting the Karmapa as a butterfly, evading a net
clutched by the Chinese Premier Jiang Zemin. The caption read,
'Hee, hee! I will come back when I get my religious instruments
and my freedom.'

Could I meet the Karmapa? I asked. A look of implacable regret
passed across the Minister's face. Alas, this was not possible. The
Karmapa was not able to see journalists, or any Westerners at
all – only Tibetan devotees to whom he was giving audiences and
blessings. But if there was anything else he could do to help . . .

Before leaving London I had been given the name of a lama
who, I was told, was close to the Karmapa and who would be able
to help me. The next morning, I took a taxi, down the winding
road from Dharamsala. In Sidbhari, the taxi turned off the road,
on to an unmade track. The monastery was set on a plain;
mountains rose in the distance behind, their peaks capped in
snow. A flag, bearing the Karmapa's insignia, in blue and gold,
fluttered from the roof. Indian soldiers patrolled the temple steps,
waving away anyone who approached. Plain-clothed Indian and
Tibetan security men lounged on a wall in the watery sunshine,
chatting. A security man stopped me before I had reached the
bottom step. I gave him the name of the lama I had been told to
ask for, presented my card and sat down on a patch of grass to
wait. The sound of construction work filled the air. On either side
of the temple, women moved to and fro, ferrying bricks and

buckets of cement while their small children trailed at their ankles or played in the piles of sand. A young monk in a maroon robe and yellow vest ambled down the steps, hawking and spitting noisily in characteristic Tibetan fashion.

At length, he was followed by another figure, moving more briskly, his robe worn with a certain *élan*, the smart silk shirt underneath signifying a degree of importance. He waved and came towards me. I had not recognized his name, but on seeing him I instantly recognized the face. It was Dzogchen Ponlop Rinpoche, the same lama I had seen ten years earlier in the centre at Woodstock, addressing the American students on the difference between emptiness and being 'spaced out'. He was exactly as I'd remembered: steel-rimmed spectacles, a broad, boyish grin, and a disarming sense of humour. 'So that's Mick, like Mick Jagger, right? Rock and roll!'

I explained that I had seen him all those years ago in Woodstock. He laughed delightedly. That was very good, he said, very propitious! We were undoubtedly joined by karma. Patiently, he explained the situation. I would not be able to meet His Holiness. Only Tibetans were permitted to see him, and purely for blessings. There was nothing that could be done. It was orders from the Indian government. He smiled, 'but maybe later . . .'

As we talked, a convoy of minibuses pulled up in front of the temple, disgorging their passengers – Tibetan pilgrims, come to pay their respects. Prayer-beads clicking between their fingers, they knelt down in supplication, facing the temple. At length, three figures emerged on to the temple's roof. One was a tall boy, dressed in a gold brocade jacket; a monk stood beside him, holding a yellow umbrella over the boy's head. Beside me, Ponlop Rinpoche clasped his hands together in the gesture of namaste, a salute to the distant figure on the roof. The boy waved back, beaming down at the crowd kneeling before him. A murmur ran through them like electricity. 'Karmapa . . .'

Six months later I returned to Dharamsala. It was August, the season of the monsoon rains. A low canopy of cloud shrouded the mountains, and water sluiced down the streets and pathways turning them to rivers of mud. At Gyuto, little had changed. The Karmapa was still there. The same police in ill-fitting uniforms

stood at the steps, the same plain-clothed security men at the door.
The Karmapa was still forbidden to talk to journalists. But this
time I had come as a pilgrim, with a supplication of my own. At
the door to the monastery, I was frisked, my passport details
entered in a ledger. I joined a group for that morning's private
audience: some Americans carrying a gift of computer equipment;
two Tibetan nuns; a family from Malaysia; and two French
women, come to discuss an education project which they wished
the Karmapa to endorse. We were led through a maze of corridors, through a kitchen, where vegetables were piled on a table, up
three flights of stairs. A notice on the wall instructed visitors not to
ask the Karmapa for autographs or signatures on any documents.
The stairs led on to the veranda. A monk stood outside the door of
the audience room with a clipboard. I stood in the sunshine
slanting across the veranda, waiting my turn. The nuns were
ushered inside first, emerging a few minutes later wreathed in
smiles and clutching protection cords. Then the Americans, then
the family. There were just the French women and myself left. I
gestured for them to go first, but instead the attendant monk
beckoned me to follow them inside. Unexpectedly, I had become a
member of their party.

The Karmapa was seated at the end of the room, his translator
at his side. Another monk and a plain-clothes Indian security
officer stood off to one side in the shadows. I was suddenly aware
that I was stepping into a minefield of ritual and protocol. In my
hand, I held the obligatory *khata*, folded in the prescribed fashion,
ready to present to him. It is also customary to prostrate oneself
three times. At no time must your head be higher than his. The two
women stepped forward and prostrated themselves three times in
front of him. Unsure what to do, and suddenly stricken by a sense
of awkwardness about kneeling in front of a fifteen-year-old boy, I
fabricated a hasty compromise, clasping my hands together in a
gesture of respect and bobbing my head. If this was inadequate,
nothing in his expression suggested it. He gestured to us to sit on
the carpet in front of him, an expectant look on his face.

The French women began to outline their request, something
about wanting the Karmapa's blessing for an educational project.
They spoke in faltering English, the translator struggling to
understand them and convey their request. The young boy studied

his visitors carefully and then, momentarily distracted, allowed his gaze to roam around the room. I caught his glance and he gave me a smile that seemed almost conspiratorial. At last they were finished. He said, 'good, good' in halting English, and smiled. They stood, offered a bunch of brightly coloured protection cords for his blessing, and then walked backwards away from him, bowing. I remained cross-legged on the floor, awaiting my turn, wondering if not having stood up when he did constituted a major infraction of protocol.

Now he noticed that I was still sitting there. His eyes widened with surprise. Although I had said nothing, clearly he had assumed that I was with them. His expression flashed – what on earth did I think I was up to? – and then . . . something else. A word that is often used among devotees in discussing the Karmapas is 'wrathful'. This is meant to suggest not so much anger as a sort of primordial power. The look that now flashed in the young boy's eyes was – and there seems no other way to describe it – like a force of nature: as spontaneous and fierce as a flash of lightning or a clap of thunder. It was unsettling, shocking.

His translator leaned forward to explain my presence. The young boy nodded and as quickly as the look had flashed in his eyes, it passed, and his face relaxed into a warm smile.

I told him that it was an honour to meet him, and congratulated him on his escape, then explained that I wished to write a book about his life and the lives of the previous Karmapas. He nodded, encouraging me to go on. I talked a little about what I hoped the book to be, to whom I wished to address it. I was not a Buddhist, I said, not a devotee. But I wanted to write a book that would be of interest to people like me, who knew little of the lives or teachings of the Karmapas, but enough to be fascinated by them.

It was impossible to tell from his expression whether he thought all of this was a good idea or a bad one. He simply nodded, acknowledging my explanation, then whispered something to his translator. 'His Holiness says, be sure your motivation is correct.' He watched my response carefully, and then whispered again to his translator. 'And he says you will meet again.' Then he rose and walked back through the door. My first audience with the Karmapa was over.

CHAPTER TWO

Signs and Wonders

While most scholars accept that Siddhartha Gautama, the prince who would become known as the Buddha (and in Tibet as Shakyamuni), was born towards the end of the sixth century BC in what is now Nepal, little is known about the fine detail of his life. There is no Buddhist equivalent of the Christian gospels of Matthew, Mark, Luke or John. The Buddha's teachings were passed down orally, in a manner that precluded individual authorship. The details of his life were considered important only insofar as they served to illustrate his teachings. Thus there are accounts – often fancifully embroidered – about his birth, his renunciation of normal life, his enlightenment and his death, but next to nothing is known about his childhood or the forty-five years of his mission after becoming enlightened.

The crucial thing about the Buddha's teaching is that he made no claim for it as revealed prophecy. It was based entirely on his own, human experience. In a sense, his importance lies in the fact that he was not unique. He taught that whatever he had realized, all beings had the potential to realize. Enlightenment, or nirvana, was a state that was entirely natural to human beings and could be experienced by any genuine seeker after truth.

The earliest biographical texts paint a stark outline of the circumstances that led to Gautama's renunciation. His father was King of the region of Kapilavastu and afforded his son every pleasure in life, making him a virtual prisoner in the palace, albeit one in a gilded cage. But the prince Gautama yearned for an existence that was 'wide open' and 'complete and pure as a polished shell'. The gods, apparently feeling he had lived for long enough in his fool's paradise, conspired for Gautama to venture out of the palace. For the first time he saw the four things – an old man, a sick person, a corpse and a monk – that would convince him to turn his back on comfort and 'go forth' in search of truth. This is a powerful metaphor. Sedated by pleasure and distraction we deny the truth of our existence; but sooner or later we must confront it.

At first, Gautama threw himself into the ascetic's regime of denial and self-mortification, until eventually realizing that rather than torturing himself into enlightenment it might be achieved spontaneously. Just as a child experiences joy without thinking about it, so our innate Buddhahood could be realized by cultivating a state of mind conducive to enlightenment. Thus Gautama arrived at 'the middle way', avoiding the two extremes of sensual pleasures or excessive mortification, finally attaining enlightenment after meditating under the Bodhi tree, and becoming the Buddha, or awakened one. Gautama's quest grew from his realization that life is *dukha* – filled with pain and sorrow and leading inexorably to ageing, illness and death. Maturity grows from recognizing the inevitability of suffering and using that to transform ourselves. What the Buddha posited was not the consoling promise of heaven to follow, but a practical psychological system to release man from the imprisonment of craving, greed and egotism, which in turn leads to the endless round of death and rebirth which is *samsara*.

Each person, the Buddha taught, should be regarded as a process, not an unchangeable entity but 'a rushing stream' which is never the same from one moment to the next, indeed one lifetime to the next. Is the flame that lights one candle from the next the same flame? But if liberation is about transcending the illusion of 'self', then what remains? By dispelling ignorance, fear, the grasping attachment to our own identity, what remains, the Buddha taught, is not 'nothing', but calm, equanimity and compassion. The corollary of enlightenment is what Buddhism calls 'loving-kindness': the realization that to live morally is to live for others.

The Buddhism that arrived in Tibet in the eighth century – some 1,300 years after Gautama's enlightenment under the Bodhi tree – incorporated three successive stages, or 'vehicles' of Buddhist teachings; the Hinayana, the Mahayana and the Vajrayana.

The first stage – the Hinayana – was the fundamental teachings about the nature of self and existence, embodied in the Four Noble Truths: all is *dukha*, or suffering; there is a reason for this suffering, which is craving or attachment; there is an alternative to this suffering, which is enlightenment; and there is a path to this alternative.

The Hinayana posited a path to personal liberation from the suffering of *samsara*. But the Mahayana went further still, teaching that all practice must be dedicated to universal liberation, since all beings are essentially inseparable. From this teaching grew the idea of the bodhisattva: a Sanskrit term meaning 'being who has awakened', but who having attained enlightenment has vowed, by dint of their infinite compassion, to forgo immersion into the eternal bliss of nirvana, and instead be reborn in the world in order to lead others to enlightenment.

The Vajrayana was revealed to only the highest yogis and spiritual practitioners. It held that enlightenment could be achieved in a single lifetime – that nirvana is here and now. The role of the guru, who could transmit these arcane teachings, helping his student to liberation by cutting through the illusions of the ego like a surgeon with a knife, was to become central to the Vajrayana path.

The first Buddhist monastery in Tibet was established at Samye by the Indian *siddha* Padmasambhava, or Guru Rinpoche as he is known. Padmasambhava is perhaps the single most important figure in the history of the development of Tibetan Buddhism, and the nearest equivalent to a patron saint in Tibet. According to legend, he was born thirty-five years after the death of the Buddha, in the Swat Valley in what is now Pakistan. He was born not in a recognizably human way, but by manifesting in a lotus in the middle of a lake. Showing no interest in worldly things, he meditated for countless years, acquiring miraculous powers, including immortality. He is next heard of in eighth-century Tibet. At that time, it seems, the spread of Buddhism was experiencing some resistance from the local deities of the indigenous, animistic Bon religion. Learning of Padmasambhava's powers, the King summoned him to Tibet to overcome these querulous spirits. By dint of these powers and the logic of the Buddhist teachings, we are told, Padmasambhava was able to convert these spirits to the Buddha dharma, or path, transforming many of them into the 'protector deities' that are to be found in Tibetan Buddhism today.

Padmasambhava laid the foundations for the Buddhist teachings that would spread throughout Tibet over the next 300 years, taking root in the four great schools of Tibetan Buddhism: the Nyingma, or 'ancient school'; the Kagyu; the Sakya; and later, the Gelug. From Samye would grow the most extensive monastic system the world has ever seen. By the time of the Chinese invasion in 1950 there would be more than 6,000 monasteries in Tibet, and it is estimated that as much as 30 per cent of the male population were monks.

But Padmasambhava also provides the great archetype of Vajrayana wisdom – the wandering yogi who turns his back on the world to search for enlightenment in the wilderness. Central to Tibetan Buddhist lore are the so-called 'eighty-four *mahasiddhas*', or great adepts. These were Indian tantric masters – spiritual mavericks and non-conformists – who rejected monastic ritual and scholasticism to live as hermits, meditating in remote mountain caves, beside rivers and in the charnel grounds.

The eleventh-century Indian yogi Naropa was one such adept. Trained at the Buddhist monastery of Nalanda in northern India, he turned his back on monastic life, setting out on a quest to find Tilopa, the guru who could lead him to enlightenment – triggering the chain of events that would lead eventually to the founding of the Karma Kagyu school, and the lineage of the Karmapas. From Tilopa, Naropa learned the teachings of Mahamudra, or the Great Seal – the ultimate instructions on the nature of existence and the path to realization. Naropa in turn passed these teachings to his student Marpa. Marpa passed them to Milarepa, and Milarepa to Gampopa, who in turn passed them to the 1st Karmapa, Dusum Khyenpa. Thus was set in motion the great lineage of the Karma Kagyu, known as the Golden Rosary, and with it the practice of identifiable reincarnation that would become the cornerstone of Tibetan Buddhism.

*   *   *

Buddhism teaches that we all have the potential for enlightenment, but that our potential is obscured by the worldly
attachments arising from the ego. We are consigned to the
endless cycle of death and rebirth, drawn back into existence
by our habits, our desires and our attachments to the illusory
sense of a discrete and individuated 'self'. According to Tibetan
Buddhist teachings a Buddha is essentially a totally uncondi-
tioned consciousness, beyond time and space, existing in a form –
an absolute reality – known as the *dharmakaya*, or the 'body of
reality'. This is the mind of enlightenment itself, the essence of
which is compassion, or *bodichitta*, which exists within the heart
of all living beings. But for the purposes of leading others to
enlightenment a Buddha may take other forms, as an archetype
of a quality in the radiant form of *sambhogakaya*, and in the
material world in which we live as a *nirmanakaya*, the Tibetan
term for which is *tulku*. The *tulku* is more than simply a living
inspiration, a teacher, an exemplar: he (or, less frequently, she) is
a living embodiment of the bodhisattva ideal. Vajrayana Buddhism teaches that bodhisattvas progress through different levels
of spiritual realization, most commonly divided into the 'ten
bhumis', or stages of awakening. At the highest of these levels a
bodhisattva acquires different powers, or *siddhis*, the most
important of which is the power to consciously choose the
circumstances of his rebirth, in order to better lead others on
the path to enlightenment. This belief in the bodhisattva, bound
by his vow of compassion to return for all time to help others,
became central to Tibetan Buddhist teachings.

The origins of the *tulku* phenomenon, as it came to be understood in Tibet, lie in the early Pali canon describing the life and
teachings of the Buddha – or as he is known in Tibet, Shakyamuni.
These teachings tell how, on his journey to enlightenment, Shakyamuni had been reborn countless times in the past, intentionally
choosing the circumstances of each rebirth in order to help and
guide others. Shakyamuni, we are told, was able to clearly
remember specific people, places and events from these previous
lives. The 'eighty-four *mahasiddhas*', who laid the foundations for
Buddhist practice in Tibet, were also held to be bodhisattvas of the
highest level, and appear 'reborn' in various identities throughout
the history of Tibetan Buddhism. But it was not until the advent of

the Karmapas, in the twelfth century, that the theory of identifiable reincarnation was institutionalized.

Born in 1110 AD in Kham, in eastern Tibet, the 1st Karmapa, Dusum Khyenpa, is said to have attained enlightenment at the age of fifty, recognizing, according to legend, 'the essential sameness of day and night, dreams and the waking state, meditation and everyday life'. His realization was said to be so great that he could pass through solid rock and mountains, and with his omniscient powers see into the past, present and future. So it was that as word of such powers spread far and wide he became known as the 'knower of the three times' (in Tibetan, *dus gsum mykhyen pa*, i.e. Dusum Khyenpa). The Kashmiri pandit Shakyashri, who had been invited to Tibet to establish a new ordination lineage, recognized Dusum Khyenpa as the 'one of Buddha activity', or Karmapa, whose coming had been prophesied 1,600 years earlier by Shakyamuni Buddha. (The word Karmapa comes from the Sanskrit *karma ka*, literally 'movement of karma'.) At the same time, he was also recognized as an embodiment of Avalokiteshvara, or Chenresig, the bodhisattva of compassion. Dusum Khyenpa died in 1193, at the monastery of Tsurphu, which he had founded ten years earlier, and which was to become the seat of all subsequent Karmapas. It is said that during his death rites mourners could observe his body in the smoke that rose from the funeral pyre, as well as seeing many suns in the sky and the dancing figures of *dakinis*. When the flames of the funeral pyre died away, Dusum Khyenpa's heart, signifying his wisdom, and his tongue, signifying his speech were found intact among the ashes, entwined as one.

Dusum Khyenpa entrusted his books, his relics and Tsurphu monastery to his principal disciple, Drogon Rechen, along with a letter predicting the circumstances of his rebirth, declaring that there would be many Karmapas in the future. It was to Drogon Rechen that Dusum Khyenpa also transmitted the teachings of the Karma Kagyu lineage, and Drogon Rechen, in turn, transmitted them to his disciple Pomdrakpa. Pomdrakpa had a young student, Chodzin, who was born nine years after Dusum Khyenpa's death. Evidently a precocious child, he could read and write perfectly by the age of six and had mastered the essence of Buddhist doctrine before he was ten. Through a series of visions, Pomdrakpa confirmed that Chodzin was the reincarnation of Dusum Khyenpa,

indicated in the letter given to Drogon Rechen, and he ordained
the young boy in the name Karma Pakshi.

It was not until the next generation, however, that the line of
Karmapa incarnations were formally recognized. The 3rd Karmapa, Rangjung Dorje, was born in 1284. Once again, he was a child
of unusual precocity. At the age of three, while playing with friends,
he demanded that they make him a throne that he then sat upon
and announced that he was the Karmapa. News of the child spread
to a lama named Urgyenpa, who had been the principal disciple of
Karma Pakshi. Through his own divinations, Urgyenpa recognized
the child as the reincarnation of his teacher. Thus Rangjung Dorje
became the 3rd Karmapa, with Karma Pakshi recognized retro-
spectively as the 2nd and Dusum Khyenpa as the 1st.

This extraordinary sequence of prophecy and self-declaration
established a precedent for the recognition of Karmapas that
would continue until the present day. Some Karmapas are said
to have declared their identity at an early age, to be confirmed
through divination by a close associate or disciple. But more often,
it seems, Karmapas have foretold the circumstances of their
rebirth in a letter of prediction, usually written shortly before
their death and entrusted to a close disciple or lineage holder of the
order. This 'last testament' would give specific details about the
Karmapa's future reincarnation, including the names of the reincarnate's parents and the time and place of his birth.

This practice of recognizing reincarnates quickly spread throughout the Karma Kagyu school, consolidating the lineage in the form
of other *tulkus*, or rinpoches (literally, 'precious ones') – the
Shamarpas; the Tai Situpas, the Gyaltsab Rinpoches, the Pawo
Rinpoches, the Jamgon Kongtrul Rinpoches and more. In time, it
spread too to the other schools of Tibetan Buddhism. In a monastic
society, where celibacy was the rule, identifiable reincarnation
served not only to affirm the bodhisattva ideal of selfless action;
it also ensured the continuity of a spiritual and political hierarchy.

As the Buddhist scholar Reginald Ray has pointed out, the
development of the *tulku* system was crucial in consolidating
monastic power in Tibet. In the early spreading of Buddhism,
monasteries depended for their survival on their affiliation to the
royal court or landed nobility, and were therefore constantly
susceptible to outside interference. The *tulku* system shifted the

balance of power, giving monasteries a way of choosing their own leaders through the clairvoyance of realized masters – by appealing, in a sense, to a power higher than that possessed by kings or landowners. *Tulkus* therefore became the repositories of social and political, as well as spiritual authority.

More than just religious institutions, the monasteries came to dominate every aspect of Tibetan peasant life. They managed land, provided public services and what little education was available, as well as serving as the fulcrum for the endless round of religious observances around which all Tibetan life revolved. *Tulkus* were at the apex of this religious system, the jewels in the crown, as it were, of Tibetan Buddhism.

The identification of *tulkus* was always an inexact science and might occur in a variety of ways across the different schools. The Karmapas were unique in being recognized either through self-declaration or by leaving a letter predicting the circumstances of their rebirth. More usually, on the death of a great practitioner, his followers would wait for two or three years before approaching a lama known for his spiritual realization and clairvoyant abilities, and who could look for indications that the new incarnation had been born and direct the followers in their search. These indications might take the form of dreams, visions and divinations, by consulting an oracle, or through particularly auspicious signs of nature.

The conception and birth of a *tulku* was often said to be accompanied by unusual phenomena, indicating that this was a special child. In his autobiography, *Born in Tibet*, the 11th Chögyam Trungpa, one of the foremost rinpoches in the Karma Kagyu school, recounts that on the night of his conception, 'My mother had a very significant dream that a being had entered her body with a flash of light; that year flowers bloomed in the neighbourhood although it was still winter, to the surprise of the inhabitants.' Trungpa goes on to recount the details of his birth in February 1939. 'I was born in a cattle byre; the birth came easily. On that day a rainbow was seen in the village, a pail supposed to contain water was unaccountably found full of milk, while several of my mother's relations dreamt that a lama was visiting their tents.' Such extraordinary occurrences are commonplace in Tibetan lore. In certain cases, the memories of a previous incarnation would appear to be very strong. Stories abound of young children making their first, faltering steps in the direction of the monastery of the predecessor, reciting mantras at a precociously early age, or identifying former friends and disciples.

The Karmapas would not only write letters describing the circumstances of their own rebirths, but also seem to have been especially proficient in using this method to identify other incarnations, usually those associated with the Karma Kagyu school. Chögyam Trungpa recounts that his discovery followed just such a course. After the death of his predecessor, the 10th Trungpa in 1938, the abbot of Surmang, his monastery, petitioned the 16th Karmapa for indications as to where the new incarnation might be found. On the basis of a vision, the Karmapa dictated a letter saying that the reincarnation had been born in a village five days northwards from Surmang. 'Its name sounds like Ge and De; there is a family with two children; the son is the reincarnation.' As Trungpa laconically notes, 'it all sounded rather vague'. However, just as the monks of Surmang were about to mount a search party, another, more specific, letter arrived. 'It said that Gyalwa Karmapa had had a second and much clearer vision: "The door of the family's dwelling faces south; they own a big red dog. The father's name is Yeshe-dargye and the mother's Chung, and Tzo, the son, who is nearly a year old, is Trungpa Tulku." ' At length a search party found a boy whose circumstances conformed to the Karmapa's letter in all the particulars except one: the name of the father. Trungpa recounts that his mother was obliged to tell the monks that the boy's father was, in fact, her first husband, who was named Yeshe-dargye. Such specific instructions left little room for doubt as to the identity of a new incarnation. But this was by no means always the case. The divinations and omens might be unclear, indicating only a vague region, not a specific place. In some cases there might be a handful of young boys, born in the same area and of roughly the same age that could possibly be the right candidate.

While theoretically the designation *tulku* would suggest that someone had been recognized as the direct incarnation of a specific person, in fact this description applied only to a relatively small number of high incarnates, those who were acknowledged to have attained the highest *bhumis*, or stages of awakening.

There was another kind of incarnation, which Chögyam Trungpa described as '*tulkus* of benediction'. In these cases, the theory held that the departed master – rather than reincarnating himself in a specific individual – would pass on his 'spiritual energy' to a chosen successor, who was already advanced on the spiritual path. This 'chosen one' would then be recognized by a close disciple of the departed master to continue the departed master's teachings – in a sense, to become the embodiment of his enduring spiritual power and influence (as opposed to the departed master himself).

In yet other cases, a child who was discerned to have particularly promising qualities might be named as a *tulku* simply to fulfil a certain religious or social position – to give them a role to live up to, as it were. Ringu Tulku, a Karma Kagyu lama, who was recognized by the 16th Karmapa in 1955, at the age of three, talks of his own recognition in characteristically self-effacing, almost dismissive terms. 'It was very simple,' he says. 'Karmapa saw me in a monastery and told my parents; you can call this boy Ringu Tulku. It wasn't very exciting! There was a Ringu Tulku before me, but I don't know if I'm that person – most probably not, because I don't remember anything! In a way, it's a blessing, and you could also call it a responsibility: it's a feeling you have to do something if you can.'

The *tulku* system was highly elitist. The recognition procedure was essentially a secret one, the system trusting to the wisdom and judgement of the lamas who were making the choice. Yet the validity of the newly recognized incarnate ultimately depended on public approval. Rumours would quickly spread about the signs and wonders that had attended the birth of a special child, the reputation of the family as spiritual practitioners, and also of the lama who had made the recognition. And a *tulku*'s authority ultimately depended on his spiritual practice. Someone who failed to fulfil his potential, and who showed himself to be greedy, self-serving, venal or corrupt would quickly lose his standing. Once discovered, the young *tulku* would usually be given up by his family to the care of the monastery to which, it was believed, he had originally belonged. In a culture in which *tulkus* were venerated above all others, to have one's son so recognized was regarded as a great honour, and it was rare for a family to raise any objections to their child being taken from them. At first, the young incarnate might be allowed to see his family on a regular basis, but gradually this contact would be withdrawn and every aspect of his upbringing would be entrusted to the monks and attendants around him.

This abrupt separation from the family home may seem, to Western standards, unfeeling and almost inhumane (if more familiar to those who have suffered the vagaries of the English public school system). The theory of the bodhisattva provided a counterargument. As a realized being, it was argued, the young reincarnate would have cultivated equanimity and non-attachment over many lifetimes, and would therefore be less susceptible to the strong emotional dependence that a child normally feels for its mother. But this was not, apparently, always the case. The Dalai Lama has written movingly of the intense feelings of loneliness he experienced as a young child in the Potala Palace, cut off from his family, his only friends his sweepers and servants. Reflecting on his own separation from his mother at the age of five, Chögyam Trungpa wrote: 'I missed her as only a young child can.'

While most monks would learn only the basics of Buddhist philosophy and practice, *tulkus* were carefully nurtured and educated to develop their potential as a bodhisattva. The *tulku*'s young life would consist of prolonged periods of intensive study; in reading, writing, calligraphy, Buddhist philosophy and the specific teachings of his school. He would be expected to master various rituals and to memorize countless texts. He would be strictly disciplined (his teachers would be obliged to prostrate themselves before him before administering punishment), schooled in manners and deportment; he would be taught to receive and bless visitors, and expected to perform with suitable bearing and gravitas religious ceremonies that to any other child would seem interminable. He would have his own rooms, with a retinue of attendants to feed and care for him. He would be denied the freedoms which children usually enjoy, unable to mix and play with the other young monks of his own age. The bearing such an upbringing cultivated in these children could leave a deep impression on all who encountered them. The English explorer Thomas Manning, who reached Lhasa in 1812, described his meeting with the 9th Dalai Lama, who was seven years old at the time, in rhapsodic terms. 'The lama's beautiful and interesting face engrossed all my attention,' Manning wrote. 'He had the simple, unaffected manners of a well-educated princely child. His face was, I thought, affectingly beautiful. He was of a gay and cheerful disposition. I was extremely affected by this interview with the lama. I could have wept through strangeness of sensation.'

All of the *tulku's* property and wealth was incorporated in the *labrang*, or administrative body, of his monastery. This was usually made up of laypeople, and headed by a manager or general secretary. The *labrang* existed to protect the *tulku* from worldly responsibilities, to make any decisions relating to secular or political matters, and to look after the day-to-day details of his activities. All the past property of that line of incarnations was the property of the *labrang*, and all new wealth and property also became a part of the *labrang*. When a lama died, the *labrang* was inherited by his successor. Like a young king, the *tulku* was therefore at the centre of an elaborate court of attendants, teachers and administrators, the object of enormous care and attention, and of an investment in manpower and money which would last for many years.

As Reginald Ray points out in *Secret of the Vajra World*, such attention would, in normal circumstances, be expected to turn any child's head; but the teachings the young *tulku* received were specifically designed to counteract this and to develop the qualities of humility, self-effacement and a detachment from the wordly wealth and power which surrounded him. For to be born a *tulku*, it is believed, does not in itself confer perfection. Rather the *tulku* can be seen as a seed of perfection, planted among the community by dint of the practitioner's past development, and the karma of his followers. But that seed must be watered, nurtured, given sunlight to grow. The intensive training a *tulku* received was designed to reawaken their innate insight and compassion, and develop their skilful means of helping others. Only after years of such training would they be considered ready to assume their role as a teacher.

'The Dalai Lama always says there are four things,' says Ringu Tulku. 'You could be a *tulku*, but not a lama. You could be a lama, but not a *tulku*. You could be a lama and a *tulku*. Or you could be none. So being a *tulku* does not mean anything much in itself. The Dalai Lama says that being a *tulku* is like a raw diamond – not worth much. You have to cut it and polish it. You have to study and practise. Being recognized as a *tulku* is the beginning of the process, not the end of it.'

'From the Buddhist point of view,' says Ponlop Rinpoche, 'everybody is a *tulku* – because everybody is the reincarnation of someone. Looked at like that, it's not a big deal, so to speak. If you really look at it historically, the Karmapa is the only true *tulku*; he founded the tradition; he is a totally realized being – a tenth-level bodhisattva. But many other *tulkus* are very much on the path. So when someone sees a *tulku* they see a tremendous potential to grow. But at the same time, if that potential is not properly developed the *tulku* will be the same as any other sentient being. Tibetans have a saying; *tulkus* are very powerful. If they do something good, it's very beneficial and influential; but if they do something bad the power is equal. So sometimes it can be very dangerous. If the *tulku* does not develop the power given to him in a positive way it can be very destructive for many people, and he can even destroy himself.'

Ponlop Rinpoche himself was recognized by the 16th Karmapa. His father, Damchoe Yongdu, was the Karmapa's general secretary. The 6th Ponlop Rinpoche, a close disciple of Karmapa, died in 1952. The present Ponlop was recognized as his reincarnation six years later. 'My father had business with His Holiness every day,' he says, 'and one day His Holiness asked him, are you expecting a child? My father was totally shocked. He said he didn't know. He came back and asked my mother, and she said, "Not that I know of". So he went back to His Holiness and told him this, and His Holiness said, you will have a son and he will be the Ponlop Rinpoche. He even gave the birth date, the fifteenth day of the fourth Tibetan month. He told my mother it was important that she not eat certain things. But she totally forgot, and ate one of the things. She realized afterwards and she got so worried – she thought she might have killed the child. She went to see His Holiness and asked what she should do. And he looked up into the sky and said, "Don't worry, the birth will be delayed by ten days." And he was right. I was born on the twenty-fifth.'

This tangled web of spiritual and familial connections was not uncommon, and can make Tibetan genealogy a bewildering science to the outsider. It was often the case that a reincarnate would be found in a family that had a particularly close connection to the deceased lama. This has a certain logic if we accept the theory of 'directed' rebirth. Where better, after all, for a *tulku* to choose to be reborn than in the community to which he had once belonged, where the conditions existed both to ensure his recognition and for his potential to be most effectively developed?

But, more pragmatically, it could also have the effect of concentrating the religious hierarchy in a small number of families, almost as if the customary hierarchy of progeny was being observed. Behind the veil of mysticism lay a bedrock of *realpolitik*. As much as *tulkus* embodied the spiritual heart of monastic life, they were also engines of political and economic power. A renowned teacher would attract the patronage of wealthy local families, and draw more pilgrims to a monastery. The secrecy of the recognition system made it susceptible to manipulation, and the period between the death of a great practitioner and his rebirth was a critical one, often marked by disputes between the *tulku*'s regents and monastery dignitaries jockeying for power. Because of the prestige and privileges that fell to the family of an important incarnate, rich families would often lobby for their sons to be recognized, and it is striking how often *tulkus* were born into high-ranking families, or seemed to favour a particular political situation.

Disputes about the authenticity of a candidate, and claims on behalf of a rival, were not uncommon. Tibetan Buddhist philosophy provided a felicitous solution to this problem. A particularly eminent practitioner might be identified in more than one reincarnation, in the different 'emanations' of mind, body, speech and action.

This theory of multiple incarnation not only served to demonstrate the efficacy of the teachings, and the spiritual accomplishments of the realized master in question; it also provided a pragmatic way of solving disputes about the identity of an incarnate. Instead of squabbling over the identity of one *tulku*, a community could consider themselves fortunate that through his boundless compassion and wisdom a great teacher had manifested in a number of forms.

It was on this curious and singular foundation of politics and magic that the edifice of Tibetan Buddhism was built. But whatever the truth of the theory of identifiable reincarnation, the imperfections of the process or the abuses it fostered, the *tulku* system provided a framework in which spiritually gifted children could be recognized and nurtured and developed into extraordinary teachers. And it became the backbone for the most extensive and developed monastic system the world has ever seen.

The main seat of the Karmapas was at Tsurphu in eastern Tibet. It was established by the 1st Karmapa, Dusum Khyenpa, and much enlarged by his successor Karma Pakshi. Over the centuries, the monastery was destroyed on innumerable occasions by earthquakes and conquerors, always to rise again, true to the prophecy of the 5th Karmapa, Dezhin Shegpa, who predicted that while Tsurphu would be destroyed and rebuilt many times, 'this monastery will be in existence until the end of this world.' Tsurphu was actually a bustling self-contained township. At its height it housed more than 1,000 monks and comprised four separate monasteries within its walls.

While the Karmapa was the undisputed spiritual leader of the Karma Kagyu, each rinpoche was self-supporting, in charge of his own monastery; autonomous and independent in every respect. The Karmapas were traditionally travelling teachers, a tradition begun by the 2nd Karmapa, Karma Pakshi, who travelled extensively through what is now Mongolia and China. The 3rd, 4th and 5th all journeyed to China, where they were teachers to the Emperors. The 9th Karmapa, Wangchuk Dorje visited Mongolia and Bhutan, and sent envoys to Sikkim, who established three Karma Kagyu monasteries in the kingdom, including one at Rumtek, where some 400 years later the 16th would take up residence. More than just spiritual teachers, the Karmapas were social administrators and reformers: the 5th, we are told, created protected reserves for wild animals and installed toll roads. The 7th constructed iron bridges and marked animals to show they were exempt from slaughter.

The Karmapas were seen as the great miracle workers of the Tibetan wisdom teachings. Accounts speak of their power to heal, to read minds, to bring rain where there had been drought, to leave footprints in rock and water, to carve statues that can speak, to foretell the future, to fly through the sky like birds. In fact, such *siddhis*, or powers, were being recorded long before Buddhism arrived in Tibet. The accounts of the life of Shakya-muni Buddha speak of his ability to 'read' his previous lives, to foresee his own death and to view the circumstances of non-human beings in other realms. What we in the West would regard as 'magic' was an experience of daily life in Tibet. As Reginald Ray puts it, 'Magic, in the Tibetan Buddhist tradition, is the handmaiden of enlightenment.' The ability of realized lamas to manipulate the elements, to prophesy the future, to have knowledge of their past and future lives, has always been regarded not as 'miraculous' in the way we understand the term, but rather as evidence of a spiritual purity and mental clarity. By removing the 'obscurations' of the ego, it was said, these great masters were able to experience reality in its pure and uncondi-tioned form, freed from the dualistic illusion that we are some-how 'separate' from the world around us.

Of all the 'miracle' stories of the Karmapas, none is more vivid and wondrous than the story of the 5th Karmapa, Dezhin Shegpa, who in 1405 received an invitation to visit China from the Emperor Tai Ming Yung-Lo. On his arrival at Nanking, riding into the city on an elephant, 10,000 monks welcomed him. At the palace, the Emperor presented him with a scarf and a precious shell, the spiral of which turned to the right – a test, it seemed. Yung-Lo had heard of the Karmapa's telepathic powers. If the stories were true, then the Karmapa would know that the Emper-or wished to be given the same gifts in return. Even as the Emperor was thinking this, we are told, Dezhin Shegpa pulled a scarf and a conch shell spiralling to the right from his pocket and gave them to Yung-Lo. For the next two weeks the Karmapa bestowed a series of empowerments on the Emperor and his wife, at the same time revealing 'the nature of enlightened energy' in a series of miracles, as Karma Thinley describes in *The History of the Sixteen Kar-mapas of Tibet*. These miracles included manifesting an iridescent cloud of fire, with colours of the most beautiful hue, expanding and contracting in various ways 'and as brilliant as the wish-fulfilling gem'. Other clouds appeared, 'shaped like begging bowls'; flowers fell from the sky, some fully open, others in bud, 'the stems and lower parts like crystal'; and heavenly beings appeared carrying begging bowls and pilgrim staffs, 'some wearing hats and others yak-tail whiskers'. On the eighteenth night, we are told, two heavenly lamps appeared, as well as other lights that illuminated the sky. In the distance gods could be seen adorned with precious jewels, riding on blue lions and white elephants. Yung-Lo was duly impressed. He presented the Karmapa with 700 measures of silver objects, bestowed upon him the title Precious Religious King, Great Loving One of the West, Mighty Buddha of Peace, and instructed his finest artists to record these miraculous events on a silk scroll, which was then sent to Tsurphu monastery (where it was to hang in the Great Hall for the next 500 years). He also expressed the view that there were too many Buddhist sects in Tibet, and offered to send his armies to unify them under the Karmapa by force (an offer which perhaps suggests he had not altogether got the hang of the Buddhist teachings of non-violence and loving-kindness). The Karmapa, we are told, refused the offer. It was Yung-Lo who also bestowed on the Karmapa a material version of the ethereal Vajra Crown, or Black Hat. Since the 1st Karmapa attained enlightenment and had – according to legend – been presented with the Vajra Crown, it has remained inseparable from all his successive incarnations as a reflection of their transcendental wisdom. The crown was said to be invisible to all but the most pure in spirit. But through the devoted eyes of Yung-Lo it could clearly be seen. The Emperor commanded that a material symbol of this celestial vision be made, to benefit all beings, and presented Dezhin Shegpa with a crown woven in black brocade and studded with precious jewels. In the seventeenth century, the 10th Karmapa's pupil, the Emperor of Jang, presented him with a replica of the Black Hat that had been presented by Yung-Lo. From then on, the original Crown was kept at Tsurphu, and the Karmapa carried the replica when he travelled. It is not known which crown the 16th Karmapa brought with him when he fled from Tibet into Sikkim in 1959.

From the time of its arrival in Tibet, Buddhism had always been inseparable from politics, its spread dependent on the patronage of local kings and warlords or the conquering armies of Mongolian or Chinese emperors. The Nyingma, or 'Ancient', school grew up during the 'first spreading' under the patronage of the so-called 'religious kings' of Tibet. The 'second spreading', which began in the eleventh century, and which coincided with the collapse of Buddhism in India under Muslim conquest, saw the growth of the Sakya and Kagyu schools. By the thirteenth century, the Sakya had become the pre-eminent school under the patronage of the Mongol emperors, not least Kublai Khan, who established the relation of 'priest and patron' that would prove so crucial to Tibet's history. With the waning of Mongol influence, Tibet came under the control of a succession of Tsang kings who patronized the Karma Kagyu school of the Karmapas. For 200 years, the Kagyu were the pre-eminent school of Buddhism in Tibet, leading to an unparalleled growth of their power, influence and wealth.

But their position, in turn, was to be challenged by the growth of a reforming monastic order known as the Gelug, which in time would become the most powerful of the four main Buddhist schools. The Gelug school was founded by a monk named Tsongkhapa. As a monk, Tsongkhapa studied with teachers from both the Kagyu and Nyingma schools, but he became disillusioned with what he regarded as the corruption and laxity among the established Buddhist orders, and set about founding a new order that advocated a return to 'pure Buddhism', emphasizing celibacy and scholasticism as prerequisites to the more advanced tantric practices. It was not until after Tsongkhapa's death that this order would take the name of the Gelugpa, or 'virtuous ones' ('Gelugpa' meaning 'those of the Gelug school'). As a symbol of purity they adopted yellow ceremonial hats, to distinguish themselves from the 'old' schools, who wore red ones. These respective uniforms would become symbols of the sectarian disputes between the 'red hats' and the 'yellow hats' that would dominate Tibetan religious life for more than 500 years.

The pre-eminent cleric in the Gelug school was the Dalai Lama. The Gelugpa secured the patronage of the Mongols, and gradually their strength and influence increased, arousing the jealousy and suspicion of the 'old' red hat schools, which saw their power under threat. The Gelug ascendancy was completed under the 5th Dalai Lama, Ngawang Lobsang Gyatso, or the 'Great Fifth' as he became known. When the 10th Karmapa, Choying Dorje, under the patronage of the King of U-Tsang, tried to resist the spread of the Gelug teachings, the 5th Dalai Lama called upon his Mongol patron, Gushri Khan, to defend his seat and unify the country under his rule. Gushri Khan's army defeated the U-Tsang king, and in 1642 the 5th Dalai Lama became the absolute temporal and spiritual ruler of an area that extended from Mount Kailash in the west to the eastern borders with China. The Mongol army sacked the city of Shigatse and the Karmapa's camp, wreaking havoc and death. The Karmapa, it is said, 'flew into space' to seek refuge in India. Those who witnessed his leave saw him in different manifestations – some as a vulture, some as a deer and others in human form. He was to remain in exile for thirty years. The 5th Dalai Lama swiftly imposed his power over the 'old' Buddhist orders. Under his rule at least forty Kagyu monasteries in central Tibet were appropriated by the Gelugpa. Tsurphu, the seat of the Karmapas, was allowed to remain intact, but forbidden from ordaining more than three monks a year. From that point on the Gelugpa would effectively rule Tibet through successive Dalai Lamas until the flight into exile of the 14th Dalai Lama in 1959. While the Dalai Lama was notionally 'the absolute ruler of unchallenged authority', in fact his prime ministers largely governed the affairs of the country. Thus the Dalai Lamas themselves were able to maintain some distance from the intrigues of politics, and to retain their position as the spiritual figureheads of Tibetan Buddhism, universally respected across all schools. But the long-standing sectarian disputes between the red hats of the old schools and the yellow hats of the new would continue to fester for centuries afterwards, right up to the cataclysmic events which followed the Chinese invasion of Tibet in 1950, and beyond.

CHAPTER THREE

The Lion's Roar

The historical accounts of the Karmapas tend not to dwell on what we in the West would regard as the salient detail of a person's life. We learn nothing of the strengths or weaknesses of their character; their idiosyncrasies or peccadilloes; whom their friends, or enemies, were; whether they were kind, generous spirited, stern, prone to bad temper or fits of depression. They come dressed in superlatives. These stories are not intended to tell us about the Karmapas' personal habits or foibles, their particular fondness for butter tea or warm baths. They exist to extol their accomplishments, both temporal and spiritual, to illustrate their role as exemplars of the Buddhist teachings on enlightenment, so powerful that nature itself bows to their presence. Rainbows appear in the sky to salute them; flowers fall from the heavens where they walk. They cure sickness and disease, fly huge distances through the sky, leave their footprints on rock or water. In these histories, apocrypha becomes fact.

The 15th Karmapa, Khakhyab Dorje, died in 1922 at the age of fifty-one. Several years before his death he entrusted the details of his next rebirth to his favourite attendant, Jampal Tsultrim, enshrined in a document entitled 'A Dying Song – the Hidden Significance of a Bamboo Flower, an Ornament for the People'. This clearly indicated the region where his reincarnation would be found, the names of the successor's parents, and the year of his birth. In accordance with this prophecy, the 16th Karmapa, Rangjung Rigpe Dorje, was born into the Althup family on the fifteenth day of the sixth month of the Tibetan Wood Mouse Year

(September 1923) at DenKhok in the region of Derge, eastern Tibet. His father was a senior minister under the King of Derge. Before the Karmapa's birth, it had been prophesied that a great bodhisattva would be born into the minister's family, and that the family should set up camp outside the walls of the Althup Palace so that the birth should not take place in a 'lazy environment'.

While still in his mother's womb the child could be heard reciting the mantra *om mani padme hung*, and immediately before his birth, it is said, he disappeared from the womb altogether, reappearing the following day. On the day of his birth rainbows appeared in the sky, the tent became radiant with white light and it was noticed that all the water in the offering bowls turned to milk. No sooner had he been born than the child took seven steps, saying, 'Mother, mother, I am going away.' Realizing his extraordinary qualities, the family took measures to protect the child, spreading the rumour that a girl had been born and keeping the new infant safely from harm. It was to be some years before the young boy would be recognized as Karmapa.

Jampal Tsultrim, the disciple to whom the 15th Karmapa had entrusted his prediction letter, was a wandering monk. Rather inconveniently he seems to have vanished shortly after the death of the 15th taking the letter with him. In the absence of the letter, the task of finding the reincarnation fell to two lineage holders, the 11th Tai Situ Rinpoche and the 2nd Jamgon Kongtrul Rinpoche. Following his own independent divinations, Tai Situ discerned the whereabouts of the child, and a party was sent secretly to Althup Palace to confirm the identity of the young boy and make offerings. It was now necessary for the 13th Dalai Lama to make his official confirmation of the reincarnation. The general secretaries from the *labrangs* of Tsurphu and Palpung, Tai Situ's monastery, made their way to Lhasa to press their case. It would take three years. In keeping with tradition, offerings were made to honour the Dalai Lama. The treasuries at both Tsurphu and Palpung dwindled dramatically. Tai Situ requested help from his patron, the King of Bhutan, who duly despatched a gift of two magnificent elephant tusks, tipped with gold and carved with the names of the Buddha. But still the Dalai Lama refused to acknowledge the recognition until he had been shown the 15th Karmapa's prediction letter. Matters were complicated yet further when a minister in the Dalai

Lama's government, Lungshawa, began to press for his own son to be recognized as the new incarnation.

It was then, just in the nick of time, that the elusive Jampal Tsultrim reappeared, bearing with him the prediction letter. For reasons that are unclear, however, the 15th Karmapa had chosen to leave a letter in a numbered code that could be deciphered only by another high lama, Khyentse Rinpoche. Happily, on deciphering the code, the letter was found to correspond exactly to the vision of Tai Situ, and so it was that the boy in Althup was recognized as the Karmapa.

The fate of Lungshawa's son was sealed shortly afterwards by his untimely death. One account has it that he fell from the roof of his home in Lhasa, another that he complained of violent pains in his stomach and died soon afterwards. Throughout these protracted events, the new incarnation was left at Althup in the care of his parents. He was recognized as a prodigiously gifted child and stories about him quickly spread. If livestock went missing he could always give an exact description of where they were to be found. On one occasion visitors brought tea in an earthenware pot to the child's room on the third floor of the palace. He threw it down into the courtyard below. Not one drop was spilled, nor was the pot broken. Laughing, the young boy squeezed the neck of the pot and sealed it completely.

In 1931, the young child finally left Althup for Tai Situ's monastery of Palpung, where he was enthroned as the Karmapa. He then set off on the long journey across Tibet to his ancestral seat at Tsurphu, visiting different Kagyu monasteries along the way, and for the first time performing the Black Hat ceremony for devotees. This, we are told, 'was like lotion to their eyes', causing the sky to be filled with rainbows and flowers to fall from the heavens. The following year, he was received in Lhasa by the Dalai Lama, who conferred his official recognition on the young reincarnate and performed the traditional hair-cutting ceremony that symbolizes the renunciation of all worldly things. It is said that before the ceremony the Karmapa was wearing a small fabric crown, which he removed before prostrating himself in front of the Dalai Lama. The Dalai Lama was heard to ask why he had not taken off his 'other hat' as well. All present protested that the young boy was indeed bareheaded. The Dalai Lama, it seems, had seen the ethereal Vajra Crown. In this way the supreme spiritual attainment of the Dalai Lama, as well as the authenticity of the Karmapa, was proved.

Thereafter, the young Karmapa's life unfolds in a series of events, which have the magical quality of fairy-tales. At the age of ten he made his first recognition of a *tulku*, the 8th Zurmang Rinpoche, foretelling such details as the place where the new incarnation would be found, the name of his family and even the direction in which the front door of their house faced. Throughout his early adulthood, he travelled extensively throughout Tibet, manifesting signs of his miraculous powers wherever he went. Once, at some hot springs, he rushed into a nest of snakes that wrapped themselves around his body. The Karmapa started to dance, saying, 'I am the king of the snakes!' His attendants, fearing for his life, begged him to stop, but the Karmapa simply laughed and the snakes fell from him like drops of rain, leaving him unharmed. Passing through the region of the Protector Nyenchen Tang Lha a white yak came straight up to him, bowed and then disappeared. All those with him were astounded, but the Karmapa said, 'It's only natural!' On another occasion, he met another high lama, Drukchen Paljor Rinpoche. The two men began to joke about their respective powers. The Karmapa took the sword of his attendant and tied a knot in its blade. Shortly afterwards, crossing a frozen river he left his footprints in the ice, and even after the ice had melted, his footprints could still be clearly seen in the water.

It was during this period, we are told, that the Karmapa received the full teachings of tantra and the Karma Kagyu lineage from Tai Situ Rinpoche. Among these teachings were the Science of All Knowledge, the oral transmission of the Treasury of the Extensive Teachings, as well as many other oral teachings, including the works of Marpa, Milarepa and Gampopa; the Indian texts on Mahamudra; the three texts of Mahakala, the Black Cloaked One, red Avalokiteshvara and Vajravarahi; and the Three Teachings called Jewel Radiance, Sun Radiance and Moon Radiance. In time, these teachings would be supplemented by others: Mahamudra, the Ocean of Definite Meaning; Mahamudra, Dispelling the Darkness of Ignorance; the 8th Karmapa's teaching on the Inseparability of Wind and Mind; Mahamudra,

Pointing A Finger at the Dharmakaya; the Six Teachings Called the Essence of Ambrosia; the Father and Mother Teachings of Secret Essence; the Peaceful and Wrathful Garlands; the Dagger of Seven Profundities, and yet more. In this way, the seed of the bodhisattva enlightenment was ripened to fruition.

Over the following years, the Karmapa carried out extensive renovations to Tsurphu monastery, which had fallen into disrepair, while continuing to travel extensively throughout Tibet, as well as making pilgrimages to Bhutan, and the holy sites of Sarnath, Bodh Gaya and Kushinagara in India. It is at this point that modern history begins.

In 1950 Mao Zedong People's Liberation Army swept across the border into the eastern Tibetan province of Kham, determined to press China's historical claim over Tibet and 'liberate' the country from its feudal practices. Within a matter of weeks, the soldiers of the PLA had taken control of the region, easily sweeping aside the resistance of the small and ill-equipped Tibetan army under the command of an aristocrat named Ngabo Ngawang Jigme. At the time of the invasion, Tibet's temporal and spiritual leader, the Dalai Lama, was just fifteen years old and the country was governed by regency. But in the face of the mounting crisis, the regency rapidly collapsed. Consulted on the danger now facing Tibet, the State oracle, Nechung, was unequivocal. The Dalai Lama must assume power. In an attempt to forestall the Chinese occupation of his country, the young leader despatched a delegation led by Ngabo Ngawang Jigme to Beijing for talks with the Chinese. Ngabo had been empowered only to negotiate. But in the spring of 1951, without consulting the Dalai Lama, the Tibetan aristocrat signed the so-called 'Seventeen Point Agreement on the Peaceful Liberation of Tibet', which effectively relinquished Tibet's independence and accepted the country's 'return' to the 'motherland', China. In truth, Ngabo had little alternative but to sign, but it was an act that led many Tibetans to regard him as a traitor. By October of that year, the first 3,000 PLA troops had arrived in Lhasa, and Tibet was effectively under Chinese control. The Seventeen Point Agreement pledged that the Chinese would respect religious freedoms, but these assurances quickly evaporated. In the eastern provinces in particular, monasteries were suppressed, monks and nuns forced to disrobe, and dissidents arrested.

In 1954 the young Dalai Lama, accompanied by a large party of officials, senior religious figures and his family, travelled to Beijing to meet Chairman Mao. The thirty-one-year-old Karmapa was among them. In his autobiography, the Dalai Lama recounts how over the course of their twelve meetings together, Mao presented a benign and paternalistic figure, even praising the Buddha for being 'anti-caste, anti-corruption and anti-exploitation'. But whatever hopes these sentiments might have stirred in the young Dalai Lama were to be dashed in their final meeting. 'Religion is poison', Mao told him. 'Firstly it reduces the population because monks and nuns must stay celibate, and secondly it neglects material progress.' On hearing this, the Dalai Lama recounts, he was 'very afraid'. Mao, he realized, was 'the destroyer of the dharma' after all. With a heavy heart, the Dalai Lama made his way back to Tibet.

By now Tibet was in turmoil. Chinese forces were engaged in fierce battles with rebels in the eastern provinces of Kham and Amdo, and refugees from these regions were flooding into central Tibet. In 1957 the Karmapa departed once again on a pilgrimage to India and Nepal. He returned through Sikkim, a country that had close historical links with the Karmapas. In the latter half of the sixteenth century, the 9th Karmapa, Wangchuk Dorje, had been invited by the King of Sikkim to build a number of monasteries, one of which was established at Rumtek, a few miles south of the capital Gangtok. Over the years, the monastery had fallen into a state of neglect. The few elderly lamas still living there requested the Karmapa to visit. He told them that the time was not yet right, but promised that he would come back one day. By the time of his return to Tsurphu, the situation in Tibet had worsened. The Karmapa began to make provisions to guarantee the safety of the young *tulkus* of the Kagyu. The 9th Sangye Nyenpa Rinpoche and the 8th Traleg Rinpoche were both brought to Tsurphu, where they joined two of the order's most senior young *tulkus*, Gyaltsab Rinpoche and the Shamar Rinpoche. The four-year-old Tai Situ had already fled from his monastery in Palpung, just three days before it was taken over by Chinese soldiers, and had also taken refuge at Tsurphu. In Tibet, the position was becoming ever more perilous and chaotic. Lhasa was flooded with thousands of refugees from across the country, seeking sanctuary from the fighting between Chinese and rebel forces.

Finally, in March 1959 there was an uprising in Lhasa, when it seemed as if the Chinese were about to seize the Dalai Lama himself. On the night of 17 March, he was spirited out of his summer palace, the Norbulingka, disguised as a soldier, and made good his escape. After a week, the Dalai Lama and his party had reached Lhuntse Dzong, some sixty miles from the Indian border. There he formally announced the repudiation of the Seventeen Point Agreement, signed eight years earlier, and announced the formation of his own government. Some two weeks later, exhausted and dispirited, the Dalai Lama finally crossed the border into India, to begin a new life in exile.

In the following months, tens of thousands of Tibetans would make the dangerous journey across the Himalayas into exile in India. The Karmapa was among them. Some nineteen years earlier, in 1940, in the quiet sanctuary of his rooms in Tsurphu, the seventeen-year-old Karmapa had composed a spontaneous verse which appeared to prophesy the threat which would engulf Tibet, and his own flight to safety, characterizing the Chinese as 'the vulture', and himself as 'the cuckoo'.

> Tomorrow, not now but around this time
> I will be known where the vulture and I will go
> The vulture will ascend the expanse of the sky
> The cuckoo will receive an invitation in Spring
> Where he will go will be known in Autumn, when the crops
>   have ripened
> There is nowhere to turn but to India, to the East

By the autumn of 1959, it was clear that he could delay no longer, and the Karmapa instructed the general secretary of his *labrang*, Damchoe Yongdu, to make preparations for their escape. Damchoe was somewhat older than the Karmapa. For many years he had been a monk at Tsurphu, rising to the position of shrine-master, responsible for preparing the shrine for various ceremonies and rituals. This included making the elaborate offerings, or *tormas* – conical-shaped cakes, decorated with elaborate discs of sculptured butter, of different sizes and shapes, each with their own symbolic meaning.

'Whatever ceremony His Holiness decided to do, my father would have to set it up,' remembers Damchoe's son, the 7th Ponlop Rinpoche. 'And he said His Holiness was very learned and strict. He would come just before the puja started, maybe half an hour before, and look around the shrine, and if he saw that a *torma* was made even slightly wrong, His Holiness would put his finger in it and it was gone, and my father would have to make it again. Right away! His Holiness was very proper, strict in the practice.'

Damchoe evidently performed his duties well. In time he became the Karmapa's personal attendant, and eventually his general secretary, his position ratified by the time-honoured procedure of casting *mos*. In this, a shortlist of candidates was drawn up, and the names inscribed on pieces of paper which were then rolled up in balls of dough. After being carefully weighed to ensure parity, the dough balls were placed in a container. As the Karmapa performed a series of rituals in front of a shrine, the container was shaken, until one of the balls fell out on the table. 'My father's name came out,' says Ponlop Rinpoche. Damchoe was a tall, powerfully built man and, like the Karmapa, a strong traditionalist. He wore a *chuba*, pendulous earrings and tied his hair in a long ponytail. He was an extrovert, with a passion for singing and acting. During festival days – at Losa (Tibetan New Year) or the Karmapa's birthday – he would dominate the monastery's opera troupe, playing a number of different parts. But he also had a fiery temper and a strongly authoritarian streak. He could be tactless and difficult; he liked giving orders and expected them to be obeyed. He was more feared and respected than loved. People said that the Karmapa had chosen him precisely because of these difficult traits, in order to curb and improve him. Without the example of Karmapa as a focus for his devotion and loyalty, Damchoe would have been trouble. At one stage he was even married to the Karmapa's sister, although she died when quite young and Damchoe later remarried.

'His Holiness invested total authority in Damchoe,' remembers Ngödrup Burkhar, who would later work as a translator for the Karmapa. '"Report to the general secretary; consult with the general secretary; don't do it without the knowledge of the general secretary." This is what His Holiness would say. Damchoe could have told anyone to do anything and it would have been no different from the word of His Holiness. If I did a hundred good things for His Holiness himself, probably he would not say thank you to me. If I did one thing that pleased the general secretary, it would please His Holiness a hundredfold more. It was a unique relationship.'

It was to Damchoe that the onerous task of preparing to abandon Tsurphu and make the long journey into exile now fell. The sacred treasures of Tsurphu were gathered together and sealed in strong boxes. Precious texts were stripped from their wooden panels to make them easier to carry and wrapped in bundles, protected by hide. (Only later would it be discovered that, in the confusion, some of the panels had been loaded and the texts left behind.) An advance party, with fifty pack animals laden with goods, set off first; travelling with them was the young Tai Situ, with his small entourage of advisers and attendants. Finally, in the autumn of 1959, the main caravan, consisting of some 160 people, horses and pack animals with the Karmapa at their head, left Tsurphu for the last time, bound for Bhutan. The journey was to take twenty-one days.

'The Chinese were very close behind them,' says Ponlop Rinpoche. 'The party would stop for a rest and light a fire, and the Chinese would come and find these places still warm, but still they couldn't catch up. My father was saying, it was Karmapa's blessing.'

Among the party was the present Ponlop Rinpoche's predecessor, the 6th Ponlop. He was a man of gargantuan girth and strength. Legend had it that, as a young man, he could ride his horse through a gate and, bracing his legs around its flanks and clasping an overhead beam, swing both the horse and himself off the ground. 'He was so huge that he needed two horses, taking it in turns to carry him,' says the 7th Ponlop with a laugh. 'And nobody could ride the other one because it was resting to take Ponlop. There were times when they were worried that he would fall too far behind and be captured, but he managed to get out.'

At length, the party arrived in Bhutan, where they were welcomed by the King. In the meantime, the Maharaja of Sikkim, Sir Tashi Namgyal, sent word, inviting the Karmapa to settle there.

He was offered several sites for a monastery. He chose the near-derelict site Rumtek. His promise of a couple of years earlier had been fulfilled. Situated some ten miles south of the Sikkimese capital of Gangtok, Rumtek's position possessed all the attributes that are believed to be auspicious for a monastery. There were seven streams flowing towards it; seven hills facing it; a mountain behind it; a snow range in front and a river below, spiralling downhill in the shape of a conch shell. The Sikkimese government gave seventy-four acres of land for perpetuity, and offered free timber and a contribution towards the costs of building the monastery. The Indian Prime Minister Pandit Nehru also promised financial assistance for building work and to feed and clothe the refugees. Work on clearing the site began in 1962. A team of more than 100 workers laboured twelve hours a day until in June 1964 the foundation stone was laid. Within two years the main temple, assembly hall and quarters for the monks had been completed. On the first day of the first month of the Fire Horse Year (March 1966) the Karmapa entered the new monastery in high ceremony.

On his arrival in India, the Dalai Lama was temporarily housed by the Indian government in the hill station of Mussoorie, but within a year Prime Minister Nehru offered him permanent accommodation in Dharamsala. In May 1960, he took up residence in a house that had been built for the former British colonial officer of the region. He immediately began to establish the rudimentary infrastructure of a Tibetan government-in-exile. In the early days this consisted of just four departments: a Council for Religious Affairs; a Department of Education; a Department of Security, and a Department of Home Affairs, which was responsible for the settlement of the tens of thousands of Tibetan refugees who had followed the Dalai Lama into exile. With assistance from the Indian government and international aid agencies the refugees were dispersed to camps and settlements scattered around the Himalayan region – at Dalhousie, Manali, Dehra Dun and Bir, as well as in Dharamsala itself.

One of the new government-in-exile's first priorities was to attempt to fashion a sense of national unity among a people whose allegiances and loyalties had always been primarily regional. In Tibet, while the Lhasa government had nominal control over the country, in fact the country was broadly divided into three regions – the central region of U-Tsang, and the eastern provinces of Amdo and Kham. Amdo, to the north, is a vast, high-altitude wilderness of treeless steppes, which the French Tibetologist Alexandra David-Neel described as a 'great desert of grass'. Its people are largely nomadic. In Kham, the landscape consists of thick, virgin forest, bordered by snow-capped mountain ranges. By comparison with their central Tibetan neighbours, the Khampas are tough, clannish, hot-tempered and renowned for their bravado. As the old Tibetan saying has it, 'From U-Tsang the best religion, from Amdo the best horses, from Kham the best men.' They carry themselves like warriors, with a swagger; a Khampa man is seldom to be seen without a broadsword hanging from his belt, sheathed in a silver scabbard and studded with coral and turquoise. They are brilliant equestrians, known for their bravery in battle and an aggression that has been only partly tempered by 800 years of Buddhism. It was eastern Tibet that had borne the brunt of the Chinese invasion, and Khampa soldiers who had offered the stiffest resistance to the Chinese forces. While Amdo and Kham paid notional subservience to Lhasa, these distant provinces tended to be effectively under the rule of local kings and chieftains. In those areas bordering China, the language and culture were principally Tibetan – but Chinese currency was used.

These geographical and cultural distinctions were also broadly reflected in religious affiliation. While the majority of monasteries in central Tibet – notably the huge monastic universities of Sera, Ganden and Drepung – were Gelug, in Amdo and Kham the predominant school was the Kagyu. And while the 'old schools' of Kagyu, Nyingma and Sakya respected the spiritual authority of the Dalai Lama, and recognised his position as the *de facto* 'King of Tibet', they retained a fierce independence in their practice, and a lingering distrust of the Lhasa government of which the Dalai Lama was the head. The old enmities between red and yellow hats had not been altogether forgotten.

Theoretically, in the crisis that the Tibetans now faced, such differences became meaningless, subordinated to the larger, collective struggle for survival in exile. But Tibetans are tenacious in their territorial identity and loyalty. Refugees flooding across the border had tended to be dispersed to settlements according to the region from which they had originally come, and the old fault-lines quickly began to replicate themselves. The newly established government-in-exile based in Dharamsala largely reflected the regional, and religious, bias of the old regime in Lhasa, which is to say that it was comprised largely of members of the aristo-cratic families from central Tibet, and dominated ecclesiastically by the Gelug school.

Mindful of the potential problems this might cause, and deter-mined to democratize the new institutions of government, in 1962 the Dalai Lama appointed the first ever Khampa to serve in government as Education Minister. He also invited representatives of the other three major religious schools to be represented in the new Department of Religion. But his moves towards integration were construed in some quarters as an attempt to impose the religious authority of the Gelugpa over the other schools, inflaming the old sectarian rivalries between red and yellow hats which had persisted in Tibet for some 500 years. Suspicious of the govern-ment-in-exile, an alliance of refugees from Kham and Amdo founded their own organization, the Tibetan Welfare Association, known colloquially as the Thirteen Settlements group, and began to solicit funds independently from the Indian government and overseas aid groups. The Karmapa was invited to become chair-man of the group. He refused, wary of being drawn into a political dispute with Dharamsala or the Dalai Lama. But at the same time he conspicuously avoided aligning himself with Dharamsala in the cause of Tibetan independence, and he declined to pledge funds to the exiled government's independence booklet *Rangtsen Lagdep*. The frictions between the government-in-exile in Dharamsala and the Thirteen Settlements group would, in characteristic Tibetan fashion, rumble on into the 1970s, but the Karmapa was to play no part in them.

Some 800 miles from Dharamsala, Rumtek functioned almost as an independent kingdom. By comparison with most of the Tibetan monasteries struggling to establish themselves in exile, Rumtek was wealthy. The Karmapas' historical role as spiritual teachers to the royal families of Sikkim and Bhutan ensured their continuing patronage. And the 16th Karmapa had a facility for attracting new patrons wherever he went. Lama Yeshe Losal, who lived for some years at Rumtek and worked as a translator for the Karmapa, tells how during a visit to Bodh Gaya in India in 1956, the Karmapa was introduced to members of the Ashok family, whose fortune had been built on a variety of businesses from manufacturing to hotels.

'They were very wealthy, but they did not have a child. So they came to Karmapa asking if he could help them. The Karmapa made a promise that their wish would be granted. By the time he escaped to India the child had been born, and from then on, wherever he travelled they provided a free chauffeur-driven car, places where his monks could stay and free food.' In 1967, says Lama Yeshe, the Karmapa was invited to Bhutan as a guest of the King. 'The King was so overwhelmed with his blessing that he offered him many vehicles – Land Rovers, jeeps, a truck. They were brought back to Rumtek, but there were no mechanics at the monastery to maintain them. Then this Indian man, he was in charge of the mechanics for all the Indian military vehicles in the area, he didn't have children either. He said, "Karmapa we hear you are the giver of everything; you can give me children and I will serve you." Karmapa said, "OK, you can have a child." And the man then had a daughter, which he gave a Tibetan name. And after that, all of Karmapa's vehicles were serviced free of charge!'

Because of the tensions with China there were a large number of Indian soldiers in Sikkim, and they were a common sight at Rumtek, queuing to take Karmapa's blessing – a fact which puzzled Ngödrup Burkhar when he first arrived at the monastery. 'They were often high-ranking officers, and one of the first things they would ask is, "Where can I get the red string?" – the protection cord which everyone who had an audience with Karmapa was given. I was very curious. So I asked someone, "Why are all these soldiers asking for the red string all the time?" They told me that one day a Captain had come and His Holiness gave him a protection cord. The Captain asked, "What is this for?" And His Holiness said, "It's for protection, like armour." He said, "It's bullet-proof", with this great laugh, so you couldn't be sure whether he was joking or not. Anyway, the Captain tied the cord around the neck of a goat and he shot the goat. And luckily it survived. So that's why all these soldiers came!' More than just a spiritual leader, the Karmapa presided over Rumtek like a benevolent patriach.

The monastic community grew to include some 300 monks, and the presence of the monastery drew increasing numbers of Tibetan refugees who settled in its immediate environs. This community was ordered in a strict hierarchy. Below the Karmapa were the four 'heart sons': Shamar Rinpoche, Tai Situ Rinpoche, Gyaltsab Rinpoche and Jamgon Kongtrul Rinpoche. For centuries, these incarnations had served as the principal lineage-holders of the Karma Kagyu teachings, sometimes as teachers and sometimes as students of successive Karmapas. These four would be expected to preserve the lineage after the Karmapa's death, and in the fullness of time to take responsibility for the discovery and education of his successor. Below the heart sons were a number of lesser rinpoches and *tulkus*, who were being educated at Rumtek under the Karmapa's guidance, in the expectation that they would eventually go into the world to found their own monasteries and teaching centres. Below them were Rumtek's monks, ecclesiastical foot soldiers, who were themselves arranged in a hierarchy of chant-masters, shrine-masters and officers.

Of the four heart sons, Shamar, born in 1952, was the eldest. Tai Situ was born a year later. Gyaltsab and Jamgon Kongtrul were both born in 1954. After the Karmapas themselves, the Shamar Rinpoches (or Shamarpas) were the oldest lineage in the Karma Kagyu order, dating back to the thirteenth century. The Shamar was the fourteenth of his line; he was also the Karmapa's nephew (the son of his brother), and, like Karmapa himself, the child of one of the old aristocratic families of Derge. The Gyaltsab Rinpoches had traditionally acted as Regents for the Karmapas, living in their own monastery within the confines of Tsurphu, and tending to affairs when the Karmapa was away. The 12th Gyaltsab escaped from Tibet with the Karmapa in 1959 and settled at Rumtek. The 12th Tai Situ Rinpoche (or Tai Situpa) had perhaps the strongest spiritual connection to the Karmapa. His predecessor, the 11th Tai Situ, had been responsible for the recognition and education of the 16th Karmapa who, in turn, had recognized the 12th Tai Situ in 1954, when the child was one year old. Tai Situ had left Tsurphu in the advance party, shortly before the departure of the Karmapa, and found sanctuary in Bhutan. Soon after his arrival, however, he fell ill with tuberculosis. He was moved to Darjeeling, in India, for treatment, where he remained with his own small entourage of attendants and advisers until 1965, when, at the age of twelve, he was taken under the wing of Karmapa at Rumtek. The youngest of the four was Jamgon Kongtrul Rinpoche who was born in 1954 and recognized at the age of one by the 16th Karmapa. People noticed that the Karmapa treated the young Jamgon with particular affection, almost as if he were his own son.

By comparison with the other monks of Rumtek, the heart sons lived like nobility. All had rooms just below the Karmapa's private apartments in the main temple. Attendants catered to their every need. But this was anything but a life of pampered indolence. Their days were spent in arduous study under the watchful eye of Rumtek's *khenpo*, or Director of Studies, Thrangu Rinpoche. It was an education that included not only religious subjects, but also such arts as painting, calligraphy, poetry and lama dancing. 'Karmapa gave all of them the best education; rooms for themselves and for their attendants,' remembers Lama Yeshe. 'He was like a father with his sons. The four of them were like brothers.' This mood of fraternal affection and solidarity would persist through the heart sons' youth and adolescence, for as long as the Karmapa was alive, but quickly dissolve into rivalry following his death.

The Karmapa was a dominating, all-pervasive presence at Rumtek. He was 'full of life,' remembers Ngödrup Burkhar, 'his laughter was the lion's roar.' The Karmapa was the sun around which life at Rumtek revolved. He rose early. 'The people serving him had a terrible time,' says Ringu Tulku. 'They would get up at four in the morning, and not go to bed until very late.' He would preside over the daily pujas, or religious ceremonies, spend time in teachings and transmissions with the heart sons, and hold court to an endless stream of visitors, his general secretary, Damchoe Yongdu, never far from his side. 'The Karmapa was an extremely kind man,' says Ringu Tulku, 'always in a happy mood. He would sit in his audience room, and anybody could come and see him and ask his advice. You just felt lifted by being with him. You would forget all your problems in his presence – and forget all your questions also! People who were not Buddhists would come and sometimes just become Buddhists, just like that. They might not know anything about Buddhism, but they would see him and say "I have to take refuge." But he was very particular about upholding the traditions, very particular about people being monks and nuns. I remember my parents telling him that in our family people would die very young when they were monks; what could they do for me to have long life? And he said, it doesn't matter if you die young as long as you are a good monk, that's better!'

The Karmapa's personal quarters were in a bungalow on the hill above the monastery. Nearby was his aviary, stocked with finches, canaries and peacocks. He was especially fond of birds and animals. One of his favourite pastimes was following the Mahayana practice of buying animals from the market and freeing them, to spare the butcher's axe. Whenever he travelled, he would make a point of visiting breeders to buy new stock for his aviary, often disconcerting them by choosing their best breeding bird. 'When His Holiness was with his birds it was a different world,' says Ngödrup Burkhar. 'The fact is that he could communicate to their basic potential. They would stand on his fingers and he would be blowing on them with his breath, murmuring something so compassionately. Sometimes I would be alone with him, when he was tending to the birds. I would have the privilege of asking him a few little things or whatever. But even then his presence was overwhelming. He was unfathomable.' Many canaries and finches, he would tell devotees, are bodhisattvas, who deliberately avoid eating seeds with worms in them 'to avoid hurting sentient beings'. Visitors to the aviary recall seeing birds that had died yet remained on their perches for days afterwards, their bodies still warm, apparently in *thug-dam*, the meditative state which certain realized lamas are said to attain at the moment of death.

Ward Holmes, one of the first Westerners to visit Rumtek in the early 1970s, recalls being in a room with the Karmapa when there was a loud thump against the window behind where he was seated. 'I went outside, and it was a dove that had flown into the window. I brought it in and Karmapa said, "Oh yes, this is a disciple of mine that wanted to die in my presence, and now he'll be reborn directly as a human." I didn't know what to say to that.'

CHAPTER FOUR

'You Can Never Be Selfish Again...'

To the bedraggled army of hippies who began to descend on India in the mid 1960s, the subcontinent offered myriad possibilities of escape and transformation. Drugs were plentiful, exotic belief systems that seemed to offer the antidote to the crushing conformity and pressures of Western materialism even more so. In this rarefied atmosphere of mind expansion and truth seeking, the names of gurus and teachers were traded like cigarette cards. What of Sai Baba – the saint of Puttaparthi, who was said to miraculously produce holy ash, *vibhuti*, from thin air? And the Maharishi Mahesh, the giggling yogi who had turned on the Beatles? To the Westerners encountering Tibetan lamas for the first time, they were emissaries from Shangri-La, a mythical kingdom concretized in the collective imagination by the writings of Alexandra David-Neel, the French writer and Tibetologist who was the first Western woman ever to reach Lhasa; by the *Tibetan Book of the Dead* which was rewritten as a handbook of the psychedelic experience by Timothy Leary; and by the fanciful narratives of 'Lobsang Rampa', a soi-disant Tibetan lama who would subsequently be unveiled as Cyril Hoskins, a surgical appliance salesman from Plymouth. For many Tibetans, their first encounter with the West was embodied in tangle-haired hippies, wide-eyed on hashish and wonder. The two parties gazed at each other across a chasm of incredulity, misunderstanding and bemusement.

In Kopan, Nepal, two exiled Tibetan lamas, Lama Thubten Yeshe and Lama Zopa, had been taken under the wing of an exotic Russian-American princess and erstwhile playgirl named

Zina Rachevsky, who was said, in the fanciful spirit of the times, to be the first reincarnation of the nineteenth-century Russian clairvoyant Madame Blavatsky, and would subsequently take ordination as a Buddhist nun. Zina established her own retreat, which became what one visitor remembers as 'a magnet for every spiritual wannabe who pitched up in the Kathmandu valley'. Among the first visitors were Aldous Huxley's niece, Olivia De Haulleville, and Michael Riggs, a 6'3" surfer from Laguna Beach, California, who had arrived in India in 1964, taken the name Bhagavan Das and was living the life of a sadhu. Bhagavan Das would assume a certain counter-culture celebrity as the man who introduced Richard Alpert, Timothy Leary's colleague in the LSD experiments at Stanford University, to his guru Neem Karoli Baba – a meeting that would result in Alpert too discarding his old identity and taking the name Ram Dass.

Michael Hollingshead, the English writer and intellectual who first introduced Timothy Leary to LSD, and who became one of the drug's most fervent proselytizers, was another visitor – and one of the first Westerners to have an audience with the Karmapa, in Kathmandu in 1970, which he recorded in vivid detail in his autobiography, *The Man Who Turned on the World*. Having spent the night preparing for the meeting by 'performing chillum and acid Sadhana', Hollingshead writes that he was 'very stoned indeed' and could barely find his way to the Mercedes which had been sent to fetch him. Ushered in to the presence of the Karmapa, Hollingshead was immediately struck by 'a beam of bright light issuing from the centre of his silver crown, or it may have been a beam of sunlight catching a reflection through the lattice-work windows. But the effect was quite startling. It really could seem that he was emitting light from his "third eye" in the centre of his forehead.' Asked by the Karmapa if he had anything to say, Hollingshead expressed his desire to see more Tibetan lamas come to the West, and particularly to open a dialogue with the Hopi Indians of Arizona, whom Hollingshead believed could prove to be 'a spiritual backbone for a future, more spiritualized America'. He goes on:

> Karmapa remained silent throughout all this. When I had fin-
> ished, he beckoned me closer and as I bent my head, his hands

touched the centre of my head, and suddenly, unaccountably, like a bolt, I experienced *samadhi*, one of the most extraordinary moments of consciousness of which man is capable. And I felt completely and utterly cleansed, as though the divine thunderbolt had gone through me like a million-volt charge . . . If ever there were a living god, Karmapa is it; of this I am utterly convinced.

Hollingshead was following in the footsteps of a Western couple that would play a more significant role in the story of the Karmapa. Ole Nydahl had completed his national service in the Danish army, where he had been an accomplished boxer, and then become an enthusiastic convert to the hippie drug culture. In 1968, at the age of twenty-seven, Nydahl and his wife Hannah set off for the East in a Volkswagen bus, following the well-trodden trail through Afghanistan into India and Nepal. The couple financed their travels by smuggling hashish back to Europe. One consignment was sent in large brass Buddha heads. Ole would later characterize himself and Hannah in his autobiography *Riding the Tiger* as, 'liberty fighters for the noble cause of inner freedom, helping people to get rid of aggression and alcohol'. Ole and Hannah had been among the 'spiritual wannabes' who had turned up at Zina Rachevsky's Kopan retreat. A visitor there remembers them as 'very tall, very blond, very loud and very dominant personalities, both of them. They were both wearing robes, and yet they were unmistakably sexual.'

And it was in Kathmandu, in 1969, that the Nydahls first encountered the Karmapa, who was there on a visit. Ole was immediately convinced that they had a bond that 'went back many lifetimes'. He later wrote in his autobiography: 'My strong recurring dreams since earliest childhood of protecting the lives of laypeople and monks, while fighting back hordes of Chinese soldiers among jagged mountains, would now make sense, as would Hannah's spontaneous Tibetan-style singing and dancing from her earliest years.' On their first meeting, Ole and Hannah presented the Karmapa with 'the most auspicious things we had' – a Danish horseshoe magnet and a piece of blotting paper with one thousand micrograms of purest LSD. Whatever bemusement the Karmapa might have felt at the Nydahls' largesse, he evidently disguised it well. The Karmapa, Ole wrote, 'looked intently at us for a while, fed us some sweets, laughed and had us repeat after him in Tibetan the colours associated with the five Buddha wisdoms'.

A year later, the Nydahls took refuge with the Karmapa at Rumtek. Ole was an unorthodox Buddhist. He was possessed of a breast-beating manner, somewhat at odds with the air of humility and self-effacement that overcame most Western visitors in the presence of the Karmapa. He enjoyed driving fast cars and powerful motorbikes. But he also had resourcefulness, boundless energy and an evangelical zeal. In 1973 he established the first Kagyu Buddhist centre in Denmark, which was quickly followed by other centres in Sweden and Germany.

Ward Holmes was another of the Westerners who made their way to the Karmapa. Holmes had grown up in Hawaii, the son of a distinguished eye surgeon, who at one time was chairman of the World Health Organization. In 1969, after leaving high school he set off for India, following the statutory stops of the hippie trail, smoking pot with sadhus in Puri, visiting Sai Baba in his ashram near Bangalore. In Darjeeling he met an elderly Chinese man named Yogi Chen. Yogi Chen was a Taoist, but he had studied meditation in Tibet, and had been acquainted with Alexandra David-Neel. Yogi Chen told Holmes that it was his destiny to meet the Karmapa. But Holmes postponed it for a year, travelling through India and studying yoga, before deciding that the time had come to return to Darjeeling.

'The day before I left for Rumtek, I spent the whole night meditating with Yogi Chen, and he wrote me a letter of introduction to take to Karmapa. I caught a bus to Sikkim and stayed a night in Gangtok. The next morning I got up and started off to Rumtek. I was already in a very unusual state because of what Yogi Chen had given to me. On the way there I had a really strong experience. I had to sit down in this little shack beside some rice fields. And suddenly a voice came to me that I should open the letter that Yogi Chen had written. And then I realized that, of course, it was meant for me, because it was written in English. Yogi Chen knew Tibetan and Karmapa didn't speak English. And as I read it I realized that after all my many lifetimes I finally was going to meet my Vajra guru – the master. At that moment, when I realized that, I felt this energy and power, like a hand coming down and pulling my heart. I leaped up and literally I couldn't stop walking for the next seven to ten kilometres up to Rumtek, with this burning desire to get there. As I was walking I had these visions that I really had to open up, surrender my ego – that if I could go there with the channel of devotion completely open, then I could really meet the Vajra guru in the proper way and receive his blessing. Because if you persist in having an inflated ego, then the power of Karmapa to reach the heart is difficult.

'So I got to Rumtek, and as I walked into the front courtyard, there were four little boys came up and all did a namaste, and it was like they were saying, "Welcome home". The next morning I was ushered in to see Karmapa. There were people in front of me making offerings, then finally it was my turn. He was on a low throne in front of me and I was on the floor. And he said to me, through a translator, "Well, what do you want?" I gave him the letter. He looked at it and said, "Yes, but what do you want?" And I said, "Please show me the right way to live," and a tear came in my eye. He said, "Come back in a little while." Two or three hours later, I came back to this room where he was going to give Milarepa initiation – to do the Milarepa meditation practice. There were just three or four others in the room. So I took Milarepa initiation. I didn't know what it was, but they just said do the mantra, it'll help. A couple of days later my visa was going to run out. Karmapa personally called the minister responsible and asked for a longer visa. So I got a nine-day visa. Then he asked me if I wanted to take refuge. I said, of course. So I took refuge alone with Karmapa, repeating after him certain things. And then at the third click of his finger this very powerful transmission happened – a very warm, blissful happiness just came shooting into my heart. It was almost like my heart was an empty cup, and he just filled it with an elixir of bliss and understanding, as if from then on I could differentiate between what is truth and what is not. It was so powerful I could hardly talk. I was shaking. There was a Western nun there, Sister Palmo. I asked her, what next? How long does this blessing last? And she said, not only this lifetime but as many lifetimes as you need until you reach the full enlightenment of Buddhahood. Karmapa will find you in whatever realm you're born into and bring you back to the teachings. It was like a bomb.'

Like most of the new Western arrivals, Holmes was sent to

study with Kalu Rinpoche, a senior lama in the Kagyu order. As a young child, Kalu Rinpoche had been recognized as one of the five incarnations of Jamgon Kongtrul Lodro Thaye – the teacher of the 15th Karmapa. But his father, himself a reincarnate lama, refused the invitation to have his son enthroned at a monastery. Instead, Kalu Rinpoche followed the example of Tibet's great wandering yogi, Milarepa, spending twelve years roaming in isolated areas, leading a hermit's existence meditating in caves and tents, finally emerging only when instructed by his own guru that it was time for him to teach. Fleeing to India after the Chinese occupation he established his own retreat centre at Sonada in northern India.

An alarmingly skeletal figure, with deeply sunken cheeks and huge, watery eyes – he was later said to be the model for Steven Spielberg's ET – Kalu Rinpoche seemed to embody the most benign and saintly aspects of Buddhism, a mixture of the profoundly wise and the curiously childlike. In the book *Enthronement*, Ngawang Zangpo, an English student of Kalu Rinpoche, tells of the lama disappearing in a department store in Vancouver, while on his first teaching visit to the West in 1971:

> Those who had accompanied him searched every floor and every department for the then sixty-six-year-old unilingual Tibetan man in monk's robes. They eventually found him sitting on the floor at play with children in the toy department. During that visit he played on the stairs of his first meditation centre with a 'slinky' and in his room with a laugh box. He amused himself with toys all his life – hand puppets, wind-up dolls, masks. During his last few years, he added to the headaches of his personal secretary, Lama Gyaltsen, by insisting that toys he collected in foreign countries be added to their already mountainous baggage, to be stored back home at the monastery, where they remained until his reincarnation was recognized.

(The next incarnation was born as the son of Lama Gyaltsen; Kalu Rinpoche had effectively been giving toys to his future father to look after for him.)

But for all his childlike innocence Kalu Rinpoche could be a stern taskmaster, and his uncompromising approach to the Buddhist teachings proved a shock to many new Western students. Being sent to Sonada was the equivalent of Buddhist boot camp. Conditions were rudimentary to the point of primitive. Deprived of any creature comforts, students were instructed in the Ngongdru, or 'foundation practice', the first stage of which involves performing 100,000 prostrations – a back-breaking exercise even for the fittest. Nor was there much comfort to be found in Kalu Rinpoche's teachings. Ngawang Zangpo recounts how he would delight in confounding his students' expectations. To strait-laced Chinese Buddhists he would describe the origins of the Buddha's teachings on tantra – a king who had faith in the Buddha but would only practise his teachings if it didn't interfere with his routine of making love with 500 queens during the day and a further 500 at night. To 'liberated' Americans he would stress the benefits of celibacy. But his greatest enthusiasm, it seemed, was for shattering any idealistic image that his students might have had of attaining nirvana, warning of the myriad torments that awaited indigent backsliders in the hell-realms. 'I came from a Swedish rational background,' remembers Dechen, an early student, and 'nothing had prepared me for that. I thought, this is incredible, unbelievable! Then I realized, this sweet little old man, he's not lying to me.'

Like many who ended up at Sonada, Dechen and her husband had come to India on the hippie trail, making the obligatory round of ashrams and beat hotels, before finding their way to Rumtek. Her husband was an enthusiastic dope smoker. At their first audience the Karmapa pointed a finger at his visitor and told him, 'If you keep using bad medicine you will become like a vegetable.'

'I don't know how he knew my husband smoked dope. We hadn't said anything.'

Within a few weeks of her arrival at Rumtek, Dechen had decided to become a Buddhist and took refuge.

'His Holiness leaned over, looked at his watch and said, you have to remember this time for the rest of your life. It was twenty-five past ten on the 10th April, 1972. And after I took the bodhisattva vow he said, now you can never be selfish again.'

In 1954, returning from his visit to Beijing with the Dalai Lama, the Karmapa had stopped at Palpung monastery in Kham, to

perform the enthronement ceremony of the new incarnation of
the Tai Situpa. Monks, lamas and rinpoches from all over Kham
had gathered for the celebrations. At the same time, the Karmapa
gave a series of empowerments, including the Mahakala, the
empowerment of the protector deity of the Kagyu order. Thirteen
young rinpoches received the empowerment; all thirteen would
subsequently escape safely into India.

Among them were Chögyam Trungpa Rinpoche and Akong
Rinpoche. The 11th Chögyam Trungpa was one of the senior-
most lamas in the Kagyu order. The abbot of the Surmang group
of monasteries in eastern Tibet, he had been found and enthroned by the 16th Karmapa eighteen months after his birth
in February 1939. The 1st Akong Rinpoche was the abbot of a
small monastery, Sowa Derma Lakum, in eastern Tibet. He and
Trungpa had been educated together as children, and become
firm friends. In the winter of 1959, both escaped from Tibet, in a
party of some 200 people which also included Akong's younger
brother, Jamdrak who would later become Lama Yeshe Losal. It
took the party three weeks to cross the Himalayas. At one stage,
attempting to traverse the Bhramaputra river, with the Chinese
in close pursuit, they had been obliged to fabricate coracles from
pieces of leather, using the gum from trees as glue. They crossed
the river under gunfire. 'We had to hide on the other side in the
trees,' remembers Lama Yeshe. 'For almost a whole week my
clothes, everyone's clothes, were frozen. We had nothing to eat.
We started to eat the leather of our clothes. Everything was
torture, and fear. But it was this fear, and the need to escape, that
kept us alive.'

Arriving in India, they were placed in a refugee camp at Baxa in
Assam. The British had built the camp during the Second World
War to imprison seditionaries. It had now been hastily made
serviceable to house some 1,500 lamas and monks from monasteries from all over Tibet. The camp was ringed by metal fences
and lookout towers. There were only a handful of wooden
buildings; the refugees slept in bamboo huts under grass roofs.
In the overcrowded and unsanitary conditions, disease quickly
spread. 'Many important rinpoches were there,' remembers Lama
Yeshe. 'Unless you were very wealthy there was nowhere else to
go. It was so hot the tar was melting. Hundreds of people died

because they could not take the heat.' It was there that Akong, Trungpa and Yeshe met Freda Bedi.

Born in 1911, the daughter of a Derbyshire watchmaker, Freda had studied politics and philosophy at Oxford, where she met a young Indian student, Bawa Bedi. A direct descendant of Guru Nanak, the founder of the Sikh religion, Bedi was a communist and an ardent Indian nationalist. The couple married and, fired by her husband's dream of independence for his homeland, Freda returned with him to India to join the struggle against the British. Bawa Bedi was to spend some four years in jail for his political activities. Freda became involved in the Gandhian non-violent struggle and was arrested on three occasions for leading demonstrations. With the coming of independence in 1947, Bawa Bedi took a position in the new government of Kashmir, which had become an autonomous state within the Indian union, while Freda threw herself into helping refugees displaced by the partition of India and Pakistan. By now, she had also developed an interest in Buddhism. She travelled to Burma to study meditation, and took Buddhist vows. Returning to India, she was invited by India's Prime Minister, Pandit Nehru, to work for the government's Central Social Welfare Board. It was this work that brought her into contact with the first Tibetan refugees who began to flood across the border into India in 1959.

Bedi took a particular interest in the fate of the lamas and rinpoches who had come into exile, and she was immediately drawn to Akong and Trungpa on meeting them at Baxa. Moved by their predicament, she invited them to live with her family. 'Trungpa was obviously very bright,' remembers Bedi's son, Kabir, who was in his early teens at the time, and is now a Hollywood actor. 'He was highly voluble, expressive – in his own way very flamboyant; a naughty boy, but a brilliant teacher. Akong, on the other hand, radiated a great calm and a great solidity. He didn't talk much about things; he just went out and did them.'

Bedi believed that it was vital that the young lamas should learn English and the basics of a Western education if they were to go into the world and engage with Western scholars and students. In consultation with the Dalai Lama she founded a school for young lamas, which was originally based in Delhi and then moved to Dalhousie, a former British hill station in the foothills of the

Himalayas. In its spirit of ecumenism, Bedi's Young Lamas' Home School was a measure of how much things would change for the Tibetans in exile. Some ten students, along with a senior lama who acted as teacher, represented each of the four major schools. As well as maintaining the respective practices of each school, students were given the basics of a solid, traditional Tibetan education – calligraphy, Tibetan history, language, poetry and Buddhist doctrine. They were also taught English. Trungpa became the school's principal, and Akong its manager. His younger brother, Jamdrak, was the school's only lay student.

By now, Freda Bedi had met and become friends with the Karmapa, and in 1964 he ordained her as a Buddhist nun. She took the name Ani Karma Khechog Palmo. Her son Kabir remembers being profoundly shocked by her decision. 'She hadn't told us in advance. She simply came home one day in her robes and said she had been ordained. She said, "An apple has no choice when it falls from the tree." I was very resentful, although later on, of course, I came to understand that it was something she felt she had to do. She was an extraordinarily compassionate woman, who dedicated her life to helping other people.' Ani Palmo left her family and moved to Rumtek, where she worked closely with the Karmapa. She would also go on to found a nunnery, Tilokpur, near Dharamsala. She died in 1977, at the age of sixty-six in New Delhi, where she was representing the Karmapa at a World Buddhist Congress.

Trungpa and Akong left India in 1963, bound for England. With the help of Freda Bedi, Trungpa had been awarded a Spalding Scholarship to study comparative religion and philosophy at Oxford. Akong took a job as a hospital porter to support them both. Another young Tibetan expatriate, Chime Rinpoche, joined them in Oxford. Chime would subsequently found his own centre in Saffron Walden, Essex. Trungpa quickly acclimatized to his new surroundings. He threw himself into his studies of Plato and Kant and at weekends travelled to London to visit museums and galleries. In 1966 his autobiography, *Born in Tibet*, was published in Britain, and afforded a respectful welcome. For Trungpa, it was all research, all to be absorbed, as he put it, 'as a learning process, always, so that everything was recorded as if in a notebook'.

Freed from the constraints of Tibetan culture, Trungpa set out to find a way to demystify the teachings of Tibetan Buddhism and make them accessible to Westerners. In 1967, along with Akong Rinpoche, he acquired Johnstone House, a property in the rolling lowlands of Scotland, near Dumfries, which had gone through various metamorphoses as a private house, a nursing home and a Theravadin Buddhist retreat. The new property was named Samye Ling, after the first Buddhist monastery founded in Tibet, by Padmasambhava in the eighth century. The first people to turn up at Samye Ling were a handful of Buddhist scholars, who had come via the English Buddhist Society, leavened with a smattering of unreconstructed hippies, veterans for the most part of the India trail. Few had anything but the most cursory acquaintance with Tibetan Buddhist teachings, and most, as Trungpa would later observe, 'seemed to be slightly missing the point'. Life at Samye Ling fell into a curious regime that combined the rigours of a monastery with the libertarianism of a commune. Morning and afternoon prayers and meditation were punctuated by long, leisurely walks through the surrounding countryside. An American cooked macrobiotic food. The distinctive aroma of cannabis hung over the house and the woodshed where most visitors slept. Local villagers traded lurid gossip about sex and drug orgies.

While Trungpa attempted to instil the basic principles of Buddhist meditation and philosophy in his students, Akong contented himself with more mundane duties. 'I was the bed maker,' he now recalls with a laugh. 'But my main job was cleaning the floors. I wasn't interested in teaching. If you want to teach, you have to know; and I didn't feel I knew enough.' While close friends, there were marked differences between the two men, which became more pronounced in the hothouse atmosphere of Samye Ling. Akong was a stolid, conservative – some said unimaginative – man; a traditionalist. Trungpa was mercurial and unconventional, a brilliant scholar who would use any tactics to get his students to pay attention. He drank alcohol and would often smoke dope. (On one occasion he and some students baked hash brownies, which they surreptitiously slipped to Akong. 'It had no effect whatsoever,' remembers one student. 'Akong was like a rock.') Trungpa also showed a distinctly unmonklike interest in the opposite sex. Akong took strong exception to what he regarded as his friend's moral slippage, and matters came to a head when Trungpa announced his intention to marry a local girl who was just sixteen. 'My own feeling was it did not suit someone who was presenting themselves as a Buddhist monk,' says Akong. 'He was still wearing monk's robes. I felt it would damage his Buddhist image as a teacher. If you're wearing a robe you have to be celibate and you don't drink. And if you want to marry you have to give up the robe.'

In his autobiography, Trungpa recounts how this was a period of anguish and confusion in his life, while he deliberated on whether his mission to teach Buddhism in the West would be best served by him remaining as a monk or giving up his robes. His quandary was resolved in a curious fashion when, driving in Northumberland, he blacked out at the wheel and crashed his car through the window of a joke and novelty shop. (Typically, Trungpa did not hold a driving licence; a student at Samye Ling had taken his test on his behalf.) The accident left Trungpa paralysed down his left side. He later wrote:

> In spite of the pain, my mind was very clear. There was a strong sense of communication – finally the real message had got through – and I felt a sense of relief and even humour. I realized that I could no longer attempt to preserve any privacy for myself, any special identity or legitimacy. I should not hide behind the robes of a monk, creating an inscrutability which, for me, turned out to be only an obstacle.

He gave up his robes and shortly afterwards married one of his students, Diana Pybus, and left Samye Ling for America. He settled in Boulder, Colorado, where a small group of students began to gather around him, and where he founded a meditation centre, Karma Dzong (Fortress of Action). Within a few years this would grow into a national Buddhist organization, Vajradhatu, including America's first Buddhist university, the Naropa Institute, which was founded in 1974. With Trungpa's departure, a more orderly regime was imposed at Samye Ling. Among the first of the new rules introduced by Akong was one stipulating that 'nobody was to break the English law'. The days of hash brownies were over.

In 1974, the 16th Karmapa arrived in the West for the first time. Travelling with him was a small entourage of monks and attendants, including Sister Palmo (the former Freda Bedi), who acted as his translator. His first stop was in London. Chime Rinpoche and a handful of his students were waiting to greet him at Heathrow aiport. Among them was the record producer Tony Visconti. 'Karmapa was whisked through with entourage in tow, one lama carrying the Black Hat in an elaborately decorated box,' Visconti remembers. 'Karmapa was wearing shades. He looked at us all individually and when it was my turn his eyes kind of zapped me and I felt as though I weighed only a few ounces. I thought I was going to levitate. When I told Chime about this, he said, "That's nothing; wait until he takes off his sunglasses." '

It was to be the first time that the major Kagyu ceremonies of empowerment had ever been performed in the West. The most important of these was the Vajra Crown ceremony, which would customarily be conducted in the main shrine halls of great monasteries, dripping with splendour, before congregations several hundred, even thousand, strong. But in Britain, Tibetan Buddhism was in its nascent stages; there were few Buddhist centres in the country, and students were obliged to hire whatever premises they could find. So it was that the Vajra Crown ceremony was performed in a conservatory at the Botanical Gardens in Edgbaston; in a rented church hall in Manchester and in a marquee in a garden in Saffron Walden.

The ceremony had remained unchanged for more than 500 years, since the Black Hat had first been presented to the 5th Karmapa Dezhin Shegpa by his disciple the Chinese Emperor. To the sound of droning horns and *gyalings* and the deafening clamour of cymbals, the Karmapa would seat himself cross-legged on a thick cushion and don the richly embroidered ceremonial meditation hat of Gampopa. The monks would then perform three prostrations in front him, and requesting that he assume the form of Avalokiteshvara, the bodhisattva of compassion, offer a silver plate heaped with rice – a mandala symbolizing the universe, and all its beauty and riches. Responding to their supplications, the Karmapa would remove the hat he was wearing and begin to enter a state of deep meditation. An attendant would then pass him a box, from which he would take the Vajra Crown, wrapped in silk. Holding it firmly in his right hand (for according to legend, such is the power of the crown that if not held it will fly away of its own accord), the Karmapa would place it with regal deliberation on his head. Holding a crystal *mala* in his other hand, he would then recite the mantra of Avalokiteshvara, *om mani padme hung*, 108 times. The Karmapa would then remove the hat, wrap it carefully in its silk covering and replace it in the box. All present would then come forward to be blessed with a touch on the head, sometimes with a small reliquary, sometimes with a ribboned stick.

More than symbolic, the ceremony is an invocation of power. In placing the Crown on his head and chanting the mantra, the Karmapa, it is believed, is actually transformed into an emanation of Avalokiteshvara. Here the literal meaning of Karmapa – 'man of activity' – becomes manifest. In this moment, it is said, the karma of all who bear witness to the ceremony, accumulated through countless lifetimes, is immeasurably 'ripened'. In Buddhism this ripening is considered extremely beneficial, for it is better for karma to manifest in this life, when you are in the presence of great teachers and able to do something about it, than to carry over at the moment of death, and perhaps dictate a bad rebirth. While few, perhaps, who witnessed the Vajra Crown ceremony fully understood its theological complexities, its effect could be nonetheless profound.

Mary Finnigan, an English Buddhist student who witnessed the ceremony in London, remembers experiencing it as 'something totally transcendental'. Finnigan had first met the Karmapa at Samye Ling, soon after his arrival in Britain. She wrote in her journal, 'He is the first human being I have ever met who has convinced me he is not entirely of this world.' Watching the Vajra Crown ceremony, she says she became conscious of:

> various, more subtle levels of awareness opening up within myself as the ceremony progressed. One moment he was a fat Tibetan dressed in wonderful regalia, holding a crystal *mala*; and the next, he was Chenresig [the Tibetan name for Avalokiteshvara]. Quite literally, he 'disappeared' to be replaced by this most glorious, translucent vision as the deity manifested. The whole room seemed to be bathed in rainbow light – every person and object in the room. People were falling on their faces in prostration. I sat there thinking, I'm not seeing this. So I closed my eyes, centered myself . . . come on, common sense . . . and I opened my eyes

again, and it was exactly the same. There was Chenresig, as depicted in Tibetan iconography, just radiating this light in all directions. And as the ceremony ended he very slowly took the hat off and put it back in the box, and became the Karmapa again and the rainbow light disappeared. I ran on the energy of that occasion for years.

Not everybody would experience the ceremony with quite the same intensity. But it seemed the Karmapa left an indelible impression on all who met him, a man who could be all things to all people. One English devotee, who spent a number of weeks driving him on one of his tours of Europe, talks of the Karmapa radiating a 'force field' so powerful that 'I was almost afraid to look at him.' To others he appeared as a figure of bountiful calm and openness. Even his appearance seemed to alter according to whoever was looking at him. While pictures show that he was a distinctly rotund figure, some talk of an appearance of 'astonishing lightness', almost as if his physical density was obscured behind a screen of some more evanescent presence. He seldom gave teachings while travelling. In fact, he seldom seemed to say very much at all. He spoke only a few words of English. Yet it was as if the Karmapa didn't have to do or say anything, he simply *was* – the walking embodiment of a principle, a palpable presence that seemed to exercise a magnetic effect on almost everyone who met him.

Ken Holmes, who was then a young student at Samye Ling and is now a Buddhist teacher, remembers accompanying the Karmapa on a visit to a cathedral in Scotland, where the dean received him. 'He showed us around, and when we got to the altar, the Karmapa asked, "What happens here?" The dean said, "This is where we pray." The Karmapa pointed to the ground and said very quietly, "Show me how you pray," and the man just fell to his knees and started praying, looking up at Karmapa like a schoolboy. Then the Karmapa said, "Thank you", and he stopped. It was like watching a little child with a great father. Karmapa had such a presence.'

On another occasion, Holmes took the Karmapa on a shopping expedition. 'At the time there was an advertisement on the television for a particular brand of luggage which showed somebody jumping up and down on it to demonstrate its strength. The

Karmapa had evidently seen this, and he got the sales assistant to jump up and down on this suitcase in the shop. The assistant was obviously quite taken with the Karmapa, completely under his spell. Then the Karmapa asked him to jump up and down on another case. Eventually the manager came down to find this going on; he wasn't at all happy. The Karmapa didn't buy any luggage, of course. In fact, he never bought very much at all.'

Edward Henning, a young Buddhist student and Tibetan speaker, accompanied the Karmapa on part of his first visit as his driver and translator in London. 'I remember somebody saying to me how extraordinary it must be to spend time with a man with no personality, because there's a misunderstanding about this whole Buddhist idea of overcoming ego. But that was completely the opposite of experiencing the Karmapa. It was as if he had personality, and the rest of us didn't, because he was so full of life. I wouldn't say full of energy – he was an older man and fairly heavy. But he was so full of *joie de vivre*, charisma, whatever you want to call it. He was absolutely radiant. There seemed to be a quality about him that reminded you constantly that you were in the presence of somebody who was not a normal human being. And if you were with him over a period of several days, so many little events would occur that would confirm that view; events that in themselves seemed quite insignificant, but taken together suggested you were in the presence of somebody who was very extraordinary.'

On his first day in London, Henning took the Karmapa to the British Library, where Chime Rinpoche worked, cataloguing the library's collection of Tibetan texts. 'His Holiness was examining a number of books,' Henning remembers, 'picking them up, touching them to his head as a mark of respect and saying "good, good". And as he was putting down one book he frowned, pulled it back up to his head and said, "This used to belong to me." He named a previous Karmapa, and passed it on. Afterwards we went through the books and found the one he'd singled out. Examining the colophon, it appeared the book had been sponsored by somebody as a gift for the Karmapa he had named. Nobody had examined the book beforehand, and the Karmapa had not examined the colophon. It appeared that he genuinely recognized it over a span of several hundred years.'

On another occasion he asked to be taken to a pet shop, expressing a desire to see a particularly rare breed of dog. Henning took him to Harrods – not, he recalls, the wisest choice. 'He told me off for having taken him to an expensive shop, he would have preferred cheap shops. As he walked in his first words were, "The ocean of suffering of *samsara*".' In the pet department, the Karmapa walked around stroking and talking to the animals. 'There was one dog he particularly liked. He played with it a little bit and then said, "Let's leave". When we got outside we realized we'd lost one of his monks, so he sent me back upstairs to the pet department to find him. I couldn't find the monk, but it suddenly struck me that the place was absolutely silent; every cat, every dog was fast asleep. It was quite eerie. I remember walking around thinking he'd done something.'

The following day, Henning recalls, the Karmapa asked him to telephone the pet department. Enquiring about the favoured dog, the Karmapa had been told by the assistant that it was priced at £90. 'Karmapa didn't think this was right. He told me to ring her up and make an offer of £65. I said, with all due respect Your Holiness, you don't barter with Harrods. He just looked at me and said, "Go and ring them." I got through to the department and the woman said, "I remember; you were with the Tibetan gentleman. I'm awfully sorry, but I made a mistake on the price of that dog; it wasn't £90, it was £65." So I went back to Karmapa and told him it was £65 and he just looked at me, basically, with no interest at all; as if to say, you don't understand . . . Of course, he didn't buy the dog.

'One of the most interesting experiences I had was during an initiation of Karma Pakshi, the 2nd Karmapa. I was sitting there with my eyes closed; Karmapa was sitting on his throne, chanting and reciting. I just happened to look up at him, and I noticed that his eyes were moving around the room, looking at everyone in the room for about two seconds each. And as he did this his whole face would change. Sometimes he would have a look of joy on his face, sometimes curiosity, sometimes disgust. It was as if he was looking right inside them. I shut my eyes before he got around to me, but that made a deep impression on me. It suggested he was capable of a deep intuition that could be related to any individual.'

From Britain, the Karmapa moved on to America. Chögyam Trungpa met him on his arrival in New York. In the six years he had been in America, Trungpa's approach to Buddhist teachings had grown even more idiosyncratic. He ran his organization, Vajradhatu, along the lines of a quasi-feudal fiefdom, surrounding himself with an élite 'praetorian guard' of his favoured students, sometimes amusing himself and his followers by dressing in a pseudo-military uniform of his own design. Hierarchy, he taught his students, was important because it creates a setting for the development of compassion and devotion. In a good society, the upper class displays compassion to its inferiors, and the lower class maintains devotion to its superiors. 'The real function of the guru,' Trungpa explained, 'is to insult you.' And his efforts to shake his students out of their complacency and what he would describe as their 'spiritual materialism' could often leave them bemused. He would frequently arrive late, and often drunk, for lectures. Sometimes he wouldn't bother to turn up at all. There were stories that he operated a form of droit de seigneur with his female students. He explained to his student, the poet and sexual libertarian Allen Ginsberg, that 'I come from a long line of eccentric Buddhists.' Ginsberg was evidently so enamoured with Trungpa that he once offered to sleep with him as a sign of his devotion. (Trungpa politely declined the offer.)

With the arrival of Karmapa in America, however, Trungpa was suddenly transformed into the staunch traditionalist. Under his watchful eye, at Vajradhatu centres in Vermont, New York, Colorado and California, new buildings were hastily constructed and existing ones refurbished in Tibetan style to accommodate the Karmapa and his party. Teams of carpenters, wood-carvers and seamstresses were mobilized to produce furnishings, fabrics and artefacts for shrine rooms and living quarters, including special tables and trays on which the Karmapa's food was carried and served. Three huge thrones were built, elaborately carved and painted and hung with dazzling brocades. American students had also been tutored in the proper protocol for receiving the Karmapa. The hippie trappings of old had disappeared. The welcoming party who greeted the Karmapa on his arrival in New York looked more like a convention of insurance salesmen, in suits, ties and neatly clipped hair. Trungpa had booked the entire top floor of the Plaza Hotel, overlooking Central Park, for the Karmapa's party.

From New York, the Karmapa travelled first to the Vajradhatu Centre in Vermont, and then to Boulder, where he recognized Chögyam Trungpa's new-born son as the Surmang Tenga Rinpoche, the first *tulku* to be identified in the West. From Colorado he travelled to Arizona, where a meeting had been arranged with representatives of the Hopi tribe of Native American Indians. The Karmapa had spoken of feeling a particular connection with the Hopi, and the meeting seemed to be the fulfilment of two prophecies. Among the Hopi themselves there is said to be a legend that many thousands of years ago, the Tibetans and Hopi were one people. With the coming of a great flood the tribe had been broken, one branch going east and the other west. An ancient Hopi prophecy held that one day, at a time of spiritual decline in the West, a brother would come from the East, wearing a red hat, and reveal himself to be a true friend of the Hopi people.

The Karmapa arrived in a gold Cadillac, which had been provided by some Buddhist students in Phoenix, Buddhist flags trailing from its radio aerial as it led an odd convoy of cars and buses across the high Arizona mesa to a reservation near the Grand Canyon. There he met with a gathering of tribal elders, among them Sun Chief Dan, Grandfather David, the tribe's lady prophet Grandmother Carolyn, and Chief White Bear. The Karmapa and Chief White Bear exchanged rings, each exquisitely wrought in turquoise, silver and coral. Those present were not in the least surprised to see that the rings were identical.

Erma Pounds ran a small Buddhist group in Phoenix. Two of her students joined the Karmapa on the expedition to the reservation. At the end of the meeting, according to Pounds, Sun Chief Dan told the Karmapa that the land was suffering drought. 'The Karmapa said, "I will pray about it." And all the way back from the reservation to the motel where the Karmapa was staying, he did pray. And the moment he got out of the car and opened the door to walk into his room, out of a perfectly cloudless sky suddenly came all this thunder and rumbling and rain like you never saw.'

Over the next six years the Karmapa would return to Europe and America several times. For his second tour, in 1976, Akong

Rinpoche had instructed some students from Samye Ling to purchase a coach, and one was eventually found in Holland. It was repainted in maroon and gold; seats were removed and a makeshift 'throne' – an armchair covered in red brocade – installed in their place. A sleeping platform was also installed, although the Karmapa never actually used it. Instead, it was quickly covered with an assortment of cages, accommodating the birds that he accumulated on his travels. The tour began in the Dordogne, in France, where a new centre was in the throes of being built on land that had been donated by the inventor Bernard Benson. From the Dordogne a small caravan of vehicles, led by the refurbished bus, set off across Europe, making stops in Holland, Belgium, Denmark, Sweden, Norway, Germany, Austria and Switzerland, finally arriving in Britain. As on his previous visit two years earlier, his itinerary took him to some curious places. On a visit to the studios of the BBC World Service, in London, he blessed all the recording equipment. One ceremony was conducted in a farmhouse on the Welsh borders belonging to a Buddhist student. Norma Levine, who had taken refuge as a Buddhist two years earlier during a visit to Samye Ling, remembers the odd spectacle of the antiquated bus, with the Karmapa seated on his 'throne' and accompanied by his retinue of monks, navigating its way down the narrow country lanes and finally pulling through the farmhouse gates.

In the front parlour, which had been transformed into a temporary shrine room, the Karmapa performed the Karma Pakshi initiation. 'Jamgon Kongtrul was travelling with the Karmapa at the time,' Levine remembers, 'and I asked him, "Why should I take this initiation?" I didn't know anything about it. And he said, "Just take it; it's good." So that's how most of us took it. Really it was just a blessing of the connection with Karma Pakshi. But it was very powerful. The Karmapa was in an altered state, if that's the phrase; there was definitely another being there, in his core. He got off this throne, and he had this skullcap filled with liquid in his hand and a spoon, and he was putting the liquid into our hands. He was barefoot, and he was dancing – this big, heavy man – as if he was in an ecstatic state of experience, completely blissed out. There was no way you could ever forget about Karmapa. Never.'

Leaving Europe, the Karmapa moved on to America, then Hawaii, where he was reunited with Ward Holmes, who acted as his driver and who had now taken the Tibetan name Yongdu. He recalls an incident when, driving along a twisting, coastal road, the Karmapa suddenly instructed him to stop the car. 'There was nothing around. I thought, why are we stopping here? But he got out and walked to the edge of the cliff, and when we looked down there was a car on the rocks below. It had turned over and there was a woman lying beside it with her head bleeding. He looked down and made some prayers and then said, "She'll be OK." Then he just got back in the car, and suddenly along came these ambulances and rescue vehicles. You couldn't see anything from the road.'

These supra-normal faculties could sometimes be used in a mischievous way, or with a motive that was not immediately apparent. The Karmapa, says Holmes, was particularly adept at avoiding certain situations by 'skilful means'. On the same visit, he had been invited by a local Buddhist centre to attend a reception which would include a performance by Hawaiian singers and hula dancers. 'He just wasn't interested. I was supposed to be driving him there, and he said, "Now we're going to go for lunch." I said, "But Karmapa, we're supposed to go to the reception." He said, "No, no, we'll go for Chinese lunch." So there was this long, long lunch, and finally it was time to leave. We drove half-way to the centre – it took maybe an hour – and then he said he'd forgotten his spittoon; he took snuff. So we had to drive all the way back; and just as we got to the restaurant, the car broke down. A brand-new car. I had just enough power to roll into a parking lot. So then I had to call up the centre and say not that Karmapa had been at a Chinese restaurant, but that the car had broken down. They had to send a van from the other side to pick us up. It turned out it was just some small fuse or something that had blown on my car. It was almost as if Karmapa had made it happen somehow, the timing was so perfect. So now we're driving in this van, and Karmapa suddenly realizes his spittoon is still back in the restaurant; we'd forgotten it in all the confusion over the car, so we have to turn round again . . . And by the time we arrived at the centre, the singing and dancing – the stuff he didn't want to see – was over, but everybody was still able to meet him.

'So this was a very skilful means of him extricating himself from the situation. Nobody for a moment thought that Karmapa hadn't wanted to come. It was mostly blamed on me – oh, Yongdu's car broke down, and he forgot this and that. And meanwhile, Karmapa was over in the corner, giggling.'

'The bodhisattva,' says Lama Yeshe Losal, 'is like a fisherman, reeling somebody in.' His own story, he said, was an example of this. Lama Yeshe himself had grown up in Tibet in the monastery of his older brother, Akong Rinpoche. But he had no interest in the religious life, and no desire whatsoever to become a monk. Nor was he any more interested when working with Akong and Chögyam Trungpa at Freda Bedi's young lama school.

When Akong and Trungpa left for England in 1963, Yeshe remained behind in India, working in Delhi as a translator for the Tibetan administration. It was there, in 1967, that he met the Karmapa for the first time. 'When I saw him my whole physical structure seemed to change,' he remembers. 'I had met many great lamas, and I was quite arrogant. I didn't have that kind of faith and devotion. But when I met Karmapa my heart was rolling with excitement and fear, as if I couldn't think this or do that without him seeing it. I really felt, whatever he said, I had to do.'

Karmapa instructed Yeshe to return with him to Rumtek. 'I was still a layperson then. He said I had to stay in the monastery. I said, "No, there's a big guesthouse out there, I'll stay there." But he said, "No, you'll stay in the monastery." So that's what I did. There was no room there. Many people, including some rinpoches, had to sleep on the floor. So I said, "I don't want to sleep on the floor." I was very arrogant. I could speak English. I thought I knew everything! And Karmapa said, "No, I'll give you a room." And he gave me a room! Nobody could understand why he was giving me special treatment. I wasn't even a monk; I was just an arrogant little boy.

'Then one day he called me and said go down to Thrangu Rinpoche – that was the abbot – and ask him to teach you the Four Foundations. And now I had to do all these prostrations for purification. I thought, I'm not going to do this! But there was nothing else I could do. I was trapped! So I ended up doing many thousands of prostrations. But my mind wasn't in it. All I could think of was escaping! I was torn between my connection to Karmapa and being drawn to the worldly life.'

When Chögyam Trungpa returned to Rumtek for a visit, Yeshe pleaded with him to be taken to England. 'I left Rumtek without seeing Karmapa. I didn't even say goodbye, because he would't have allowed me to go.' Yeshe arrived at Samye Ling in 1969. 'It was even more crazy than I expected.' Dope smoking was rife among the students. 'I took some interest in these sort of things.' He grew his hair, acquired a motorbike and took up the electric guitar. 'People called me the Tibetan Jimi Hendrix!' With money borrowed from his brother, Akong, he opened a boutique in the nearby town of Dumfries. 'I stayed in Samye Ling for five years, and never one day in the meditation room. I thought, this is for crazy people, and I'm not crazy! I thought, now I've escaped! But karma is so strange . . .'

In 1974, when Karmapa visited the West for the first time, Yeshe met him once again in London. 'He was smiling, saying, "Now you will not escape!" ' He told Yeshe that he must accompany him on his tour of America. And at the tour's conclusion, he instructed him to remain behind to work with another lama establishing a teaching centre in upstate New York, in a house that had been donated by a wealthy Chinese devotee, Mr C.T. Shen. 'Karmapa didn't ask me whether I wanted to stay or not,' says Lama Yeshe. 'He just told me, "You will be the secretary and treasurer and help build the centre there." There was no question about what I wanted. But I could never say no to Karmapa.' He was joined by Ward Holmes and a handful of Tibetan monks, and they laboured to convert the house into a teaching centre. After two years, however, they received word from Karmapa; he had decided the site was unsuitable. The house and land were sold, and a new property purchased in the small town of Woodstock in upstate New York, made famous by the huge rock festival which had taken place there in 1969. It was named KTD, Karma Triyana Dharmachakra. Yeshe was to remain there for the next three years. In 1980 he finally succumbed to the inevitable and took ordination from Karmapa as a monk. The good fisherman, he says, had reeled in his catch. And so he became Lama Yeshe. 'Karmapa told me I must go into solitary retreat. But before I did that, I heard that he was in hospital in

Chicago. I had $15,000 in the bank, and many religious objects. I thought, this is the time for me to offer everything I have, so I sent it all to His Holiness. And then I received a message. He said, "If Yeshe is sending me everything, why didn't he send me his bed too?" I had a very beautiful, fancy bed in my room, which I liked very much. Karmapa had never been to my room, but he knew!' Lama Yeshe went into retreat in 1981. He would not emerge for the next five years. Nor would he ever see the 16th Karmapa again.

The Karmapa had long been susceptible to health problems, but in middle-age his condition went into a marked decline. Like many Tibetans, a lifelong diet of butter tea had played havoc with his arteries. His weight ballooned, he moved ponderously, and he began to show symptoms of diabetes. In 1976, during the Karmapa's visit to Hawaii, Ward Holmes' physician father checked his blood sugar levels. 'My father said it was three times over what it should be and Karmapa should get to hospital straight away,' Holmes remembers. 'The Karmapa said not to worry, and that he was controlling it by yogic means and knew what he was doing. My father was shocked.' On another occasion, C.T. Shen arranged for him to be examined by a top consultant. To everybody's bemusement, the examination suggested he was in perfect health. 'People couldn't understand,' says Lama Yeshe. 'But he was giving a lesson in the nature of impermanence; one minute he would be sick, the next minute nothing could be found.'

By 1980, however, it was clear that his health was worsening. He had lost weight, and his physicians began to suspect that he was suffering from cancer. He flew to Singapore, where a gastrectomy was performed and part of his stomach removed. A pathology examination confirmed that he was suffering from cancer. But the operation appeared to be successful, and later that year he flew to America to undertake another tour of teaching centres. In New York he stopped to take more tests. Here he was joined by the young American doctor who was to act as his personal physician up to the moment of his death. Mitchell Levy was a specialist in critical care medicine. He was also a Buddhist, a student of Trungpa Rinpoche, and Trungpa's personal physician. He now took charge of the treatment of Karmapa. From New York, the Karmapa continued on his American tour. He had now developed Bell's palsy, a condition commonly associated with cancer, causing one of his eyes to droop, and giving his face a distressingly lopsided appearance. Ward Holmes, who accompanied him for part of the tour, recalls that the Karmapa would hardly eat. 'He'd say, let's go for ice-cream, but it was really just for the people around him. He'd have a lick or two, then pass it on and people would be so happy to get the ice-cream of Karmapa.' Holmes recalls being with him on another occasion when he was trying on some new shoes. 'I asked him, how do the shoes fit? And he said, shoes fit good, but body doesn't fit good any more.'

He returned to Rumtek, but his condition continued to worsen. Now he ordered craftsmen to construct a number of wooden and metal cases, to store the monastery's most precious treasures, including relics which had been passed down from the ancestors of the lineage, Naropa, Tilopa, Marpa and Gampopa. Among them was the most precious relic of all – the Vajra Crown.

'He knew that he was going to die,' says Lama Yeshe. 'He called the four heart sons and told them, "If you want to see the relics you must see them now." ' The treasures were placed first in wooden cabinets; in turn these were placed in cabinets made of steel. The locks were sealed with wax. The Karmapa instructed that they should not be touched by anyone, and should be opened only by his next incarnation. It was now clear to everyone that the Karmapa's condition was becoming critical. He wanted to stay at Rumtek, but he ceded to the wishes of his those around him to be flown to Hong Kong for further treatment.

'His stomach cancer had spread,' remembers Mitchell Levy, 'and he was also suffering from TB. It was the opinion of his Western doctors in Hong Kong, including myself, that the situation was very bleak, and that any further surgery or chemotherapy would not be productive. It was terminal. It was very, very hard for the heart sons to hear this. He had raised them – he was their spiritual father, and in many ways their physical father, in the sense that they were just kids when he first started taking care of them. There was a period when I was at clear odds with them. I had these two hats; the spiritually devoted Buddhist, and the Western doctor who was trusting to his skills. I said to them, His Holiness is going to die, and the best thing you can do is take him to Rumtek and allow him to spend the rest of his days in his monastery. But they felt they hadn't

done all they could do, and it was very important for them to feel
they had done everything they could. It was also very important to
His Holiness that they felt that too.'

Levy flew back to America. In his absence, every possible
treatment for the Karmapa was considered and employed. Chinese doctors were consulted on herbal remedies; a faith healer
laid on hands; another swung a pendulum over the Karmapa's
stomach. Finally, an American working in alternative therapies,
who claimed to have had some success treating Hollywood
personalities, prevailed on the Karmapa to be flown to America
for treatment.

In October 1981, the Karmapa flew from Hong Kong to Seattle,
where he was met by Mitchell Levy. The Karmapa was suffering
from low blood pressure and in a state of shock. Levy stabilized
his condition, and accompanied him on the last stage of his
journey to Chicago, and then to Mount Zion, Illinois, a thirty-
minute drive from the city, where he was admitted to the American International Clinic. The Karmapa was given a private room
in the Intensive Care Unit. The room next door became a dormitory for his closest disciples. Jamgon Kongtrul had accompanied
him from Hong Kong; Tai Situ had come from England where he
had been giving teachings, and Shamar Rinpoche also flew to
America to be at his side. Of the four heart sons only Gyaltsab
Rinpoche was absent; the Karmapa had instructed him to remain
in Rumtek, to take care of things in his absence.

Almost from the moment the Karmapa arrived at Mount Zion,
says Mitchell Levy, everybody in the hospital became aware of a
peculiar paradox. 'It was as if he'd come in to cheer everyone up.
You would expect somebody in his condition to be very weak and
sick and experiencing a lot of pain. But in fact he was his usual
beaming, magnificent self. All those things you read about in the
books about the great masters – openness, warmth, equanimity –
he would sit there in bed and radiate all those qualities. The staff
in the ICU [Intensive Care Unit] – and these are people who are
not easily impressed – just fell in love with him. They called him
'grandfather'. He didn't speak any English – Jamgon Kongtrul
was usually his translator. The doctors and nurses would ask,
"Are you having pain?" And Karmapa would laugh, and ask
them how they were doing. Everybody was just amazed that he

genuinely was more interested in how they were, than how he was himself. The fact that he was ill didn't appear from his demeanour to be the reason that he was in the hospital. We all get sick; you wind up in hospital, and there's no doubt that the reason you're there is for you. You're not there to find out how the doctors and nurses are doing. But Karmapa's demeanour almost made you wonder, are we here looking after him, or is he here looking after us? And, day by day, that really began to have an effect on the staff. They'd go to his room to bring him food and end up sitting there telling him their life story – "Well, I'm married, and I've got a couple of kids . . ." '

What the Karmapa was demonstrating, Levy now believes, was an exemplary lesson in the art of preparing for death. 'I think you could say that His Holiness was someone who understood how to bring to bear the resources of his attitude and his spiritual life to working with a physical illness. And in many ways that's the whole message. It's not, "Oh God, that was His Holiness; I could never deal with my illness like that." The foundation of Buddhist principles is that everybody possesses *bodhicitta* and the possibility of becoming enlightened and, moment to moment, you have the possibility of discovering something of that in yourself. And because they lived with his example every day, the staff understood that. They didn't feel they were witnessing a miracle; they realized that here was a guy who was setting an example of how to deal with this. It was just inspiring to see someone really able to make peace with their illness and care about others as much as himself.'

Throughout the four weeks that he lay in the ICU, says Levy, the Karmapa refused all sedatives or painkillers. His English, limited to only to the most basic pleasantries, now included a new phrase: 'No pain.' On one occasion, the Karmapa's usual surgeon was off duty and Levy was late arriving at the hospital. The covering physician, unable to believe that the Karmapa was not in acute discomfort, administered morphine. 'He immediately got very groggy and drowsy, and his blood pressure went down. It was a very striking example of the way his state of mind was controlling his body, because once you interfered with that with the morphine, his physical condition deteriorated very rapidly. I came in and very quickly gave him an agent that reverses morphine, and he was absolutely fine.'

In these last days, a succession of senior lamas from the Kagyu order made the pilgrimage to his bedside. There was unfinished business to settle. In the years since they had been together at Samye Ling, the discord between Akong Rinpoche and Trungpa Rinpoche had festered. Trungpa had published a revised edition of his autobiography, *Born in Tibet*, in which he had talked about his disagreements with Akong at Samye Ling and made disparaging remarks about his old friend. Others had encouraged Akong Rinpoche to reply. Now, in his last moments, Karmapa called them both to his bedside and told them there should be no more disputes between them. 'He said, "I consider both of you as my sons," ' remembers Akong. ' "Now you have to promise there are no more bad feelings between you, only friendship." ' He told Trungpa to remove the references to Akong in his book, and made Akong promise never to speak of it again. 'So we both agreed. And Karmapa was very happy.'

He also made a decision that some would interpret as being an important indicator about his feelings towards the respective heart sons. There was a Buddhist conference going on in Belgium, to which Tai Situ had been invited as the Karmapa's representative. But the Karmapa said he wanted Tai Situ to stay with him, and that Shamar should go to Belgium instead. Akong was told to go with Shamar.

On the day of Akong's departure for Brussels, the Karmapa again called him to his side. 'He asked me to draw the curtain,' remembers Akong, 'and then he said, "All the Kagyu lineage have been here to see me, so now I can die." I didn't reply. I asked him to repeat it, because I wanted to be sure what he'd said. And he repeated, "I'm going to die." Then I called [Tai] Situ Rinpoche, and he and Jamgon [Kongtrul] Rinpoche came in, and the Karmapa told them also, now he would be dying soon. They were very upset. They said, you cannot die. And they offered long-life prayers, and Karmapa said, "yes, yes", but it was not a very strong response.' By now pneumonia had set in and doctors inserted a tube into his lungs to help him breathe. 'We asked him if he wanted that,' says Mitchell Levy. 'He said whatever the heart sons and I felt was necessary he would do. He never once expressed to me that he wanted any of it; but he made it very clear that he put his faith and trust in the heart sons and in my medical recommendations. That made it harder in a way, because as a physician you want to do what your patient wants you to do; you want to act as a patient's advocate. But His Holiness was basically saying, it doesn't matter to me what happens to me, I'll do what you want.'

At last, on the evening of 5 November 1981, the Karmapa suffered a massive cardiac arrest. It was clear, says Mitchell Levy, that there was no possibility of resuscitation, and he was allowed to die. 'The staff were just devastated,' says Levy. 'They'd come to regard him as their grandfather, and they were just devastated.'

According to Buddhist teachings, realized practitioners, at the moment of death, go into a state of *samadhi*, in which consciousness continues to reside in the body. This state of *samadhi* is regarded as a critical moment in the transition of consciousness into the *bardo* – the intermediary state between death and rebirth. It is regarded as a great blessing to be in the presence of an enlightened being in such a state, 'like the first rays of light from the spring sun', and it is considered important that during this time the body is not disturbed.

The normal hospital rules were waived. For three days, the body of the Karmapa lay where he had died, as his disciples gathered around. In this period, Mitchell Levy witnessed the remarkable physiological effects of spiritual realization. 'I think Tai Situ and Jamgon Kongtrul wanted me as a witness in some way, and also because I had gained their trust and was devoted to His Holiness, they didn't feel that my being near His Holiness would disturb him. So once or twice a day, they'd bring me in to put my hand over his heart, or feel his skin texture. And for three days I could feel there was some warmth coming from his heart-centre. [Three days is] a little bit too long to explain from a medical point of view. Also, there's a pliancy, a resilience to normal skin, and that was definitely still there after three days. As a physician I have no explanation. And as far as the heart sons were concerned I was the scribe, the witness. It was like, let's show these white boys what it's all about. There would be these knowing, pleased glances when they would see the astonishment on my face.'

Levy describes caring for the Karmapa up to the moment of his death as 'much more of a spiritual education than all my years of

Buddhist practice'. The Karmapa, he says, 'allowed you the illusion of taking care of him, when what he was really doing was teaching on a very deep level what it means to offer care. As a doctor you want to form a partnership with someone to help them get better, but ultimately it's up to each individual. And that was particularly true taking care of His Holiness. I would come in in the morning and he'd have a bowl of grapes in front of him. I'd say, "Those are grapes!" And he'd say, "That's because I can't eat sugar." I'd say, "That's still sugar . . ." And he'd just laugh, because he knew that. The day after he died, Jamgon Rinpoche and Situ Rinpoche sat me down and said, "We realize His Holiness did all of this for our benefit. We realize now that he knew he was dying and that it was his compassion that brought him to Chicago. He allowed us to do this for him so that we would feel we had done everything we could." And I think that's absolutely true. He knew they needed to feel they had done everything they could for him.'

In accordance with tradition, the Karmapa's body was placed in a casket packed with salt. A flight from Chicago took the casket first to New York, where in the VIP lounge at JFK airport some forty Buddhists from local centres sat in meditation as the casket was transferred to another flight, for the Karmapa's long and final journey home to Rumtek.

Among devotees, who sought intention and meaning in all things, the Karmapa's death was a cause not only of grief but also of bewilderment. What did it mean that he had died of cancer, and in America? If he was omniscient, as the Buddhist teachings said, why had he succumbed to illness, and at such a relatively young age?

In fact, history suggests that the Karmapas had tended to die young. The 4th Karmapa, Rolpe Dorje, died at the age of forty-three; the 5th, Dezhin Shegpa, at the age of thirty-one, and the 11th, Yeshe Dorje, when he was just twenty-six. But rather than being a sign of physical frailty, it was said that this was a sign of the bodhisattva's compassion, taking on the illnesses, the bad karma, of others. Tibetan legend provided countless stories about this. The great Tibetan yogi Milarepa was said to have once demonstrated just a small fraction of the pain that he was carrying on behalf of his disciples by shattering a wooden door with a single glance.

For Mitchell Levy, caring for the Karmapa up until the moment of his death was a lesson in the bodhisattva ideal. 'I think it's true of a lot of Tibetan lamas, and it was true of Trungpa Rinpoche as well, that they take a lot of cultural and karmic illnesses on themselves, and they definitely show the effects of it. There is no question of this. And that's why historically a lot of them don't live very long. But the human body is the human body. If you get hit by a truck, you bleed. If you get diabetes it eventually takes its toll. In many ways, the gift these people give is a message that enlightenment is enlightenment and it's timeless; but when you're born, there's birth, old age, sickness and death, and that's inevitable. And it's coming to grips with that inevitability which allows us the possibility of discovering the enlightened mind.'

Others consoled themselves ~~them~~ with the thought that, as painful as his death may have been, it was surely intentioned, the unfolding of some greater karmic design, the true meaning of which would be revealed in the fullness of time. Ponlop Rinpoche, the son of the Karmapa's general secretary Damchoe, remembers his father's distress on first learning that the Karmapa was dying. 'This was in Hong Kong, before His Holiness was taken to America. His Holiness told me father that soon he would be going into *paranirvana* [dying]. My father was very upset. He was crying and begging with His Holiness not to die. But His Holiness told him, you don't have to worry; I will come back. And I will appear even more powerful, much greater, much more learned. So it seems like there is this purpose. Times change, maybe he can benefit more in the body of a young, energetic Karmapa.'

On 9 November, a helicopter carrying the Karmapa's body landed at a military airstrip near Gangtok. A Mercedes truck carrying his coffin, with the four heart sons squeezed on to the front seat, wound up the narrow, twisting roads to Rumtek. A group of people, including Ole Nydahl, carried the coffin into the monastery.

His body was enshrined in an upstairs hall, in a posture of sitting meditation, surrounded by a shimmering sea of butter lamps. For the next forty-nine days the sound of chanting, the beating of drums and the drone of *gyalings* and long-horns echoed through the monastery as the four heart sons led pujas to purify obstacles and request the speedy return of the Karmapa's reincarnation. On 20 December a crowd of more than 10,000 people, including political dignitaries from India and the Bhutanese royal family, gathered at the monastery. At midday, the body was carried in ceremony to the roof of the main balcony and placed in a newly built clay stupa, constructed in the shape of a mandala. In the grounds below, trumpeters from the Sikkimese division of the Indian National Guard sounded the last post, and a contingent of soldiers fired a twenty-one-gun salute. Tradition demands that someone who has not received teachings from the Karmapa should light the funeral pyre. A monk who had recently arrived from Tibet stepped forward with a torch to ignite the dry sandalwood heaped at the foot of the stupa. Within minutes, it was enveloped in flames, which leaped twenty foot high.

Norma Levine, who had travelled from Britain for the funeral, found herself carried up to the roof of the monastery in the throng, barely able to breathe because of the crush. Watching the stupa burn she was struck by 'a feeling of some kind of light going out of the world'. As the smoke spiralled upwards, mourners were astonished to see what Levine describes as 'a halo' appearing to encircle the sun in an otherwise cloudless sky. Some claimed to have also seen a flock of birds circumambulating the monastery roof, as if in tribute.

The four heart sons, clad in ceremonial robes and crowns, had taken up positions around the stupa in the four cardinal directions, to make pujas and offerings of water, oil and ghee at the 'gates' of the stupa. As Tai Situ stepped forward to make an offering, something suddenly seemed to leap out of the blazing stupa. Unsure what to do, Tai Situ despatched a monk to the most venerable lama in the gathering, Kalu Rinpoche. A few minutes later, the monk returned to tell Tai Situ that the object was undoubtedly something very sacred and should be preserved. It was placed in a silver chalice and carried away. The object, it was declared, was the Karmapa's heart and tongue, *tug jag jensum*, representing his speech and mind, fused together in the heat of the funeral pyre but only partially charred. It was the same sacred object which, legend had it, had been found among the ashes of the funeral pyre of the first Karmapa, Dusum Khyenpa, and in the funeral pyre of Gampopa. The ceremony completed, the stupa was sealed. Small sachets of the salt in which the Karmapa's body had been packed for its journey from America were handed out to devotees. Some people said that it would guard against cancer, so great was the Karmapa's power. The silver chalice containing the Karmapa's heart and tongue was placed in a shrine room.

On the following day, the senior lamas and rinpoches of the Karma Kagyu school and representatives from centres all over the world gathered together in the meeting hall of Rumtek's Nalanda Institute. The heart and tongue, said Tai Situ, signified the Karmapa's heart transmission to his four heart sons and the fact that he was still with his followers and 'all sentient beings'. He would take it to his monastery at Sherab Ling and construct a stupa of solid gold, 'at least two or three feet high', and place the heart inside it. Then Damchoe Yongdu spoke: the stupa, he said, should be at least five feet high, and built at Rumtek. They would need to collect gold. People began to take off wedding rings, necklaces, and earrings and pass them forward, the offerings jangling in a box that had been hastily provided.

CHAPTER FIVE

The Golden Rosary

Sherab Ling: August 2000.

The death of the Karmapa left a gaping void at Rumtek, and an immediate necessity – to find the instructions pertaining to his next incarnation. Tradition held that a Karmapa would entrust his prediction letter, or some indication of his next birth, to a trusted disciple. But the 16th, it seemed, had left no such letter, no such instructions. With the ashes from his cremation pyre not yet cold, Damchoe Yongdu and the youngest of the heart sons, Jamgon Kongtrul, made a systematic search of the Karmapa's rooms and belongings, but without success. Among the inner circle, consternation began to grow. Tulku Urgyen Rinpoche, a close friend of the late Karmapa and one of the four heart sons' most respected teachers, suggested that they say nothing about having failed to find a letter. The Karmapa, he argued, would not have died without leaving some form of instructions. Finding them was just a matter of time.

Over the centuries the task of deciphering the Karmapas' prediction letters, and finding and enthroning the new incarnations, had fallen to any one of a number of the senior-most lineage holders. The four heart sons, the 16th Karmapa's closest disciples and lineage holders – Shamar, Tai Situ, Jamgon Kongtrul and Gyaltsab – were now in their twenties. All of their previous incarnations had, at some time, been involved in bringing Karmapas to the throne, and it was to them that the responsibility fell, not only of ensuring the recognition of the Karmapa's next rebirth, but of fulfilling his dying wishes.

Before his death, the Karmapa had inaugurated a series of major projects. Of these, the construction of a new monastic college at Rumtek, the Nalanda Institute for Higher Buddhist Studies, was almost completed. In Delhi, foundations had been laid for another college of Buddhist studies, which would be called the Karmapa International Buddhist Institute (KIBI), on land which had been donated to the Karmapa by the Indian government. The Karmapa had also set in train the printing of 500 sets of the Tengyur, the complete collection of commentaries on the Buddha's teachings, to be distributed to major Buddhist libraries and universities around the world. It was agreed that Jamgon Kongtrul would supervise the completion of the Nalanda Institute, while the construction of the new school in Delhi would be the responsibility of Shamar Rinpoche. The printing of the Tengyur was also to be completed in Delhi.

In 1961, the Karmapa had also established the Karmapa Charitable Trust, with the broad aim of maintaining Rumtek, raising money for medical and educational projects and supporting refugees. It was the responsibility of the Trust to manage the affairs of Rumtek. But the Karmapa had left no specific instructions as to who should serve as his Regent until such time as his next incarnation was found. It now fell to Damchoe Yongdu to devise a plan whereby the four heart sons would share the responsibility for the management of Rumtek and the Karmapa's affairs until the coming of age of the 17th reincarnation. Each of the heart sons, Damchoe decreed, would hold the office of Regent for three years, by rotation, supported by the other three. Shamar Rinpoche, as the senior of the four, would be the first to hold office. For the first three years, this plan held good. Then, as one lama would put it, 'things began to go wrong'.

To reach Sherab Ling, the monastery of the Tai Situpa, I took a two-hour taxi ride from Dharamsala. The road snaked through the Dhauladhar valley, the foothills of the Himalayas visible on the northern horizon. The driver drove as if he were playing an arcade game, at breakneck speed, throwing me from side to side as we sped through small hamlets and across bridges under which the water, sluicing down from the mountains, foamed and tumbled, swollen by the summer rains. At every turn of the road, men stood to piss, apparently incapable of either bladder control or embarrassment. Occasionally, flocks of cyclists passed by in the opposite direction, red and gold flags flying from their handlebars – pilgrims effecting a laborious circuit of all the temples in the region. The road narrowed as we passed through small villages, little more than a single street of shops and stalls; scrums of pedestrians, dodging the traffic; music jangling from shop doorways; the smell of wood-smoke and cooking; the inevitable stand-off between trucks and buses, fighting to squeeze through. At the village of Baijnath we turned towards the mountains, the narrow road winding ever upwards, twisting and turning on itself. Swathes of white cumulus cloud had settled into the folds of the mountains ahead of us, completely obscuring their peaks. Now we passed into a pine forest, the driver down-shifting gears to accommodate the precipitous climb. Tattered prayer flags, their blessings bleached by the rain and sun, were strung in the trees and across the road, signalling that we were nearing the monastery. We rounded a corner, and lurched to a sudden halt.

A truck stood in our path, skewed at an angle across the road. Coming down the hill, it had seemingly come off its rear axle. Only a miracle had prevented it swerving off the road into the ravine. The driver and his mate stood beside the truck smoking, apparently at a loss as to what to do next. The prospect of it being moved in the immediate future seemed remote. I hoisted my luggage out of the taxi and set off on foot up the hill. After a few hundred yards I passed under a white arch. To the right, visible among the trees were a cluster of magnificent stupas, some more than thirty feet high, moulded in white plaster, and surmounted by cupolas of gold. The road forked down the hill towards the roofs of some monastery buildings, crowned by a shining gold pagoda, visible at some distance through the trees.

Sherab Ling had been built in two stages. Half-way down the hill were the original monastery buildings, shrouded in scaffolding and evidently under reconstruction. At the bottom of the hill was the new monastery, a huge building three storeys high, its fascia decorated in the traditional Tibetan style. Passing through an archway, I emerged into a wide flagstoned courtyard, flanked on three sides by barrack-like blocks containing dormitories, offices and classrooms; on the fourth side, a broad flight of steps led up to the doors of the temple itself. Two carved, golden lions stood guard. The heavy wooden doors, elaborately plaited tassels hanging from their huge brass handles, would have served to repel invaders in a medieval castle. On either side the walls were covered in vividly coloured frescoes depicting protector deities – a dazzling bestiary of scowling, bulging-eyed creatures, crowned with aureoles of fire, draped in tiger skins and necklaces of skulls, striding through mythical landscapes of foaming rivers and mountains under billowing psychedelic skies. Stepping through the doors I was assailed by a smell of incense and wood polish. The temple was bathed in a half-light. Brightly coloured *thankas* – highly detailed religious paintings, framed in silk – decorated the walls, and ornate tapestries hung from the ceiling. At the far end stood a forty-foot-high statue of Maitreya, the Buddha of the next *kalpa*, or age – so high that its head protruded into the floor above. Climbing the stairs to the next floor brought you level with the statue's eyes. The head was undergoing restoration and was swathed in scaffolding, its pendulous ears already gilded, but its exquisitely shaped features were yet to be painted.

I took a seat outside the room where Tai Situ was receiving visitors. A handful of monks was also awaiting an audience, along with a Tibetan family, a husband and wife and teenage daughter, clutching *khatas*, looking nervous. One by one, they were ushered into the room, emerging after a few minutes until, at length, it was my turn.

The Tai Situpa sat cross-legged on an elevated platform. He greeted me with a warm smile, but did not get up. Protocol. He was dressed in a yellow sleeveless silk shirt, a shawl of fine buttery cotton thrown over his shoulder. His skin was pale, almost white; his complexion smooth and unlined. He looked to be in his late twenties, although he was twenty years older. His hair was cropped short, accentuating his long sideburns – an intimation, perhaps, of vanity. His large gold-framed spectacles seemed as much a signature as a necessity.

I crouched down in front of him to present my *khata*, which he draped around my neck before beckoning me to take a

seat beside him, set at a lower level than his own. An attendant
stood silently to one side, holding a string of red silk protection
cords.

I asked Tai Situ, 'How are you?' – a pleasantry, but he sighed
deeply, apparently weighing the question at face value.

Being a rinpoche, he said, was a great responsibility. He smiled.
'Perhaps I would have been better off if I had been born as a
shoeshine boy.'

Did he actually say shoeshine boy? I was unsure how to
respond.

'Not so much responsibility, perhaps,' he went on, 'but then
again, hard work.'

'At least you would develop your arm muscles,' I said, disarmed
by the direction the conversation was taking and clutching for
something to say. He gave me a querulous look.

'Arm muscles?' He mimicked shining shoes. 'Wrists
perhaps . . .'

The conversation moved on. I had come armed with questions
about Tibetan Buddhism, Tai Situ's life, the question of the
Karmapa, but, for the moment at least, he clearly had no
intention of answering any of them. I sensed he was sizing me
up. Somehow, over the next twenty minutes our conversation
hopped from the vicissitudes of monastic life, to the rarity of
women rinpoches, to Roman gladiatorial combat. Women rinpoches may be rare, I said, but did he know that there were
women gladiators in Rome. (What on earth was possessing me to
say these things?)

'Really?' Tai Situ laughed uproariously. 'Very good! Equality!'

I had been told that he had a light humour, but this was
positively surreal.

And how long, he asked, did I intend to stay in India? We
discussed my travel arrangements, the possibility that I would be
changing my itinerary, the availability of seats of trains.

'You know they keep allocations for foreigners,' he said.

'I think it's been stopped . . .' I said.

'Oh, that's a pity.'

'More fair, perhaps . . .' I ventured.

Tai Situ laughed. 'Why should you think that? You're a
foreigner!' I should stay in the monastery as long as I liked,

he said. I was his guest. He gestured to his attendant to give me a protection cord. 'And come and see me on Wednesday.'

The meeting was apparently over.

I took a room in the monastery guesthouse, located a brisk twenty-minute stroll through the woods from the main monastery building itself. There was hot water in the showers, an obliging staff in the kitchen providing rice and vegetables and endless cups of sweet tea. It was evident that by usual monastic standards Sherab Ling was a wealthy and extremely well-ordered institution. It accommodated more than 400 monks, the majority, it seemed, in their teens and twenties. There was a large *shedra*, or school, and a medical institute; a huge satellite dish sat on the flat roof of the administrative offices; smart four-wheel drive Armada jeeps – India's luxury utility vehicle – came and went down the rutted road at regular intervals, laden with monks and monastery dignitaries. Outside the monastery wall was a large patch of dusty ground where the monks played volleyball, or lounged outside a small cafe, selling food and basic provisions.

It is a fallacy that monasteries are places of quiet and tranquillity. From dawn until dusk, Sherab Ling echoed to the sounds of workmen hammering, the chatter of young monks as they crossed back and forth across the courtyard, running between classes and pujas. The mournful sound of horns and the clatter of drums drew me to the temple. Some thirty monks were seated cross-legged on the floor, enacting one of the obligatory daily rituals, chanting from prayer sheets balanced in front of them on wooden lecterns. A boy monk, no more than eight years old, measured time by banging on a drum hung from an ornate wooden frame. Another noisily coughed up phlegm into a scrap of cloth and amused himself by furtively flicking grains of rice, dropped from the offerings tray, at a friend. The chant went on for about thirty minutes, incessant and rhythmic, gathering in pace until, at some unseen signal, it climaxed in a cacophony of horns, drums and cymbals. The monks gathered their robes around them and filed out of the temple. Walking back across the courtyard, I caught a drift of the distinctive monastery smell: a peculiar compound of incense, wood-smoke, the pungent aroma of kitchens and latrines.

Before Tai Situ came here, there had been only jungle where the monastery now stood. That was in 1975, he explained. He was twenty-two, and having spent the past nine years at Rumtek, growing up under the protection of the Karmapa, he had been invited to visit Ladakh by another senior Kagyu lama, Drupön Dechen Rinpoche. On his way from Rumtek to Ladakh, Tai Situ stopped at Bir, a few miles from where Sherab Ling now stood and where there is a large Tibetan community. There, the local people offered him a large tract of jungle which had been given to them by the Indian government, but was too far away from the encampment to be turned to good use; furthermore, there was no electricity, no water, and no road. Tai Situ hiked into hills to reconnoitre the site. 'And it was very interesting. As I was climbing this little hill I met a Tibetan girl, walking towards me from the forest. She was leading a donkey, packed with firewood, and she was carrying a bundle of peacock feathers. I felt this was very special. Our protector deity is Mahakala, and Mahakala's consort is Mahakali. Mahakali is always depicted riding a donkey, and she also has a peacock feather on her crown. So that was very auspicious. I asked the girl her name, and she said Tsering Tara. Tseringma is one of the five deities of Mount Everest, Milarepa's deity. When Milarepa was doing meditation in the caves, these deities offered food for him. And Tara is a very important deity for the Tai Situs. The 8th, 9th, 10th and 11th all did Tara practice. Then, wood is my element – I am horse, but a wooden horse.' He paused and smiled. 'We Tibetans are maybe a little eccentric about these things . . .

'And then, when we got to the site, there were three families living there, and one old lady gave me yoghurt; yoghurt is one of the eight auspicious ingredients. Then she brought a naked boy to me to be blessed – a little fat, naked boy, maybe one year old, and he looked like a frog. I don't mean that in a bad way! I asked her, "What is his name?" And she said "Frog!" Later he became my monk. So all this was very interesting . . .'

'And it was all these signs,' I said, 'that convinced you to build the monastery here?'

'Not only that. It was a quiet place, very beautiful, and the land was there. So why not? Even if there had been no signs I would have taken it!' Tai Situ burst into laughter.

It was our second meeting, this time in his office, high above the temple, adjacent to his private quarters. A small white lapdog was tethered to his door. Tai Situ was seated behind a laminate desk, surrounded by filing cabinets and bookshelves. A complimentary calendar from a stationery supplier hung on the wall behind him. This was the rinpoche as administrator. At one point, to check a date, he riffled through his desk and produced an *Economist* diary, red, pocket-size, embossed in gold letters 'H.E. Tai Situ'. (I was always struck by these strange cultural non sequiturs; also for instance the fact that the monastery's telephone answering machine played a particularly treacly version of the theme from *Love Story*.)

A monk brought tea and biscuits. I asked Tai Situ to tell me something about the historical relationship between his lineage and the Karmapas.

He smiled and settled back in his chair. 'In Tibetan culture, you never talk about yourself. But nowadays everybody has to put their résumé up there; and it is not a shameful thing, but an expected thing to do, so I'll try. I'm supposed to be 12th Tai Situ. The first Tai Situ was actually a reincarnation of a great Tibetan master whose line goes back many generations. During the time of the 1st Karmapa he was Drogen Rechen, the first Karmapa's disciple [and to whom he entrusted his prediction letter]. Before that there's one, then another one, and then there's Marpa . . .'

So he was the reincarnation of Marpa?

He shrugged. 'Well that's what they say. And then before Marpa it goes back to India . . .' He waved his hand, suggesting a lineage stretching back into the mists of time. 'So in that way, for each incarnation of Gyalwa Karmapa there was a Tai Situ, always a disciple; and for quite a few times he was the guru as well as the disciple.'

Then he spoke about the Golden Rosary, the series of teachings transmitted from the Karmapa to his disciples, and back again, in an unbroken chain over the course of more than 900 years. 'The Karmapas are the backbone of the Golden Rosary; then there are other masters who are in the Golden Rosary according to their service to Karmapa.' Some Tai Situs were in the Golden Rosary, he said, some were not. Sometimes Shamars, Gyaltsabs or others were in it. 'But all of the masters who were at least once in the Golden Rosary in their incarnation are considered to be in the

Karma Kagyu lineage of what we call "The Glorious Father and Son".' The cement that held the lineage together, he said, was *samaya*, a bond of trust, loyalty and devotion to the guru (in this case Karmapa) which ensured the purity of the teachings and their benefit for all. To break *samaya* was the equivalent of a cardinal sin, threatening not only the destruction of the lineage but also one's own future rebirths.

The teachings of the Golden Rosary comprised innumerable different practices, and there was a lineage for every one of them – for each initiation, every ritual, for a multitude of meditation practices. The heart and essence of it all were the Mahamudra teachings on the true nature of mind. This was the highest form of transmission from master to disciple, likened to nectar being poured from one vase into another and back again. At the heart of this teaching, he said, was the belief that every action, every experience has an ultimate, essential and sacred value, a potential far greater than it may appear. 'And that is regardless of whether something is supposed to be holy or unholy, good or bad. And also we don't believe that our essence and the Buddha is a separate thing; we are Buddha, always – but we just don't realize that.'

'So our true Buddha nature,' I said, 'is obscured, like a diamond covered in mud?'

'Actually, that is one example used by Lord Maitreya. There are nine examples that describe Buddha nature; another one is that an Emperor is in the womb of a beggar lady. This lady is so poor, she has nothing, not even to eat, and she is begging, but she is carrying the Emperor.' He smiled. 'That's wonderful, isn't it?'

Our talk turned to the 16th Karmapa. Tai Situ had come to Rumtek when he was thirteen years old, and said he had spent virtually every day with Karmapa until he left Rumtek at the age of twenty-two. 'I think he thought highly of me. He always described Jamgon Rinpoche and I as his gurus' incarnations, because the 11th Tai Situ, my predecessor, was his main guru; and the second Jamgon Kongtrul was his guru as well. So that way he really always took very special care of us. Of course, he took very special care of Shamarpa and Gyaltsab Rinpoche, equally actually. But because he had tremendous respect for the previous Tai Situ, that was a tremendous encouragement for me; I felt, I have to do well, I have to study hard, I have to practise well, because I have this responsibility. I can't let him down. I felt that very strongly.' The Karmapa, Tai Situ went on, was 'a warm man – really like a father, but more than a father. But also very strict! Maybe, in the first place it was because Rumtek monastery was very new, with lots of monks and everything just starting to be established. I think he had to be severe for everybody to start well. But for me it was a great inspiration that he was strict. I was there [for] studying.'

In the years between leaving Rumtek in 1975 and the death of the Karmapa in 1981, he had seen Karmapa many times. 'He was travelling too, but we would meet – in Delhi, Calcutta, Rumtek, many places. I would talk about my projects and he would give me advice, and he would give me teachings.' When the Karmapa fell ill in Hong Kong, Tai Situ was in Britain, on a teaching tour. He flew to Hong Kong to be at the Karmapa's side. 'Then I had to go back. His Holiness was supposed to go back to Sikkim, that's what he told me. I was in London when I heard he had been taken to America, so I cancelled everything and flew to America. I was with him all the time until he passed away. And then bringing his body back to Rumtek . . .' He fell silent.

Thinking about the teachings on the intermediary state between death and rebirth, I asked, where did the Karmapa 'go' after his death?

He laughed. 'I don't know! He could be gone somewhere else, or maybe stay in some meditative state. He could be reborn in another universe. Maybe only he knows that . . .'

So does he 'choose' to reincarnate in the form of Karmapa, or is that reincarnation spontaneous?

'It's the same thing. We believe Karmapa is omniscient, and omniscience transcends any dualism. And in that case there is no difference between intention or spontaneity.'

My confusion must have been apparent.

'It's like this. Whatever time Karmapa dies is the right time; whatever time he is reborn has to be the right time too. There can be no doubt in this.'

According to the tradition, Tai Situ too was a bodhisattva. Did he, I wondered, see the world in a non-dualistic way?

He pondered the question. 'Sometimes. When I do meditation and practice in my shrine, on my cushion, in front of my Buddha, and when everything's going well I have glimpses of these things. But glimpses does not mean very much. It's like a very good kung fu master who can break bricks and all these things, but when he gets attacked by four big men he forgets everything, and the only thing he knows is how to run away!'

But isn't it the case, I asked, that he was believed to be Maitreya, the Buddha to come?

'That's what they say! But that's a long time in the future. Do you have a pen?' I passed him one and he scribbled some figures on a scrap of paper. 'It's written in the Abidharma and the Bhadrakalpa Sutra when Lord Maitreya will attain enlightenment. Roughly 20,000 times 100, a little bit more – so maybe two to three million years from now! But that's if I am the real incarnation of the Lord Maitreya himself – if I am not the incarnation of his sandal. Although when he attains enlightenment, I think even for his sandal something will happen!' He laughed. 'You have to be a little bit pragmatic about these things. You can never become Buddha by mistake. I'm very happy. If I can improve by just one per cent in my lifetime, then in 100 lifetimes perhaps I will be Buddha. What more can I ask?'

Growing up in Rumtek, Tai Situ told me, the four heart sons were 'like brothers' under the fatherly gaze of their spiritual guru, Karmapa. He and Jamgon Kongtrul were linked by their common affiliation to Palpung, Tai Situ's seat in Tibet, where the Jamgon Rinpoches also traditionally resided. He was close to Gyaltsab Rinpoche because they studied together, and because their previous incarnations had been friends.

'But Shamarpa,' he said, 'was the real friend of mine. He and I are from the same region in Tibet, Derge. I am from – how do you say it? – ordinary people, but Shamarpa's father was one of the top four ministers of our King. His father was Karmapa's brother. So I have lots of respect for him from that point of view. Although I am Tai Situ, we are Khampas so we respect our King and Lords. We consider loyalty very, very important. But at the same time we were really friends. We would spend hours together playing and sharing many many things.' Tai Situ's particular interest was drawing and calligraphy. The Shamarpa, he said, was also very artistic. 'He likes flowers. I think he liked to draw. He is very good at poetry, and his calligraphy is really good. And his lama dancing is very good, really the best. He's very, very talented; very intelligent. We would draw together, read epics and play chess – all kind of things. Sometimes we'd even have little cooking parties and things like that. We were teenagers and you cook something . . . it doesn't mean you're hungry, you know!' He laughed. 'It's not as if we could order pizzas.'

Behind this idyllic picture of shared childhood pleasures, however, lay a more uneasy relationship, rooted in the tangled web of reincarnation, family connections and theological politics which constitute Kagyu history. The present Shamar Rinpoche – the 14th – was recognized by the 16th Karmapa in 1956, when he was four years old. The recognition was important for two reasons. Firstly, the new Shamar was the Karmapa's nephew. Secondly, it marked the return to the fold of perhaps the most controversial figure in the history of the Karma Kagyu school.

The Karmapas and Shamarpas had a relationship going back to the beginning of the fourteenth century when the 3rd Karmapa, Rangjung Dorje, bestowed the title Shamarpa upon a monk named Khedrub Drakpa Senge, giving him a ruby-red crown, which was an exact facsimile of his own black crown. The Shamar Rinpoches quickly rose to become the second most important lineage in the Kagyu hierarchy. In the Byzantine world of theological hierarchy, status was measured by the height of the throne. By the time of the 5th Shamarpa in the sixteenth century, it is said that his throne had been raised to a height only four fingers less than that of the Karmapa himself. But the Shamarpas had a political as well as a spiritual importance. While the Karmapas tended to avoid wherever possible the labyrinthine intrigues of Tibetan politics, their reputation resting on their skills as teachers and miracle workers, the Shamarpas showed a distinct proclivity and talent for political machination.

The 4th Shamarpa acted as cardinal-counsellor to the Phamo Drupa dynasty that ruled central Tibet at the time, and whose patronage established the Karma Kagyu as the dominant religious school in Tibetan affairs. After the Gelugpa wrested political control in the sixteenth century, under Mongol patronage, the Shamarpas proved a constant thorn in their side. Matters came to a head with the 10th Shamarpa and an event that would have consequences that would resonate into the twenty-first century. The 10th Shamar Rinpoche was born into a wealthy aristocratic family in the U-Tsang region of central Tibet in 1742. Even by the querulous standards of identifiable reincarnation, he was born into a particularly blessed family, for his two elder brothers were also recognized as reincarnates. One was the Chungpa Hutuktu Tulku a Gelugpa rinpoche; the other, more significantly, was the 6th Panchen Lama – the second most important figure in the Gelugpa hierarchy after the Dalai Lama himself. The 10th Shamarpa was a brilliant scholar; fluent in Chinese, Nepali and Hindi, he travelled extensively throughout the Himalayan region, cultivating close relations with the Nepalese royal family. It was these connections that were to lead, ultimately to his downfall. There are conflicting accounts of what actually occurred. In 1780, the Panchen Lama died of smallpox in Beijing, where he was visiting the Chinese Emperor. As tribute, the Emperor made a gift of a large quantity of gold coins to the Panchen Lama's family. But the Chungpa Hutuktu, who was also the Panchen's Regent, supposedly refused to share the gift with the Shamar on the grounds that he was of the Kagyu school, maintaining instead that the money belonged to the Panchen's monastery of Tashilhunpo, in the town of Shigatse. Considering himself ill-served, the Shamar fled to Nepal, where, it is said, he incited the King to invade Tibet in order to secure the spoils from Tashilhunpo. Evidently, not much incitement was required. Tibet's relations with Nepal had been strained ever since the Gurkhas had seized power in Nepal in 1769, festering in a long-running dispute over currency and customs duty. In 1791 the Gurkhas attacked Tibet, reaching as far as the town of Shigatse, where they looted the homes of aristocratic families and Tashilhunpo monastery. It was at this point that the Chinese Emperor intervened.

Historically, the Tibetans had always regarded their relationship to the Mongol and Chinese emperors as one of 'Cho'yon', the term given to the relationship between a religious figure and a lay patron. The Chinese, however, regarded Tibet in a more proprietorial light, and stationed ambans, or envoys, in Lhasa to protect their interests. Early in 1792, the Chinese Emperor despatched 13,000 troops to join the 10,000 Tibetans already amassed against the Gurkha invaders. Together, the combined Chinese and Tibetan force drove the Gurkhas back across the border into Nepal. As a condition of truce, the Gurkhas were ordered to hand over the Shamar Rinpoche, his family and his followers and to return all the treasure taken from Tashilhunpo. By this time, however, the Shamar was already dead; one account has it that rather than being handed back to the Tibetans he had taken his own life by poison. The government in Lhasa branded him as a traitor. His estates were confiscated, his monastery at Yangpachen handed over to the ruling Gelugpa sect, and a law enacted forbidding any future Shamar incarnations – a punishment that the Tibetan historian Tsering Shakya likens to 'freezing the assets of the company and stopping it trading'. The Shamar's red crown was buried under the steps of the courthouse in Lhasa as a mark of disgrace.

There is another interpretation of this story, however. Some Kagyu historians hold that rather than being a traitor to his country, the 10th Shamarpa was actually the victim of a plot by the ruling Gelugpa political establishment. Fearing the Shamar's influence, and seeing the opportunity to rid themselves of a long-standing political rival, the Gelugpa took advantage of his presence in Nepal at the time of the Gurkha invasion to brand him as a traitor. According to this version, the Shamar did not take his own life with poison, but died of jaundice.

Whatever the truth, the banishing of the Shamar Rinpoche was to leave a lasting legacy not only for his own lineage and the Karma Kagyu school, but also for the fate of Tibet itself. For one thing, the intervention of the imperial army to help repel the Gurkha invaders gave the Chinese Emperor greater leverage over Tibetan affairs – a fact which 200 years later the communists would cite as a historical precedent for their occupation of Tibet. More immediately it led to the Chinese intervening in the recognition of reincarnates. The fact that the Panchen Lama, Shamar Rinpoche, and Chungpa Hutuktu Tulku had all been born into the same family – and the trouble this had caused – apparently prompted the Emperor to wonder whether the clairvoyant procedures traditionally used in recognizing reincarnates could altogether be trusted.

In 1793 he introduced a system of divination known as the Golden Urn, to be used in the event of any disputes over the recognition of the Dalai and Panchen Lamas. In this system, the names of the candidates would be inscribed on ivory tiles and drawn from a Golden Urn. The Tibetans accepted the Golden Urn on the understanding that it would be used along with the other traditional forms of divination, but they attached no great significance to it, and it was used only occasionally. It was to be a further 200 years before the precedent of the Golden Urn would be fully exploited by the communist Chinese in the recognition of the 10th Panchen Lama.

Whether the Shamar Rinpoche had been justly punished or was the innocent victim of an act of political revenge, the consequences were the same – a complete loss of the authority of his lineage: no monasteries, no land holdings, no *labrang*, no power. Commenting on this period, the 16th Karmapa said, 'Merit was becoming smaller and smaller. There was much political interference. Black was becoming white. The real was becoming unreal. At that time it was not practicable to have any Shamarpas recognized or enthroned. Everything was kept secret. The incarnations appeared, but were not revealed.' The Shamarpas were to play no further part in the recognition, enthronement or education of the Karmapas for the next 150 years and their incarnations constitute barely a footnote in Kagyu history. By the present Shamar's account, the 11th of the line lived a hermit's existence in northern Tibet. The 12th, born in 1880, was one of the sons of the 15th Karmapa (who was not a celibate monk); while the 13th supposedly died when only a year old.

In 1956 the line of the Shamarpa was finally reinstated when the 16th Karmapa formally recognized his four-year-old nephew as the 14th Shamar Rinpoche. However, it was not until 1963 that the Dalai Lama's new government-in-exile in Dharamsala finally gave its official imprimatur, and the 14th Shamar Rinpoche was enthroned at the age of eleven at Rumtek. Reinstated he may have been, but the Shamarpa no longer possessed the power and prestige that he had enjoyed in earlier incarnations. Having been banished for more than 150 years, his place in the Karma Kagyu lineage had been usurped by other figures, not least the Tai Situpas. The previous Tai Situ – the 11th – had been responsible for recognizing the reincarnation of the 16th Karmapa, and had been his guru and the crucial link in the Golden Rosary. The 16th

Karmapa, therefore, understandably looked fondly on the 12th and present Tai Situ. It might be argued, then, that the Shamar had good reason to resent both the Gelugpa establishment who had banished his line 200 years earlier and the Tai Situ who had supplanted him in the Kagyu hierarchy. Equally, it might be argued that the Tai Situpa had good reason to view the return of the Shamarpa with unease. But whatever suspicions might have existed between the two rinpoches were kept in check for as long as the 16th Karmapa was alive and in charge of Rumtek.

Everybody who met the Shamarpa agreed that he was an extremely bright, intelligent boy. 'He was very astute, with a very cheeky sense of humour,' remembers Edward Henning, who spent several months with him in Kathmandu and Rumtek. 'He had a boundless curiosity about the world around him.' Another Western visitor, who taught the young Shamar English for a number of months, recalls that, in a curious echo of his previous incarnations, the Shamar was 'absolutely fascinated by politics'. He apparently demonstrated a particularly keen awareness of Kagyu politics, the harsh treatment that had been meted out by the Lhasa government to his predecessor, the 10th Shamarpa, and his traditional position as second in the Kagyu hierarchy, which he seemed anxious to reaffirm at every opportunity. 'Previously Shamar's lineage was very high, but then when the lineage was lost the Situ's took that place,' says Lama Yeshe. 'And I think Shamar was finding it difficult to fit in after losing his place.'

He also seemed to have an ambivalent relationship with his uncle, the Karmapa. 'His Holiness always had a particular feeling for Tai Situ, because the previous Tai Situ had been Karmapa's root guru [principal spiritual teacher],' remembers Lama Yeshe. 'So Situ was honoured in this respect. But with Shamar, His Holiness was always jokingly smacking him all the time. But we would consider this as a blessing, a purification. Whatever the Karmapa did, it was always for the best.'

For all four heart sons, the death of the 16th Karmapa and their own coming of age presented a further, pressing necessity – that of financial survival. It was, of course, a problem that all lamas coming into exile had been obliged to face. In Tibet, an important rinpoche could rely on the patronage of local nobles, the income from their monastic estates. In exile, they had to look elsewhere for support, using all their initiative and ingenuity to survive. There were two directions to look; to the East, to wealthy Chinese Buddhists in Malaysia, Hong Kong and Taiwan; and to the West.

The arrival of the first Tibetan lamas in Europe and America in the late 1960s and early 1970s consummated the West's long-running infatuation with the mysteries of Tibetan Buddhism. As the American scholar Donald Lopez has put it, Tibetan Buddhism appeared to offer 'the cure for an ever-ailing Western civilization . . . a tonic to restore its spirit'. The more feudal aspects of Tibetan Buddhism – its rigidly hierarchical structure, its chauvinism – tended to be overlooked in this romantic embrace; so too were the complex, and often bloody, internecine rivalries that have marked Tibetan history. Tibetan lamas provided an idealized image of perfect humility and compassion for Westerners; the West, in return, provided the atmosphere of aspiration, unquestioning belief and financial support the lamas needed to flourish. Rinpoches would be invited to teach, to give initiations and empowerments, all costs paid. These tours in turn opened the doors to more wealthy donors, eager to support the dharma and to gain personal merit in the process. The lamas of the Karma Kagyu school were to prove the most energetic and industrious in this spreading of Buddhist teachings, and by the early 1980s the majority of the major dharma centres in Europe and the USA were Karma Kagyu.

On his travels through Europe and America in the 1970s, the 16th Karmapa had established a string of centres, small and large, in his wake. Under the direction of Akong Rinpoche and his brother Lama Yeshe, who had moved there after emerging from his lengthy retreat in 1985, Samye Ling grew to be the largest Tibetan Buddhist centre in Europe, a fully-functioning monastery with a growing complement of monks and nuns, most of them young Westerners, and a large community of laypeople. Almost as large was the Karmapa's American 'seat', KTD. The Karmapa had established another centre in the Dordogne, France, which was now under the control of the Shamarpa's brother, Lama Jigme. Kalu Rinpoche had also established a number of centres on his Western travels. Following the traditional model in Tibet, these institutions, while all belonging to the Kagyu school and recognizing the ultimate spiritual authority of the Karmapa, were self-determining and financially independent.

As they came of age, all four of the Karmapa's heart sons – Tai Situ Rinpoche, Jamgon Kongtrul Rinpoche, Shamar Rinpoche and, to a lesser extent, Gyaltsab Rinpoche – travelled extensively throughout Europe, America and the Far East on teaching tours. Shamar, in particular, established a reputation as a brilliant scholar and teacher who could convey the essence of Buddhist teachings in a readily accessible way to Western students. He also had a gift for raising funds. One Western devotee recalls being with him in New York, in an apartment on 5th Avenue, with a wealthy sponsor, 'and he extracted this $25,000 donation, just like that. He had enormous charm and personality. It was just his way.'

Shamar became close to Ole and Hannah Nydahl, the Danish devotees of the Karmapa who had been energetically establishing their own centres throughout Scandinavia and Europe under the banner of 'The Diamond Way'. Shamar was regularly invited to teach at Ole's centres, and reciprocated by lending his imprimatur to Ole as a bona fide Buddhist teacher. The Karmapa had written letters giving his formal blessing to Nydahl opening centres in Europe, but in 1983 Shamar went further, issuing a letter to Ole certifying him as 'an appointed Buddhist master', authorized to transmit the 'blessing and activity' of the Karma Kagyu lineage, citing as Ole's qualifications the fact that he had taken initiations and Mahamudra teachings from the Karmapa and the highest Kagyu lamas, which he had practised accordingly. The 'authorization' was unusual to say the least. Traditionally there is no such position in Tibetan Buddhism as 'appointed Buddhist master', but the title brought Nydahl valuable credibility among Western students. He displayed it prominently in the first volume of his autobiography, *Entering the Diamond Way*.

Under the 'rotating regency' scheme devised by Damchoe, Shamar Rinpoche remained in occupancy of Rumtek, acting as the Karmapa's surrogate in official duties and the titular head of the Kagyu school. Jamgon Kongtrul also stayed at Rumtek, developing the Nalanda Institute in accordance with the Karmapa's wishes. Tai Situ was mostly to be found at his own monastery at Sherab Ling. Gyaltsab had also established a monastery of his own, in Sikkim. For the first year, the rotating regency worked smoothly enough. But then, in 1982, Damchoe Yongdu died, and a new general secretary, Topga Yulgal, was appointed to take his place. Like Shamar he was a nephew of the Karmapa; he and Shamar were cousins. More than that, they were to become the closest of allies as the unfolding events of the next few years drove an irreparable rift into the Kagyu school.

CHAPTER SIX

Honey on the Razorblade

Gyuto: August 2000.

In Dharamsala, it seemed you could see the Karmapa everywhere, or at least his image. His photograph hung on the walls in shops and restaurants, and was reproduced in several variations on the postcard stalls in the market, among the images of the Tibetan national flag, the sundry Hindu deities and the ubiquitous portraits of a smiling Dalai Lama. (The most charming picture was a portrait of the Karmapa and the Dalai Lama together, photographed shortly after the young boy's arrival, clasping hands like father and son, and smiling broadly into the camera.)

Yet the Karmapa himself remained, as he had been for the last eight months, imprisoned behind the wall of security at Gyuto. The mood of astonishment and celebration which had greeted his arrival had given way to a more sober one of frustration and bemusement. The Indian government had still not made a decision on whether or not to allow him to remain in the country. His application for refugee status had been filed and greeted with silence. Permission to travel to his ancestral seat at Rumtek had been categorically refused. Nor was he allowed to travel to the nearby monastery of Tai Situ at Sherab Ling. Confined in Gyuto, he could make only the occasional visit to Dharamsala to meet the Dalai Lama, and then only with the permission of his Indian minders.

In his office at the secretariat of the government-in-exile, Tashi Wangdi, the Minister of Religion and Culture, was his usual welcoming, smiling and opaque self. The Karmapa's status, he said, remained uncertain. He had not been told he could stay in India; but then again nobody had actually said that he could not stay either. But it was just a matter of time. One had to be patient. The government of India was a huge bureaucratic machine; so many ministries, and so many agencies. The Dalai Lama had made representations to the government of India, emphasizing that the Karmapa had fled to India for purely religious reasons, and pleading for him to be given permission to travel. These representations had been acknowledged, but . . . Tashi Wangdi's shrug spoke volumes, its message clear enough. The Tibetans, after all, were guests in India; they could make polite requests. But they could not push.

There had, he said, been many rumours about the Karmapa's escape. It was said that the Tibetan government-in-exile had been responsible. That was not the case. 'The Karmapa came on his own.' There had been rumours that the CIA was involved. All nonsense. Then there was the suggestion that his escape was all some kind of Chinese plan or ploy; that if the Karmapa goes to Sikkim he will create problems there and stir up public agitation. Indian intelligence officials had questioned the Karmapa and the other members of the escape party, he said; they would recognize that he was not a Chinese spy. Tashi Wangdi gave a deep sigh. 'Really, it's all nonsense. Right from an early age the Karmapa has been a strong nationalist, and put his faith in His Holiness.' He paused. 'His heart led the Karmapa away from the Chinese. At the end of the day, everything will be quite normal.' He said it again. 'But these things take time.'

At Gyuto, the same soldiers patrolled the monastery steps, carbines slung over their shoulders; the same plain-clothed security men stood poker-faced at the door. The population of the monastery had been further swollen by other new arrivals, monks and administrative staff from Rumtek, lending the tiny, cramped quarters the provisional and shambolic air of a refugee encampment. Monks were sleeping up to four to a room.

My attempts to interview the Karmapa had not been altogether successful. Since my first meeting ('Be sure your motivation is correct') I had met him only once, a fleeting encounter in one of the private audiences. He remained shut off behind a wall of Indian security and Tibetan protocol. The Indian government had forbidden him to give any press interviews. My audiences were ostensibly as a devotee. At the door, the guards confiscated my tape recorder. The members of his immediate circle were unfailingly polite, yet at the same time unmistakably distant. Tenzin Namgyal, the general secretary of the *labrang* had arrived from Rumtek and was billeted in a room at the back of the monastery. I was introduced to him one day whilst waiting outside the audience room. I outlined my plans to write a book, and hoped that he would be kind enough to talk to me. He smiled, pondered, nodded. The next time I saw him he ignored me.

Everywhere there were rumours. The Karmapa was said to be growing restless and unhappy in his confinement, so unhappy that he had considered walking out of Gyuto in disguise. Occasionally he would be driven to Dharamsala for a meeting with the Dalai Lama. But for the most part his days were spent in a monotonous round of lessons and public and private audiences. He was not allowed even to walk outside. Other than pacing the corridors of the monastery or stretching his legs in the sunshine on the roof, he received no exercise. For most fifteen-year-old boys the constraints would have been intolerable. Yet among his inner circle the mood remained stoical. 'From the human point of view, the Karmapa's conditions are difficult,' Ponlop Rinpoche told me. 'But at the same time it doesn't mean that it's driving him crazy and making his mind go insane. That is not going to happen. His Holiness is a realized master.'

Ponlop Rinpoche told me how one day, shortly after Karmapa's arrival at Gyuto, in the midst of pujas, he had suddenly turned to Ponlop and told him to fetch his laptop. 'I was surprised, it was so kind of . . . not respectful; and also some older monks get upset; they think we're playing or something. But it was his command, so I fetched the computer.' While continuing with the ceremonies, the Karmapa had begun to recite a poem. It was only as Ponlop was typing it into the computer that he realized that the verse was actually the instructions concerning the discovery of a new incarnate. 'It was in the traditional form. It mentioned the first syllables of the region and town where the boy was to be found, the parents' initials and different details. It didn't specify a

country. Usually these letters will give you a direction – north
from here or south from here, so perhaps this letter meant from
Gyuto, in whichever direction he wrote. I was shocked. The
Karmapa wasn't meditating, or checking his dreams or anything
. . . maybe he did have a dream before, I don't know. But it
seemed completely spontaneous. Really, it was quite remarkable.
After the puja when His Holiness showed that to his attendants,
they were really happy. It was not really a surprise for us, knowing
that's what a Karmapa does. But at the same time there was
tremendous joy, because it's proof of the truth of the teachings,
and the truth of the reincarnation. This is not really something you
can train in. You can be trained in the scriptures, or to be a good
sitting practitioner, but to train in recognizing new incarnates is
impossible. It's the quality of the 16th or the 15th or the 14th that
continues . . .'

The Karmapa's appointments diary was managed by Lama Phuntsok, one of the party who had arrived from Rumtek. Phuntsok was
the uncle of Ponlop Rinpoche. (The more familiar one became with
the circle of people around the Karmapa, the more one was
reminded of the fine network of familial relations on which the
hierarchy of Tibetan Buddhism is built.) Phuntsok was responsible
for arranging audiences with the Karmapa; in short, he was the
gatekeeper between Karmapa and the outside world. He was a
serious-faced man in his forties, with hooded, melancholic eyes,
who seemed perpetually harassed by his responsibilities.

   In the ante-room of the monastery, a group of people had
arrived for the Karmapa's morning audience; a handful of devotees from Taiwan, dressed in their best silk suits, wrapped gifts
under their arms. Some Tibetan monks and nuns, patiently
navigating the labyrinth of red tape at the door. A Westerner
in a suit was badgering Lama Phuntsok with a request. There was
a big rock concert coming up in Brazil. Could the Karmapa be
persuaded to tape 'a message of hope . . .'?

   Lama Phuntsok looked pained and shook his head. 'Not in the
present circumstances . . .'

   I was led upstairs and left to wait on the veranda outside the
interview room. Half an hour passed, and finally I was ushered
inside. The Karmapa sat on a dais at the far end of the room, a

wooden lectern holding some papers in front of him. A monk attendant, and a plain-clothes Indian security officer stood off to one side. The Karmapa gave a slight smile, a nod of recognition. His head had been freshly shaved and he was wearing a pair of rimless reading glasses, the brand name stamped on the bottom of the lens. He looked in every way heavier than the last time I'd seen him; the glow in his cheeks, which had been evident on his arrival from Tibet, had given way to a dull pallor. He looked like an athlete who, unable to train, was quickly falling out of shape.

I sat cross-legged on the carpet in front of him and reached for my notebook, aware once again of the gaze of the security guards boring into me. I felt, more than ever, as if I was talking to a prisoner.

He was, he said, frustrated. 'My main reason for coming out was to fulfil the wishes of my devotees, many of them related to the 16th Karmapa, throughout the world. Many tried to come and see me in Tibet, but not all could come. That is one reason for my frustration, but there are many reasons which I cannot say right now.' He did not know, he said, why he had consistently been refused permission by the Indian government to leave Gyuto. 'Maybe they still have some doubt about my escape, or maybe because of the security situation, or maybe there's another reason I don't know.' His administration had made several requests, and he had personally written to the Prime Minister of India, requesting permission to leave. 'So far there is no reply.'

He spoke quietly and deliberately, watching the interpreter as my questions and his answers were translated, occasionally shifting his gaze to the back of the room, mindful perhaps of how his every word was being overheard and mentally noted. Watching him, I found myself once again trying to separate the boy from the legend that surrounded him. I had not met the 16th Karmapa, but from the early pictures of him it was clear that the young man in front of me bore a striking physical resemblance to his predecessor; the same broad face, the same steady expression with a suggestion of sternness in the eyes; the same big-boned physique.

Ponlop Rinpoche told me that he had first met the Karmapa in Tsurphu monastery when he was nine years old, and immediately recognized 'imprints' from the 16th in the young lama. 'He spoke of things which are personal to me, which I had discussed with the

16th, and which no one else knows, but which [came] from his memory or something. There is no doubt in my mind. His qualities, his wisdom, everything is exactly like the 16th, except that he has a different body, a different age.' He laughed. 'Sometimes it's a little difficult to relate to that. Suddenly you realize, I am older than him! That's hard to take! Sometimes I find myself acting younger than him in front of him and realize how stupid I am.'

I could understand this. He was, patently, a fifteen-year-old boy; yet like no fifteen-year-old I had met before. His air of composure and authority was disconcerting. Tai Situ had told me that even he at times felt himself quailing under the Karmapa's stare. 'Honestly, I get very scared in his presence most of the time.' Being with the young Karmapa, Tai Situ said, was 'very much' like being in the presence of the 16th. 'His movements, the look, his way of thinking, his perceptions – even though he's a teenager his reactions to important things are unbelievable, like someone of eighty. No, not eighty,' he laughed. 'Eighty would be senile most of the time! Like fifty. Its really unbelievable.'

The Karmapa tapped his fingers absently on the lectern. 'I am still trying to think positively,' he said. 'India is a very big country. They have lots of things to deal with, not just my situation. I am a very minor subject. I am not thinking negatively towards anyone, and not fulfilling my wishes does not mean they are not doing what they should do.' In the meantime, he said, he was continuing with his studies. Four hours each day with his tutor, sessions of meditation and prayers. 'On a personal level, I have an intention to study a lot. But knowledge does not mean just staying in one room. To be a scholar and to benefit others you must have freedom . . . For the individual, freedom is the most important thing. There are many things I can do, but still there are boundaries.'

He gave a sad smile. 'Living like this, it's like trying to touch the sky.'

After several requests, Tenzin Namgyal had agreed to an interview. Once more I took a taxi down the hill from Dharamsala to the monastery.

It was a glorious, sun-struck day. Pilgrims had arrived in a caravan of taxis and minibuses from another Tibetan settlement to the east; a party perhaps 100-strong. The mood was distinctly festive. The men in tunics and boots, beards combed and hair braided; the women in their most colourful silk blouses and *chubas*. Laughter and greetings filled the air. Some sat on the grass, improvising picnics. A line of people stood at the door to the monastery, clutching gifts for the Karmapa: packets of biscuits and incense, small devotional statues, bolts of fabric, banknotes of varying denominations tucked into envelopes or wrapped in white silk *khatas*. A monk sat at a wooden table, carefully noting each offering in a ledger, and issuing receipts. I pressed through the crowd and presented myself at the security desk. The plain-clothes officer noted my details in his register for the umpteenth time, showing no sign of recognition.

Tenzin Namgyal was in his sixties: a dusty-looking man, squinting myopically through thick eyeglasses. He wore an ill-fitting suit jacket over an open-necked shirt. He had the weary, beleaguered air of a housemaster in a minor English public school. He led the way through the corridors to a small room at the back of the monastery. There were two camp beds, a battered desk strewn with papers. Every other available inch of the room seemed to be filled with trunks and cardboard boxes, a detritus of pots, pans, clothes and provisions piled in the corners. This, explained Tenzin Namgyal, was his bedroom and his office. He shrugged as if to acknowledge the preposterousness of attempting to admin-ister the affairs of the Karmapa in the midst of such chaos. He gestured for me to sit on one of the beds, cleared some papers from a chair and pulled it up beside me. The general secretary spoke no English. His assistant and translator, Gompo, a slim, moist-eyed man dressed in a tweed jacket and tie, perched at the other end of the bed.

Tenzin Namgyal explained that he had known the 16th Karmapa since he was a boy. He had come with him from Tibet in 1959, and had worked as his private secretary, assisting Damchoe Yongdu. 'His Holiness was a great bodhisattva,' he said. 'His leadership was excellent. And he was a very generous, compassionate man, very spacious-minded. People could open their hearts to him and he would listen.'

He pulled a *mala* from his pocket, and began to methodically work the beads through his fingers as he spoke. 'His Holiness taught me a lot. One example: when we escaped from Tibet we had so many difficulties such as illness, difficulties with the climate. We had no medicine, no doctors. But whenever there was a problem, His Holiness was the doctor, the guide. Always we were bringing him problems, and he would always have the answer. It is because of him that we survived. I owe my long life to him.'

He paused, obviously moved by the memory. 'I loved him very much. The Karmapa is the highest of all reincarnated lamas, spiritually speaking he is perfect. And within human society, I have never met anyone else like him. He was the most perfect man in the world. Always smiling, always the same. If I think about him, I feel tears because his body has gone. If I think back on him and his qualities, there's no question, I just cry because his kindness was beyond words.'

He paused, reached into his pocket and took out a small snuffbox. He carefully took a pinch, spread it on the back of his hand, sniffed deeply and launched into a prolonged sneezing fit, then wiped his eyes with a handkerchief.

At that moment, the door burst open and a monk came in, a bulging sack thrown over his shoulder. He upturned the contents unceremoniously on the general secretary's bed. It was the gifts for the Karmapa which, an hour earlier, the monk had been fastidiously recording in his ledger. Now he began to sort through them. The sticks of incense, the small gift shop statues, the packets of biscuits and other foodstuffs, he put to one side; the *khatas* were tossed into a corner, a snowdrift of white silk, presumably to be recycled in the endless round of audiences and devotions. Now the monk set to tearing open the envelopes, pulling out crumpled rupee notes. Beside the bed was a small strongbox with a slit in the top, like a letterbox. The monk began to methodically feed the notes, one by one, into the box. Tenzin Namgyal tutted in irritation, gestured for me to turn off my tape recorder and rose to help him. The meeting, it was clear, would take some time.

In the aftermath of the 16th Karmapa's death, Tenzin Namgyal went on, his old general secretary, Damchoe Yongdu, did his best to maintain equilibrium at Rumtek. But then Damchoe Yongdu died, and Topga Yulgal became general secretary. And that, said Tenzin Namgyal, is where the trouble started.

Topga and Damchoe could hardly have been more different.

The years in exile had done nothing to dampen Damchoe's conservatism or his grouchiness. He had continued to favour the traditional *chuba* and long hair, to tongue-lash anyone who incurred his disfavour. Topga was in his early forties, smooth and polished, a man who favoured well-cut Western suits, spoke fluent English. 'He was a tall, handsome man – he carried himself very well – and he was very, very charming,' remembers one American student. 'From a distance there was a real charisma, but get close to him and it felt like someone had opened a refrigerator door – this draught of cold energy. He was the perfect Mephistopheles.'

'Topga,' says Ngödrup Burkhar, the 16th Karmapa's translator, 'was honey on the razorblade.'

As a young boy, Topga had been a monk at Tsurphu, and he was among the party that escaped with the Karmapa into Sikkim in 1959. At Rumtek, he rose to the position of Dorje Lopon, or Ritual Master, a position that entitled him to use the honorific Rinpoche, although he was not, in fact, recognized as a reincarnate *tulku*. But in 1966 he gave up his robes and married Ashi Choeki Wangchuk, the sister of the King of Bhutan, Jigme Dorje Wangchuk, and a devotee of the Karmapa whom Topga had met on her visits to Rumtek. However, he retained the honorific, and continued to be known as Topga Rinpoche. It was not that unusual for a monk to leave orders to marry – but it was somewhat out of the ordinary for a monk to take a princess as his bride. But Topga, it seemed, had always set his sights high.

'He and I were together since childhood,' Tenzin Namgyal told me. 'I knew him very well. [From] the personality that he wears externally, you would think he was a wonderful person; a very pleasing personality. He had been a monk, it's true, but studying the dharma is one thing and practising it is another. In every individual, human nature is for desire, to be a big man. But Topga had more ego, more pride, more desire. He was always up to some mischief.'

Topga's marriage incensed the Karmapa, who regarded the monastic life as the highest possible calling and took a dim view of those who gave up their robes. It is said that in the courtyard at Rumtek he smashed his nephew's seat to smithereens, and ordered the debris to be thrown down the mountainside, proclaiming, 'Let not a mote of dust rise up here again.' But in 1968, when the

Karmapa travelled to Bhutan, Topga pleaded with him for forgiveness and to be given a title that would lend him some status in his new life. The Karmapa apparently relented, partly for sentimental reasons, perhaps – Topga was his nephew after all – and partly for pragmatic ones, as the Bhutanese royal family were generous patrons of Rumtek. He conferred on Topga the title of honorary general secretary. It was basically a sinecure. Topga's duties consisted mostly of maintaining good relations with the Bhutanese royal family and notionally keeping an eye on the Karmapa's interests in Bhutan. These included not only two new monasteries, which were under development, but also a small portfolio of businesses, including shops and a cinema that had been donated to Karmapa by the King of Bhutan. 'His Holiness never assigned him any official work,' Tenzin Namgyal told me, 'and Topga never once showed up at Rumtek before the Karmapa's death. But after the Karmapa died, then he started to show up. Topga was really a businessman.'

What sort of business? I asked.

Tenzin Namgyal laughed. 'Smuggling!'

This aspect of Topga's activities was well known to the Indian authorities. In March 1980, customs at Calcutta intercepted seven packages belonging to Topga containing silver worth 400,000 rupees (around £50,000) which he was attempting to smuggle out of the country into Hong Kong. But following the intervention of the Bhutanese royal family, the silver was returned to Topga and no charges were brought. In May 1982, he was once more in trouble when he was again stopped by customs at Calcutta airport, this time arriving on a flight from Hong Kong, along with his wife the princess, and her daughter by a previous marriage. Indian officials had been watching Topga for some time, noticing his frequent movements in and out of the country and the inordinate amount of baggage he seemed to require for his travels. On this occasion he (or rather his attendant) was carrying eight extremely heavy suitcases, which, when questioned, Topga claimed contained only clothes. In fact, they were to found to contain 150 kilograms of gold, which, at that time, would have cost around £1.26m in Hong Kong and been valued at £2.6m in India. His luggage was also found to contain twenty expensive wrist-watches – and a well-pressed monk's robe. The gold was confiscated and a prosecution brought against an Indian business-man whom Topga claimed had financed him and for whom he was carrying the consignment. But again, after a request from the Bhutanese royal family, no charges were laid against Topga himself and he walked away scot-free.

Topga's skirmish with the authorities was widely reported in the Indian press, yet he proved remarkably resilient in the face of scandal. Following the death of the 16th he began to appear more frequently at Rumtek, sweeping into the monastery in a motor-cade with a posse of flunkies, cultivating his connections with Rumtek's trustees, and, most noticeably, with his cousin the Shamarpa, who was now installed as acting Regent. Topga's increasing involvement in Rumtek's affairs put him at loggerheads with the general secretary Damchoe Yongdu. The first argument came over the construction of the new Karmapa Institute in Delhi. The land on which the Institute was being built was owned by the Indian government, but had been granted on lease to the Karmapa for a period of ninety-nine years. However, the Karmapa had died before the lease could be signed. Topga called a meeting of monastery officials and accused Damchoe Yongdu of trying to put the name of his son, Ponlop Rinpoche, on the lease. Damchoe fiercely denied the charge. In fact, according to Ponlop Rinpoche himself, his father Damchoe had gone through a protracted legal procedure attempting to put the Karmapa's name on the lease, *post mortem*, which had involved soliciting testimonies from the governments of Sikkim and Bhutan about the history of the Karmapas' reincarnations. Faced with the evidence, Topga withdrew his allegations, but the rift between the two men continued to fester.

In December 1982, Damchoe travelled to Bhutan, to check on the accounting of the Karmapa's business interests and to seek a loan from the Bhutanese government to complete the building of KIBI in Delhi. Travelling with him were his assistant Gompo and two other attendants. On 10 December, Damchoe visited Topga at his home. Gompo and the two attendants were shown into a waiting room upstairs, while Damchoe took tea with Topga in another room. Less than an hour later, Damchoe was dead. A doctor was summoned who declared that the general secretary had died of a heart attack. 'There was talk,' said Tenzin Namgyal, choosing his words carefully, 'of suspicious circumstances.' It was said that blotches could be seen on Damchoe's body, perhaps consistent with the use of certain poisons. There was, however, no evidence of foul play or of Topga having been responsible for Damchoe's death. He was sixty-two, and like many Tibetans, reared on a lifetime of butter tea, susceptible to high blood pressure, but otherwise in good health. There was no post-mortem. Damchoe's body was carried back to Rumtek, where he was ceremonially cremated.

At that time Tenzin Namgyal was Damchoe's deputy. He might have expected to be considered for the position of general secretary on Damchoe's death. But while nobody doubted Tenzin Namgyal's devotion and dedication, Topga was a man of the modern age: educated, charming and urbane. His history as a smuggler was overlooked. In January 1983 the board of trustees appointed him as general secretary of Rumtek. Sixteen years after leaving the monastery under a cloud, he returned firmly holding the reins of power.

Tenzin Namgyal's chagrin was still evident almost twenty years later, as he sat in his cramped room at Gyuto, reliving the events. From the moment of Topga's arrival at Rumtek, he told me, the new general secretary had only one ambition: to assert the primacy of the Shamarpa in the Kagyu hierarchy, and to further his own ambitions in the process. 'Topga wanted to make Shamar Rinpoche as high and as powerful as he could, and he wanted 100 per cent control of Rumtek. It was also very important for them to have a Karmapa who was their own Karmapa. . . . Topga led Shamarpa by the nose.' Shortly after Topga's arrival, Tenzin Namgyal went on, he was approached by Topga and Shamar. 'They told me that Shamar Rinpoche was the only Regent of His Holiness and therefore he was the only owner of Rumtek. They tried to impress on me that Shamar and Karmapa were of one mind and each have equal right to the properties and treasures of Rumtek. I could not accept this. I said, "No you're not." ' Those people who did not recognize Shamar as having equal status, Tenzin Namgyal said, gradually left. Among the first to leave was Tenzin Namgyal himself, along with his assistant Gompo. He was followed by Thrangu Rinpoche, who had been *khenpo*, or teacher, to the four heart sons, and whose sister was married to

Tenzin Namgyal. A new abbot was appointed at Rumtek, Khenpo Choedrak Tenphel Rinpoche, Shamar Rinpoche's cousin.

With Topga now in control, the dispute about the new Karmapa Institute in Delhi flared once more, this time amid allegations that Shamar Rinpoche was attempting to alter the deeds of the property to make himself the leasee as the successor to Karmapa. Tai Situ, Jamgon Kongtrul and Gyaltsab threatened a lawsuit. But the Shamar vociferously denied the charges, and the threat of a lawsuit was eventually dropped. In the ensuing argument, the agreement about the rotating regency was also dissolved. Shamar emerged from the debacle as the sole holder of the regency. A cloak of fraternal harmony was thrown over the row for the benefit of Karma Kagyu followers around the world. But below the surface, the battle lines were drawn.

New Delhi: November 2000.

When I contacted the Shamar Rinpoche in Delhi to arrange a meeting, I expected him to suggest the Karmapa Institute. Every meeting I had ever had with a Tibetan lama had taken place in either a monastery or a teaching centre. The Shamarpa suggested the Hyatt Regency Hotel. In the lobby of the hotel I was met by one of the Shamarpa's assistants, a young Tibetan, dressed in grey slacks and a blazer. He was carrying an attaché case and a mobile phone. We took the lift to an upstairs lounge where Shamar Rinpoche was waiting. He greeted me warmly, beckoned me to sit down, make myself comfortable. He was a short, powerfully built man, wearing a simple yellow shirt, a red robe draped around his shoulders. His crumpled features were set in an unwavering smile, his manner warm and expansive, as if to say, we are both men of the world who understand a thing or two. 'More coffee? Of course, you can smoke, yes. I'm not one of those conservative lamas!' Another assistant, a young, smartly dressed Indian, also clutching a mobile phone, hovered in the background; an Austrian woman in her mid-forties, well turned out in a brown suit and high heels, sat down beside him, a notebook in hand. The Shamarpa spoke in a fluting, broken English, occasionally turning to the woman for help in translating difficult terms. Behind us on the wall, a flat-screen television was tuned to the BBC World Service. It was all very surreal.

Could he, I asked, tell me something of the history of the Shamarpa lineage? He launched into a lengthy monologue about Tibetan history, the rise and fall of the Sakya school, the role played by the Mongolian khans and Chinese emperors, the emergence of the Karma Kagyu as the dominant school in Tibetan affairs. Shamar was evidently a keen historian, although I sensed his perspective was somewhat subjective.

Had I realized, he asked, that during the fifteenth century the 4th Shamarpa of the day had 'ruled' central Tibet? 'This was during the Pagdru dynasty. The Pagdru King passed away, the Crown Prince was too young to rule, and so according to the will of the King the 4th Shamarpa took the position of ruler. So he sat on the throne for four years and ruled Tibet. And he did very well – he ruled very peacefully. But after four years he said he was a spiritual teacher so he did not wish to be King. The Crown Prince assumed the throne, but the Shamarpa was behind him, the actual power was in his hands, and he ruled for another seven years.' And that, said Shamar, was how the Karma Kagyu became the most powerful school in Tibet.

Then, some 200 years later, came the rise of the Gelugpa and the ascendancy of the Dalai Lamas. Under the 5th Dalai Lama, twenty monasteries belonging to the Karmapa and twenty-one belonging to the Shamarpa had been forcibly converted to the Gelug school, leaving only the principal seats of the Karmapa at Tsurphu and the Shamarpa at Yangpachen. Eventually, the 10th Karmapa had to flee for his life, flying through the sky so the legend had it, and landing in Arunachal, in India. He then travelled through China, living as a beggar. The Chinese Emperor, a devotee, offered to send an army 300,000-strong to restore his power. 'And Karmapa said no, I don't want to harm even a little bug! He said there will eventually be benefit. And then, when he was almost eighty, the Dalai Lama finally allowed him to come back to Tsurphu, because everything was already suppressed, so what could an old man do? Poor Karmapa!'

Shamar gave a wistful smile, sat back in his chair and called for more coffee. He had given me this history lesson, I sensed, to clearly establish the rightful place of his lineage in Tibetan history, the persecution of the Kagyu, the iniquity of the Gelugpa.

Many people in the West who harboured more romantic

notions about Tibet, I suggested, would find this litany of dispute, warfare and double-dealing intensely disillusioning.

The Shamar gave me an indulgent smile. 'Yes, I understand. Actually, I'm quite critical of the non-Tibetan people's concepts about Tibet. Not only Tibet, but all Asians. You have to know how to judge the Asian culture, and especially Himalayan culture. Not everything is as it seems. You see something is green, it does not mean it is always green. I give you an example.'

In the period of the present Dalai Lama's minority, Tibet was governed by his Regent, the Reting Rinpoche. The Reting, said Shamar, wished to pursue his spiritual practice for some years, so he asked his friend and teacher the Taktra Rinpoche – 'his good friend, his spiritual friend', said Shamar emphatically with a smile – to take his place until he returned. After three years, the Reting was ready to resume his position, and it was then that Taktra Rinpoche had him killed. 'He didn't want to sacrifice his position now! Taktra Rinpoche's image was of a very, very learned lama, a great spiritual master. But the heart is still hungry for power! How could he kill this Reting Lama? Hypocrisy is very big in Asia . . .'

Our talk turned to the 16th Karmapa. He, I said, was a man of whom I had heard only good things.

'I am his nephew,' said Shamar. 'His brother's son. Yes, he was a very good man. He opposed the Dalai Lama very strongly!' He laughed, delighted at his own joke. Seated beside him, the Austrian woman gave a thin smile. 'In 1962 the Dalai Lama started saying that all the four schools should unify. And Karmapa challenged that. Many Nyingmapa lamas didn't agree with Dalai Lama. But the Nyingmapa lamas were weak and Karmapa was powerful. So they appealed to Karmapa to lead them, and he happily accepted.' This was a story I had heard before, but with a difference. My understanding was that Karmapa had done his best to avoid any direct political confrontation with the Dalai Lama.

But what sort of man, I asked, was Karmapa himself?

Shamar sighed. 'Actually, I like to be frank. I will not give special support to Karmapa because he is Karmapa. If there are any mistakes I will say so. Karmapa was like many high lamas in Tibet. His moral conduct was excellent – no hypocrisy. But he was very conservative, very stubborn, and very strong on hierarchy and protocol. And authoritarian. I order; they should follow me; do as I say . . . He was that kind of person.' He shrugged. 'He did not understand modern life.'

As a young boy growing up at Rumtek, Shamarpa went on, he had been very impressed by the teachings of Mahatma Gandhi. 'I am the son of a lord! Very, very dictatorship! But I am in favour of democracy. When I was younger I always liked the Dalai Lama's attitude because he said he followed Gandhi. I liked that! I didn't agree with my uncle Karmapa's attitude.' He laughed. 'I thought the Dalai Lama's idea of unification and democracy and Gandhi's view was excellent! Why was Karmapa opposing this? But later I found out that the Dalai Lama is actually very attached to his leadership. He made a future constitution for Tibet based on democracy, but in fact the Dalai Lama decides everything. What kind of democracy is that? He doesn't want to give up his leadership. Karmapa also. They're all the same – very attached to their position.'

I had the impression, I said, that growing up together in Rumtek, the four heart sons were like brothers. Shamar shot me a look, as if to say, where had I got that idea?

'No, no, not like that! In Karma Kagyu history there was always a hierarchy. Karmapa is the spiritual leader. Shamarpa is the second, Tai Situpa is the third, Gyaltsab is the fourth, Pawo Rinpoche is the fifth, and Dawo Rinpoche is the sixth. This system was known as the six spiritual leaders. So we continued that.'

But at Rumtek, I said, you and the other heart sons were friends?

'Yes, we were very close friends. And then the 16th Karmapa passed away, and the general secretary formed the regency. And that invited politics. So in 1984 we dissolved that. And then we remained as before – number one, two, three, four.'

Why, I asked, was the regency dissolved?

Shamar shrugged. 'It invited politics. And politics still continues. There were people running back and forth making slander and making trouble. Enormous trouble was made. So we dissolved it.'

Who dissolved it?

'The suggestion was made by me. And then agreed by Jamgon

Kongtrul. Then Gyaltsab Rinpoche agreed finally. And then all three of them signed to dissolve, giving two reasons: because it was not traditional, and because it invited politics.' He paused. 'You know, you might have a group of people who are very much renowned for proper conduct. And within that group you will have some who really only want power. It's very confusing.' He smiled. 'And you never know which is which . . .'

We had been talking for more than an hour. Now the Shamar's Indian assistant appeared at his shoulder, to remind him that he had a luncheon appointment. His guests were waiting downstairs.

'Please, you will join us for lunch . . .'

His guests were already seated at a table in the hotel restaurant: a corpulent, florid-faced German in his sixties, and his Chinese wife, pretty, expensively dressed, and perhaps twenty years younger. The Shamarpa and his party sat down. The German explained that he was a businessman who had owned a factory in Hong Kong making garments; now he had sold his business and retired to travel the world. The lunch passed in desultory conversation about exotic destinations, the Hong Kong economy; Shamar smiling, the members of his party saying little. At the end of the meal, the German reached for the bill. The Shamar led his guests out of the restaurant and into the lobby. 'Now we must go upstairs,' he said. He turned, smiled and shook my hand. I had been dismissed.

CHAPTER SEVEN

The Letter

The ten years of the Chinese Cultural Revolution from 1966 to 1976, instigated by Mao Zedong, had seen the decimation of Buddhism in Tibet. In an attempt to tame what the Chinese called the 'wild animal' of religion, thousands of monks and nuns had been subjected to imprisonment, torture and execution. More than 6,000 monasteries and *gompas* were destroyed; books and manuscripts burned or thrown into rivers; precious bronze images melted down and cast into guns. But this barbarism was unable to extinguish the Tibetan spirit. The death in 1976 of Mao Zedong allowed the return to a more pragmatic approach to engineering social change. The regime which replaced Mao and his 'gang of four' was initially led by Hua Guofeng, but in 1977 Deng Xiaoping, who had suffered disgrace and humiliation during the Cultural Revolution, was rehabilitated and returned to senior positions in both party and government, and by 1978 he had triumphed in an internal power struggle to become China's paramount leader.

Under Deng, the Cultural Revolution was denounced as 'ten years of catastrophe'; the new priority became economic modernization, and with it an attempt to salve the raw wounds of past excesses. For Tibet, this meant that force was abandoned in favour of a policy of co-option. The first symbolic gesture of this new approach came in February 1978, with the release of the Panchen Lama after fourteen years of imprisonment. The Panchen had been the most senior figure in the Buddhist hierarchy to remain in Tibet following the flight into exile of the Dalai Lama in

1959. The Panchen had initially welcomed the Chinese occupation, arguing that it offered the best prospect for a modernized, progressive Tibet. The Chinese had rewarded his enthusiasm by appointing him as acting chairman of the Tibetan Autonomous Region (TAR).

Yet within a couple of years, as the full consequences of Chinese rule became apparent, the Panchen had begun to experience serious misgivings. In 1962 he submitted a confidential report to the Beijing government outlining a range of criticisms of Chinese policy in Tibet. The report, known as the '70,000 Character Petition' criticized the arrests and executions which had been carried out by the Chinese to avenge the 1959 uprising, and attacked the collectivization policies of Mao's 'Great Leap Forward', which had resulted in famine and death across Tibet. (It would later be estimated that the famine arising from the Great Leap Forward caused the deaths of some thirty million people throughout China.) Chinese policies within Tibet, the Panchen Lama warned, would result in the complete extinction of Tibetan culture and religion. The letter was tantamount to a suicide note. Mao Zedong described it as 'a poisoned arrow shot at the Party by reactionary feudal overlords'. The Panchen Lama was ordered to undertake a period of rigorous 'self-criticism', and a year later he was sent to Beijing, where he was to spend the next fourteen years in detention and then under house arrest.

His release signalled a watershed in the new 'enlightened' liberal policy. In June 1978, Beijing announced that for the first time since 1959 Tibetans would be permitted to contact and possibly visit their relatives abroad, and that exiles would be permitted to return to Tibet to visit their relatives. In the same year, the Dalai Lama received an invitation from Deng Xiaoping to return to his homeland. He cautiously replied that he would first like to send a series of fact-finding delegations to investigate conditions in Tibet. The first delegation arrived in Tibet in August 1979 to a hero's welcome. The discomfort this occasioned their Chinese minders was amplified with the arrival of the second delegation the following year, when the cheers from the crowds in Lhasa gave way to shouts for Tibetan independence. The visit was quickly cut short. The third delegation, led by the Dalai Lama's sister Jetsun Pema, was already in the country and had completed its mission, but a planned fourth delegation was postponed. It would not arrive in Tibet until 1984.

Encouraged by these exchanges, in September 1980 the Dalai Lama made a further overture to Beijing, offering to send fifty trained teachers from the exile community to help with the development of education in Tibet. He also suggested opening a liaison office in Lhasa, to build trust between the Chinese government and the Tibetans in exile. There was no response, but in July 1981 the Chinese government raised the stakes still further by issuing a direct invitation to 'the Dalai Lama and his followers' to return to their homeland, but with the stipulation 'not to go to live in Tibet' [i.e. within the TAR, including Lhasa] or hold local posts there. 'His followers,' the Chinese statement went on, 'need not worry about their jobs and living conditions. These will only be better than before.' The Dalai Lama refused the offer. While the visits of the delegations from Dharamsala had achieved very little in terms of reconciliation between Beijing and the Tibetan government-in-exile, they did have the effect of signalling to the Chinese leadership the deep level of popular dissatisfaction within Tibet.

In 1980, the Party secretary in Tibet, Ren Rong, was sacked, and a senior government minister Hu Yaobang was despatched from Beijing with the duty of sorting out the Tibet 'problem'. Hu's appointment opened the door for a revival of the influence within Tibet of the United Front – China's 'party within a party'. The United Front had more or less dictated policy in the early years of Chinese occupation, employing a tactic of co-opting Tibet's old ruling class with promises of official jobs and large salaries, thereby attempting to create a loyal and docile Tibetan élite through which the country could be ruled. The United Front had all but vanished during the Cultural Revolution, but in the changing political climate its influence began to revive.

A loyal disciple of Deng's reformist philosophy, Hu Yaobang moved swiftly to implement a new policy of 'Tibetanization'. On his first visit to Lhasa in 1980 he ordered the immediate recall of one third of the Chinese officials stationed there, paving the way for the return to local leadership of the older generation of Tibetans who had been thrown out during the purges of the Cultural Revolution. There was official encouragement for the revival of Tibetan culture, and money was allocated to rebuild

monasteries that had been destroyed during the ravages of the
Cultural Revolution. Later, a new language law would be introduced, making Tibetan the official language of the TAR administration (although this was never properly implemented). In this
new climate of liberalism, lamas who had fled into exile were
allowed to return to develop projects within Tibet and rebuild
their monasteries. Akong Rinpoche, the abbot of Samye Ling in
Scotland, was among the first. In 1983, Akong made his first
journey back to Tibet since his escape twenty-four years earlier,
and with the permission of local officials he began to set up a
number of schools and welfare centres for Tibetans under the
banner of his charity Rokpa. In 1984, Tai Situ also returned to
Tibet for the first time since his escape, visiting his ancestral seat of
Palpung and a number of its subsidiary monasteries in the region.

Elsewhere in Tibet, another important monastery was undergoing renovation: the Karmapa's ancestral seat of Tsurphu.
Drupön Dechen Rinpoche had been the retreat master at Tsurphu
before the exile of the Karmapa. He had left Tibet with the 16th in
1959 and taken up his position in Rumtek, then gone on to
establish his own monastery in Ladakh. One of the Karmapa's last
instructions before his death entrusted Drupön Dechen with the
reconstruction and administration of Tsurphu, if and when circumstances permitted. In 1982, Drupön Dechen made his first
visit to the old monastery, and two years later he returned to
assume the position of abbot.

The once great monastery was now in ruins. In 1966, at the
height of the Cultural Revolution, Chinese soldiers had forced
local villagers at gunpoint to tear down the monastery buildings
brick by brick. They had also destroyed Tsurphu's most important
monument, a fifty-five-foot-high statue of Shakyamuni Buddha,
cast in brass, and said to contain relics of the Buddha himself and
his disciples. Chinese soldiers had initially used the statue as a
target for their field artillery, finally ordering a monk to demolish
it with dynamite. The priceless relics sealed in the statue had been
blown to smithereens and scattered around the valley. When
Drupön Dechen arrived at Tsurphu, the monastery comprised
just one habitable building. With a small community of some
twenty or thirty monks, he began the slow, painstaking process
of restoring it to its former glory.

In 1986, Ward Holmes arrived from America. Following the death of the Karmapa, Holmes had spent three years in a meditative retreat. On his arrival at Tsurphu, Drupön Dechen pointed him to a cave above the monastery where successive Karmapas had meditated over the course of the previous 800 years. 'I spent a month there,' says Holmes, 'just sitting. Karmapa came to me every night, saying this was my work, to be here and to help rebuild the monastery by raising money. I argued with him that I didn't know how to fundraise. He said, "But you were treasurer at my monastery" – I'd been the bookkeeper at KTD for three or four years. I knew all the wealthy people, what money came in. Still, I said, I didn't want to do it, I didn't know how to do it. But he said, start small . . .'

Holmes began by selling Chinese-made prints of the Buddha to friends and Buddhist centres for $10 a piece. In 1989, Holmes's father passed away, and he came into a small inheritance. With the money, he founded the Tsurphu Foundation, and began soliciting donations from America, Malaysia, Hong Kong and Taiwan. Slowly, Tsurphu began to grow from the rubble until, thirty years after the Karmapa's departure for India, it was fit for his return. But where was the Karmapa?

Sherab Ling: August 2000.

In his office at Sherab Ling, the Tai Situpa called for more tea. 'And then,' he said carefully, 'things began to get more difficult. For me, it was very confusing, and very difficult, but at the same time, very clear and very easy. It's strange . . .' He paused. 'Let's just say, we were trying to do our best.'

The wheels turn slowly in Tibetan Buddhism. The 16th Karmapa had died in 1981. A search of his rooms and belongings had revealed no sign of his prediction letter, no indication of when his reincarnation might appear, or where he might be found. But history suggested these things did not work on a timetable. There had been long interregnum periods before. All that was required was patience. The four heart sons went about their business, travelling and teaching. Having assumed control of the regency, Shamar Rinpoche had based himself at Rumtek. So too had Jamgon Kongtrul. Tai Situ was busy establishing Sherab Ling. The disagreements and the air of mutual distrust among the heart sons were kept effectively secret from the legions of Kagyu followers, who were waiting with growing expectancy and impatience for news of the Karmapa's reincarnation.

In the absence of any announcement from the heart sons, each passing month seemed to bring a new rumour. In 1983, word spread that a boy born in Bodh Gaya who had been brought to Tai Situ's monastery at Sherab Ling was the Karmapa. But the child was subsequently recognized as the reincarnation of another lama, Gongkar Rinpoche. The following year, the King of Bhutan gave birth to a son. Topga (who, of course, was married to a Bhutanese princess) happened to be at his home in Bhutan at the time. He despatched a letter to Rumtek, stating, 'Considering what everyone is saying from all sides, you can trust that the precious reincarnation of our protector and refuge, His Holiness the Gyalwang Karmapa, has arrived. After consulting the calendar for an auspicious day, all monks and laypeople should put up prayer flags and perform *sang* and *solka* (offering pujas made outdoors).' The Bhutanese royal family were obliged to issue a statement denying that the child was the Karmapa.

In February 1986, the four heart sons convened once again in Rumtek to discuss the situation. They now faced an impossible quandary. The Karmapa had been dead for more than four years, and the clamour for some announcement about his reincarnation was becoming deafening. Yet none of the heart sons was any the wiser about when or where the reincarnation might be found. If they were to announce publicly that they had been unable to find a letter, or any sort of instructions about the rebirth, the result would be widespread pessimism and despondency. And what if, having made that announcement, the letter suddenly turned up? Then there would be wholesale confusion. What was required was a holding plan. In the absence of a letter, perhaps they could at least find something written by the 16th Karmapa himself, which would serve as a surrogate until the letter itself turned up. But it seemed that nothing suitable could be found.

At length, Gyaltsab Rinpoche remembered that he had a verse on the nature of mind that the Karmapa had written and given to him some years earlier. Gyaltsab made a thorough search of his quarters, only to report back that he was unable to find the original document. However, he could recite the four-line verse from memory. Jamgon Kongtrul dutifully wrote it down; the verse was sealed in an envelope and then put into a *gau*, or relic box. Together, the four rinpoches swore that they would never disclose the ruse to anyone, and would take the secret with them to their graves. They then announced that two letters had been found pertaining to the reincarnation – an 'inner one' and an 'outer one'. The inner letter, it was explained, was supposed to be opened on 'a certain date' in the future (which was not specified), but only after a number of religious ceremonies, described in the outer letter, had been performed to remove obstacles.

The logic behind this curious exercise was purely Tibetan. It was to give hope. 'If the Regents had told people there was no prediction letter, that would have been a lie,' says Ponlop Rinpoche. 'Just because they couldn't find a letter didn't mean it didn't exist. It was just a matter of time.' At Kagyu centres throughout the world, devotees dutifully applied themselves to performing the rituals supposedly specified in the outer letter: 100 million recitations of the 100-syllable Dorje Sempa mantra, a practice believed to be particularly efficacious in the removal of obstacles. An instruction from Rumtek also encouraged devotees to chant the Karmapa Chenno mantra ['Karmapa, heed me'] 'as many times as you can'. At Samye Ling, the recitation of Dorje Sempa became the central practice at puja every evening. Each devotee would count the number of mantras they had recited on their *mala*, and the totals were entered in a record book, to be eventually despatched to Rumtek. For the next two years, the same ritual would be enacted at Kagyu centres and monasteries around the world.

At last, in May 1988, an announcement came from Rumtek that the rituals were complete, and the obstacles to opening the 'inner' letter had been overcome. The reincarnation of the Karmapa, it was announced, would be found 'very soon'. Notwithstanding, of course, the simple fact that nobody appeared to have the faintest idea where he might be.

In 1989, Tai Situ was approaching his thirty-seventh year. In Tibetan Buddhism, thirty-seven is regarded as an 'obstacle year' – a time when unforeseen difficulties might arise, and when it is regarded as expedient to make a retreat. With this in mind, Tai Situ cancelled his teaching commitments for the year and

embarked on a series of month-long retreats at his monastery in
Sherab Ling. It was then, he told me, ruminating on the matter of
the Karmapa's prediction letter, that he suddenly remembered
something.

Eight years earlier, in December 1980, he had been in Bodh
Gaya, laying the foundation stone for a new monastery that was
being built by another Kagyu lama, Khyentse Rinpoche. From
there he had travelled to Calcutta to meet with the Karmapa, who
was returning from Singapore. Cancer was raging through the
Karmapa's body. Nobody wished to accept the fact, but he was
dying. The Karmapa was occupying the Presidential Suite at the
Oberoi Grand Hotel, and he asked Tai Situ if he would share his
room. 'I was very surprised. Of course, in retreats I had shared a
room with him, but never anywhere else. But it was what he
asked, so of course I agreed.' While Tai Situ moved into his guru's
bedroom, Gyaltsab Rinpoche and another lama occupied the
living room. Over the next few days, the Karmapa gave teachings
and advice to his protégés.

On the last night, before going to bed, said Tai Situ, the
Karmapa presented him with a gift of a protection talisman: a
pouch, sewed in brocade; this would normally contain a square
piece of paper, with a mandala printed on it, blessed and folded in
a specific way and tied with a cord. 'I don't remember exactly
what Karmapa said when he gave it to me,' Tai Situ told me. 'This
will protect you, or this will be very beneficial in the future –
something like that. It was little bit unusual, I thought, but nothing
that would make me think about what was really inside there.'
Ten months later, the Karmapa died in Chicago.

For a year or so after his guru's death, Tai Situ said, he
continued to wear the pouch on a cord around his neck. 'Then
I went to South East Asia and in those places it's very, very
difficult. It stinks, and you can't wash, you know! So I made a
special belt with zips and I put it in there. And all this time we had
many meetings and talked about where to find the prediction
letter, but we didn't find anything. We made our decisions to keep
everybody calm, and we did many things, and some things were
not that wise but, you know, we were kids. And we were very
sincere. We were just doing our best.' He gave a rueful smile.
'Actually, our best was a little bit weak.'

In 1989, in his retreat quarters in Sherab Ling, Tai Situ's thoughts turned to the events in Calcutta. 'It wasn't that I was in a meditative state; I did not have any voices or anything like that. I was simply thinking about this and wondering, and for some reason I opened the amulet.' Inside, he said, was an envelope. Written on it, in the Karmapa's handwriting, was the instruction that it should be opened in the Iron Horse Year – 1990. 'Ninety per cent sure, or maybe more' that it contained the prediction letter – 'I thought, what else could it be?' – Tai Situ drafted a letter to the three other heart sons, and to the general secretary Topga. It read, 'I am writing concerning a particular issue, namely H.H. 16th Karmapa's instructions indicating his next reincarnation. I will come to Rumtek on the fifteenth of the first month of the Tibetan Iron Horse Year [i.e. March 1990] to discuss this.' There is a saying in Tibet that when peacocks hear the sound of thunder, heralding the cooling summer rains, they sing with happiness. 'I have good news,' Tai Situ wrote, 'similar to the joyful cries of peacocks.' The ambiguity was necessary, Tai Situ said. 'I could not say exactly "I've found the letter!" because we had been making so many stories. We'd been telling people that we'd already found the letter.'

But his news was not received with quite the unconfined joy that he might have anticipated. In February 1990, members of the Karmapa Charitable Trust gathered in New Delhi for the official opening of the Karmapa Institute, the project that Shamar Rinpoche had steered to completion, and which had been the subject of such acrimony in the past. Neither Tai Situ nor Gyaltsab Rinpoche was in attendance. After the ceremonies, a meeting was convened to discuss Tai Situ's letter and his request for a meeting. The next day, Topga despatched a reply. Its tone was curiously equivocal: 'If at this point there is reliable information concerning H.H. the 16th Karmapa's reincarnation, I rejoice,' wrote Topga. 'If not, a premature announcement concerning this would create rumours and doubts . . . Therefore the Trust decided that for the time being it is preferable to wait before presenting yet another report on the progress to date.' However, he went on, if there was 'reliable information' as to the reincarnation, it would be 'like a cure for the blind, like the sun which illuminates all'.

Had Topga guessed that Tai Situ was about to produce some

crucial news of the Karmapa's reincarnation? What was clear was that the general secretary was in no great hurry to find out. Tai Situ, on the other hand, could apparently contain himself no longer. In his room at Sherab Ling where he had first looked inside the pouch which the Karmapa had given him, he now opened the letter itself. A cursory glance, he told me, was enough to confirm that it was indeed the prediction letter of the 16th Karmapa. 'I was overjoyed. I was almost in a state of grace.' The letter, he went on, was 'very simple to understand. But of course, interpretation takes time. I did not go that far.' Instead, he said, he carefully put the letter back in the envelope, and placed it in a safe place with his crown and other relics. 'I didn't dare to carry it any more.'

By the beginning of 1990, it was clear even to those outside the closed circle of the four heart sons that all was not well with the search for the next incarnation of the Karmapa. It had now been almost four years since the heart sons had announced the discovery of the inner and outer letters at Rumtek; two years since the completion of the pujas which were said to be necessary before the inner letter could be opened, and the announcement that the reincarnation of the Karmapa would be found 'very soon'. Yet since then there had been only silence. Despite the urgency of the situation – what, after all, could be more important than to find the reincarnation of the Karmapa? – the four heart sons had apparently been unable to find time in their busy schedules to meet and discuss the matter. In the absence of any new developments, the rumour mill had continued to churn ever more wildly. Whispered doubts about the existence of the letter in the Rumtek *gau* box grew ever louder. From all sides, letters, petitions and gossip accused both Tai Situ and Shamar Rinpoche of following their own agendas.

In March 1990, Shamar, Tai Situ and Jamgon Kongtrul convened once again for an informal meeting in New Delhi, at the Oberoi Hotel, where Tai Situ Rinpoche was staying. Gyaltsab Rinpoche was teaching in Taiwan. Theoretically, there could only have been one thing on the agenda, but curiously, the matter of Tai Situ having news 'similar to the joyful cries of peacocks' seems not to have been mentioned at all. Tai Situ would later explain that it would have been 'inappropriate' to have raised such a

serious matter in a hotel, rather than in the sanctified environs of
Rumtek. But nor, it seems, did Shamar and Jamgon Kongtrul see
fit to mention it either. Instead, the heart sons issued what
amounted to a 'holding' statement to the Karmapa Charitable
Trust, reaffirming their belief in the procedures by which previous
Karmapas had identified themselves, and emphasizing the need
for patience and for all to 'remain firm in all circumstances, until
we arrive at the appropriate time'. The statement went on to
request the trustees to 'give serious thought' as to whether it
would be appropriate to make any kind of public announcement
concerning the current state of the efforts to find the Karmapa's
reincarnation. No announcement was made.

In November, responding to what they described as 'persistent
enquiries' from all quarters, the four heart sons issued yet another
statement, this time publicly, attempting to quell the growing
unrest. 'We do not have intentions to obtain personal gain, which
would be divisive,' it read. 'There have been false and unfounded
rumours claiming that one of us has personal intentions and that
there is no testament. We advise everyone not to listen to or follow
such rumours.' The letter went on to reiterate that the 'indestructible instructions' of the Karmapa would be the basis for the
recognition of the next reincarnation, and to plead for patience. 'If
all of you are able to . . . exert yourselves in being patient there is
no possibility of the Karmapa's activity failing you, he will appear
at the appropriate time.' But the appeals for faith were beginning
to wear thin.

In September 1991, Tai Situ journeyed once again to Tibet, to his
ancestral seat of Palpung monastery. The monks of Palpung and
other Kagyu monasteries throughout the region had been requesting Tai Situ to give one of the major initiations of the Kagyu lineage,
Dam Ngak Dzo. For four years, the Chinese had refused Tai Situ's
requests for a visa, but now, at last, it had been granted. *En route* to
Tibet, Tai Situ stopped for a week in Beijing, where he met with a
number of Chinese and Tibetan officials. From Beijing, Tai Situ
continued on his way to Tibet. Finally arriving at Palpung, he took
his place on the Red Throne. The throne had survived the sacking of
the monastery during the Cultural Revolution after a Red Guard
hid it in the storeroom, and had recently been restored and replaced
in the temple.

Thousands of monks, lamas and *tulkus* from all over Kham and beyond had come to Palpung. The empowerments lasted for six weeks. Each day pujas were conducted in the main shrine room. As part of his duties, it was also incumbent on Tai Situ to ratify the recognition of a number of new incarnates. In the quiet solitude of his rooms above the main shrine room, Tai Situ meditated and made divinations, watched for signs, then made his decrees. Over the course of a few weeks he would recognize almost 100 new *tulkus*. Most were Kagyu, but the number also included Nyingma, Gelug and Sakya *tulkus*. Not all of them were young boys. Some were the reincarnations of masters who had died during either the Cultural Revolution or the subsequent famines which had swept Tibet under Chinese occupation – monks who were now in their twenties and thirties and who had no inkling of their special status.

Among those recognized by Tai Situ was the reincarnation of Chögyam Trungpa, who had died in America four years earlier. One story had it that before his death Trungpa, in character-istically idiosyncratic fashion, had announced his intention to reincarnate not as a recognized *tulku* but as a Japanese factory worker. But evidently, there had been a change of plan. Tai Situ had received the first request to find Trungpa's reincarnation from the monks in Trungpa's traditional seat in Tibet, Surmang Dutsithil, a few months after his death. In March 1991, Tai Situ gave his first instructions to the monks, telling them how to conduct the search and what rituals should be performed. They responded by submitting a list of names resulting from the search, and the new incarnation was confirmed. The new Trung-pa, the 12th was born into a family of nomadic herdsmen. On the day of his birth, it was reported, the local water source had run white, like milk, for several hours. Now the two-year-old boy had been brought to Palpung, and was among the hundreds of monks who, taking advantage of Tai Situpa's presence, came forward to be ordained, and to have a lock of their hair cut in the traditional manner.

Among the youngest of these monks was a six-year-old boy, the son of a nomadic family from Kham. He was small for his age, with the vividly ruddy cheeks of a Khampa, and noticeable for his unusually fierce and penetrating gaze. For the past two years he had been living in a small monastery, or *gompa*, called Karlek, where he had been recognized as a *tulku*, but not yet identified and formally named. Instead he was known simply as Apo Gaga. Nobody could have guessed quite how important he would prove to be.

In January 1992, Jamgon Kongtrul and Gyaltsab Rinpoche issued a joint communiqué. They had heard rumours, they said, that acting on 'a vision' Shamar had gone secretly to Tibet to investigate indications about a child whom he believed might be the new incarnation of Karmapa. Other rumours, they said, had suggested that Tai Situ was also working independently of the other three rinpoches. They dismissed these rumours as being of 'a political nature'. 'Furthermore, all kinds of rumours prevail and all kinds of letters are distributed here and abroad. We see a danger that these will obstruct our goal which is to find the incarnation of His Holiness.' It was a desperate attempt to stitch together the thin fabric of unity between the Regents which was now being inexorably torn apart. An attempt to disguise the fact that Tai Situ and Shamar were now pursuing quite separate agendas.

On 21 January – some three weeks after the letter from Gyaltsab and Jamgon Kongtrul – Shamar wrote to Tai Situ Rinpoche. Topga, he said, had called a meeting of the Karmapa Charitable Trust in Rumtek for 25 March. Because Tai Situ had been in Tibet, Topga had been unable to contact him, so Shamar was writing instead to inform him of the meeting. It is a measure of the deep enmity and mutual suspicion between the two lamas that while both were in Hong Kong at the time, they did not meet personally. Shamar sent his letter by messenger. On 1 February, Tai Situ replied, in a letter addressed to Shamar, Gyaltsab and Jamgon Kongtrul, requesting the heart sons to meet in Rumtek the following month. At the same time, ceremonies were being held at Rumtek to consecrate a new fourteen-foot-high Buddha statue in the main assembly hall. Shamar had sponsored the casting and gold plating; Jamgon Kongtrul had provided the funds for the gold leaf. During the consecration rituals, liquid started dripping from the statue's forehead. It was taken to be a bad omen.

On 15 March, Tai Situ arrived at Rumtek, carrying with him

the prediction letter. Jamgon Kongtrul was waiting to greet him; Gyaltsab and Shamar had yet to arrive. That evening, Tai Situ called a meeting of the monastery's administrative staff. Saying nothing about the letter, he informed them only that he brought good news about the reincarnation of the Karmapa, and that he would be entering a three-day retreat in the shrine room, meditating in the presence of the 16th Karmapa's relics in the hope that Gyaltsab and Shamar would arrive in the meantime. Before entering retreat he took Jamgon into his confidence and showed him the letter. 'He was very, very happy,' Tai Situ told me. 'He even cried, actually.'

On the morning of 19 March, Tai Situ emerged from his retreat. Leaving the shrine room, he saw three children from the village, two boys and a girl, approaching, each carrying a full jar of milk. Tai Situ took this as a propitious omen. Gyaltsab and Shamar had now arrived at Rumtek, and that morning the four heart sons finally convened in the sitting room of the Karmapa's residence behind the monastery. The atmosphere was distinctly strained. Tai Situ asked each of the others in turn whether they had found the instructions of the Karmapa. They replied that they had not. Then Tai Situ rose from his seat and walked over to the empty chair where the Karmapa used to sit, made three prostrations and unfurled a long silk *khata*, which he placed on the chair. From his robes he produced a yellow silk pouch. 'The letter is here,' he said. He then gave his account: of how, in his suite at the Oberoi Grand Hotel in Calcutta the Karmapa had given him the protection pouch; of how he had worn it first around his neck and then in a belt, for eight years without once suspecting the true nature of its contents; and of how, in his room at Sherab Ling he had finally opened the pouch to discover the prediction letter. The three other Rinpoches gathered round to examine it. There are sharply conflicting accounts of what happened next.

'When I showed them the letter, Gyaltsab Rinpoche was very happy,' Tai Situ told me. 'But Shamar Rinpoche showed some unhappiness. I was very shocked. That was the first time, like that. But then later when we discussed everything, all the details, he was not showing any dissent or disagreement.'

Sitting in the lounge of the Hyatt Regency Hotel in New Delhi,

Shamar Rinpoche told a different story. 'Tai Situ said, "The letter is here." And Jamgon Kongtrul said, "Oh, very good, very good! The letter!" Jamgon Kongtrul was quite innocent . . . Then Tai Situ opened the letter. I am quite good at noticing these things, everybody knows this. I was the first person who took it. And I noticed that Tai Situ's name was there, in the letter, it was saying that Karmapa should follow Tai Situpa.' Shamar shrugged. 'OK . . . that doesn't matter. But the letter was clearly in Situ Rinpoche's handwriting. He had tried his best, but he could not disguise it. And then the signature was definitely not Karmapa's signature. I have so many examples of Karmapa's signature. In Rumtek, when we passed examination, every subject we pass there is a signature of Karmapa. And there were water stains on the signature, almost disguising it, as if they had been put there deliberately.

'I said, "How can this be?" And Tai Situ said, "Because of my sweat!" He said, "I have been wearing the pouch for the last eleven years, all the time, and it went through my clothes." Then I said, "But the envelope is very new! There is only water here in the corner. But the letter inside is terribly damaged. So how?" He said, "I don't know: you must ask my sweat!" On the envelope it was written, it should be opened in the Iron Horse Year. So then I said, "You opened this pouch just recently?" And Tai Situ said, "Yes, just recently." So I said, "You don't know any boy who answers the description written here?" So he said, "Now, according to these instructions, the general secretary and a party should go to search for the boy. Here it is mentioned that the boy should be in the East region somewhere." I said, "In India or Tibet?" He said, "I don't know where it is." This is what he said. He could have said that according to the letter I've searched, found the boy, this is the letter, the boy is there. But he didn't say that. I suspected that the boy had already been found. That's why I said, "Where is the boy?" And he said, "I don't know." So I said again, "I don't think this is Karmapa's handwriting." Gyaltsab Rinpoche, even before he read the letter, he was saying, "Oh, that's the authentic letter." I said, "You didn't even see the letter. How can you know it's authentic?" "No, no, authentic letter," he was saying. That showed me that he and Situ Rinpoche were already together in this.

'Then Jamgon Kongtrul went to his room to get an example of

Karmapa's handwriting. I had a letter from Situ Rinpoche with me. So word by word we tested. There was one character in particular which was very different from how the Karmapa wrote. And there was a spelling mistake which Situ Rinpoche had made in his letter which also appeared in the Karmapa's letter. So now I said, "Rinpoche, you must tell the truth, whether you have written this letter or not. If you have written this, then we will tear it up and we will say nothing. And if you really have a remarkable boy, we will follow you. You should say now." I said this. But he didn't reply.' Shamar shrugged. 'Perhaps he didn't trust me. I said, "If we reveal this letter, hundreds and hundreds of lamas and rinpoches will make research on this. And then later people will say, Karmapa's letter is a fake! It will ruin the principle of our history. So if you won't reveal this, then it has to go to forensic scientists. In London there is a forensic science test centre. In London the law is applicable for India also, so we go to London." "Oh," he said, "you'd have to spend $11,000." I said, "I don't mind. We can raise the funds." He said, "It would take us ten years." I said, "We have no choice." Then he said, "I will die nine times before I let this go for a foreign forensic test. I will die nine times for this . . ." '

The prediction letter read as follows:

Emaho
Self-awareness is always bliss;
the dharmadatu [1] has no centre or edge
From here to the north [in] the
east of [the land of] snow
Is a country where divine thunder
spontaneously blazes [2]
[In] a beautiful nomad's place with
the sign of a cow [3],
The method is Döndrub and the
wisdom is Lolaga [4]
[Born in] the year of the one
used for the earth [5]
[With] the miraculous far-reaching sound
of the white one [6]
[This] is the one known as Karmapa

He is sustained by Lord Dönyö Drupa [7]

Being nonsectarian he pervades all directions
Not staying close to some and distant from others,
he is the protector of all beings;
The sun of the Buddha's Dharma that benefits others
always blazes

'We worked on it for almost a whole day,' Tai Situ told me. 'There were a few interpretations, but all pretty much the same. It was really very clear. Once we really sat down, very clear . . .'
The interpretation was made as follows:

[1]: *Chos kyi dhying*, the expanse of all phenomena and equivalent to *sunyata* or emptiness.

[2]: In Tibetan, divine is *lha* and thunder (in the text poetically called '*gnam chags*', or 'sky iron') is *thok*. 'Divine thunder' was therefore taken to be Lhatok, the Karmapa's birthplace.

[3]: The name of the nomadic community where the Karmapa was born is Bakor: *ba* means 'cow' (the dharma term for 'cow', used in the text, is *dodjo*).

[4]: Method refers to the father, and wisdom to the mother.

[5]: 'The one used for the earth' was taken to refer to the Karmapa being born in Wood Ox Year: a tree lives from the earth and an ox is used to plough it.

[6]: The 'white one' is a conch shell, often blown on holy occasions.

[7]: Refers to the Tai Situpa.

'And then,' Tai Situ said, 'we made a calculation . . .'
Jamgon Kongtrul had been invited to go to Tsurphu in a few weeks' time to give a series of initiations. He would take a copy of the letter with him, and instruct the abbot of Tsurphu, Drupön Dechen Rinpoche, to organize a search party to investigate the instructions in the letter. In the meantime, the heart sons would say nothing publicly about the contents of the letter or the possible whereabouts of the new Karmapa. They would say only that a further announcement would be made in October, by which time the investigations should have been completed. Jamgon Kongtrul

made a photocopy of the letter, and the original was carefully placed inside a *gau* box.

Throughout the day, as the four heart sons deliberated over the letter and its contents, a large group had gathered outside. Among them were devotees from Ladakh and Nepal, a delegation from the six major Buddhist associations of Sikkim and some Western devotees who happened to be on pilgrimage to Rumtek. Also there was Akong Rinpoche, who had been summoned by Tai Situ from Scotland. Finally, at three o'clock, a group of delegates was invited into the sitting room. Whatever discord had erupted between Tai Situ and Shamarpa was now carefully concealed behind a veneer of unity.

The long years of waiting, it was announced, were at an end. The prediction letter of the 16th Karmapa was here. There was a murmur of excitement from the delegates, then Kunzang Sherab, the chairman of the Sikkim Buddhist Association, stepped forward. Could they see the letter? Jamgon and Gyaltsab removed it from the golden relic box. Explaining that such a sacred object should not be touched by anybody, Gyaltsab held the letter gingerly between two fingers as people jostled around to inspect it.

There were nods of approval, then another question. The date on the envelope specified that the letter was to be opened in Iron Horse Year [1990] – that was two years ago, said one delegate. 'Perhaps,' the delegate said, 'the Rinpoches don't love His Holiness so much since they had not opened the letter till now . . .'

Jamgon Kongtrul rose from his seat to reply: 'Was it the job of the Rinpoches to find the reincarnation, he said, or the job of the delegates?'

Then Akong Rinpoche spoke up. 'Wasn't this the same letter that the Regents were supposed to have found six years ago, in the relic box? If so, why was the envelope so oily, and why did the letter look so old and worn?'

'We have answers for that,' said Tai Situ, 'but not at the present time.'

With the meeting at an end, the delegates and heart sons filed out of the room. Among those waiting outside was the German film director, Clemens Kuby, who was filming in Rumtek at the time. Jamgon Kongtrul was filmed after the meeting, speaking straight to camera and saying, 'The instructions are very clear.'

The following day, 20 March, there was an official meeting between the four heart sons and members of a hastily formed delegation made up of representatives from the government of Sikkim, members of the Sikkim Legislative Assembly (the Singha) and a representative of the monasteries of Sikkim. Here it was formally announced that the prediction letter had been found, and that the new incarnation would be identified and enthroned within six to seven months. This time, the heart sons declined to show the letter, explaining that it would lose its *jhinlap*, or blessings, if it was handled indiscriminately. Michele Martin, an American Buddhist scholar, who was in Rumtek helping Jamgon Kongtrul with translations, translated the prediction letter into English. 'I have no doubt whatsoever that [Jamgon Rinpoche] totally believed this was the Karmapa's letter,' she remembered. 'Everybody was just ecstatic. We'd been waiting for so long. And the fact that the four heart sons were together and this announcement had been made . . . everybody was just glowing with excitement.'

Not everybody. Topga was incandescent with rage. In a meeting with the four heart sons he echoed Shamar Rinpoche's accusation that the letter was a forgery, and threatened that he would do everything he could to prevent a 'false' Karmapa assuming control of Rumtek.

The following day, Tai Situ left Rumtek for a meeting in Dharamsala with the Dalai Lama. Tai Situ would later describe the meeting in a speech at Rumtek. He had informed the Dalai Lama, he said, about the discovery of the prediction letter, and the discussion that had taken place between the four heart sons. The Dalai Lama had then told him that he himself had experienced a sacred vision pertaining to the Karmapa's rebirth. In this vision, the Dalai Lama was in a place that was green and had no trees, a very beautiful place. The mountains were not high, and there were small streams flowing on each side, right and left. He said he did not see any people or any animals, and he heard the sound 'Karmapa' in the air. 'His Holiness,' Tai Situ recounted, 'felt very, very happy when he woke up from that sacred vision.' During that meeting, Tai Situ went on, he had told the Dalai Lama that it was clear from the prediction letter that Karmapa had decided to be born in Tibet. Since that was the case, the Dalai

Lama replied, there was undoubtedly a sacred meaning to it, adding that 'everything should be done very carefully'.

On 26 March, Tai Situ issued a letter from Sherab Ling addressed to 'followers of Buddhism and particularly the Kagyu lineage', stating that 'the organization and recognition' of the 17th incarnation of Karmapa was now in place, and that 'with the prayers and blessings of His Holiness the Dalai Lama and other Vajrayana leaders, the final confirmation of the incarnation will be made and announced.' The agreement to say nothing until October had lasted less than a week.

Sitting in his room at Sherab Ling, Tai Situ outlined the plan that, he said, the Regents had devised in their discussions at Rumtek. Jamgon Kongtrul would go to Tibet to initiate the search for the Karmapa. A party would be despatched from Tsurphu to investigate the instructions contained in the letter. Once the boy had been found, the findings would be reported back to Tai Situ himself, who would then inform the Dalai Lama. 'And if he approves then we will send the party back to collect Karmapa; if he doesn't approve, we will have to search again.' In the meantime, Tai Situ went on, Jamgon Kongtrul would talk to his grandfather, Ngabo Ngawang Jigme, and request him to talk with the Chinese and Tibetan officials to arrange a visa for the new Karmapa to come to India. He would then be taken to the Dalai Lama for the hair-cutting ceremony, and finally enthroned in Rumtek.

It all sounded too good, too easy, to be true. 'We were not sophisticated politically, you know,' Tai Situ told me. 'We thought all these things were going to work! Just like you get a visa and go to America, you know? You need somebody to help get all your stuff, but then you go there and do your things. We almost thought like that. Because when I went to Tibet also, that's how I functioned; not hiding anything.'

It was then that Jamgon Kongtrul died. In late April, in the midst of making preparations for his journey to Tibet, Jamgon took delivery of a gift – a new BMW 525 – from his brother, a businessman. On the morning of 26 April, Jamgon decided to test-drive his new acquisition. With him was his driver, a friend Lama Kunga, and Jamgon Kongtrul's personal secretary Tenzin Dorjee.

Driving north of Siliguri the car suddenly veered off the road and struck a tree. The speedometer on the wrecked car was stuck at 110 k.p.h. Jamgon Kongtrul died almost immediately. The driver and Lama Kunga died in hospital. Only Tenzin Dorjee survived the crash.

Five days later he issued a lengthy statement on the accident. The tragedy, he wrote, had 'befallen us due to our lack of merit and for purposes beyond our sight or comprehension'. He went on to describe how the car had been speeding along the National Highway north of Siliguri when the driver had suddenly swerved to avoid a flock of birds. As the road surface was slightly damp, the vehicle went into a skid and 'fishtailed' for some thirty or forty metres before colliding with a tree. All of the occupants were thrown from the vehicle by the impact. Dorjee had regained his senses straightaway and gone to Jamgon Rinpoche who was lying near the vehicle. 'While I was holding him,' he wrote, 'he seemed to breathe his last.' After flagging down a passing vehicle, Dorjee recounted, he took the body of Jamgon to the stupa at Salugara, a few kilometres away, where Kalu Rinpoche had once lived, and placed it on Kalu Rinpoche's bed. '[Jamgon Kongtrul] Rinpoche looked completely lifeless, but when I cleaned his face with a damp cloth, his expression changed to one which I have often observed while Rinpoche slept. Rinpoche's heart area was also warm and I began to feel relief that he would survive. This was about two hours after the accident. A doctor was called in to examine Rinpoche, but he stated that Rinpoche had expired.'

The first of Jamgon's fellow heart sons to arrive on the scene was Shamar Rinpoche. That morning he had been visiting a local school when he received a telephone call from a Sikkimese government official informing him about the accident. He rushed to the scene. He told me, 'When you see a person who is dead by accident then . . . great shock. Then tears were coming out. It was very disturbing. I almost become mad, tears keep coming . . .' Examining the body, he declared that Jamgon was in *thug-dam*, or *samadhi*, a state of luminosity. Gyaltsab and another high lama, Bokar Rinpoche, arrived shortly afterwards. Because of the rising heat of the day, it was suggested that Jamgon's body should be taken immediately to Rumtek. Together, the Rinpoches made prayers requesting Jamgon to emerge from his state of *samadhi*.

'As they did so,' Tenzin Dorjee wrote, 'Rinpoche's *thug-dam* concluded, and his face became as before.'

Jamgon's body was carried in state back to Rumtek where it was placed in the Crown Ceremony Shrine Hall. That night a hailstorm rained down on Rumtek, burying the monastery and the surrounding countryside under two centimetres of hailstones. 'It seemed,' remembered one Western visitor, 'as if the sky was crying.' Vistors quickly began to arrive from all over the world to participate in the forty-nine-day funeral pujas. Rumtek was in a state of shock, 'awash', as one person remembered, 'in grief and disbelief', the atmosphere heavy with fear and trepidation. A story began to circulate that before Jamgon's fatal accident, Gyaltsab Rinpoche had had a dream of the upper shrine room in Rumtek – the Kashi Dung Gye, or 'four-pillared, eight-beamed room' – in which two of its pillars had collapsed, causing the roof of the monastery to cave in. The four pillars, it was said, were the four heart sons, and clearly the collapse of one of them signified Jamgon's death. What would happen next? Jamgon had been just thirty-eight. He had been universally loved and respected, and his sudden, terrible death left everybody shaken, 'as if something impossible had happened, something unspeakable'.

Indeed, so shocking – so *inconceivable* – was Jamgon's death that it was hard to believe it could actually have been an accident. What possible forces of karma could have made it so? Rumours quickly began to multiply. Photographs showed that the engine had been found some thirty yards away from the crashed car, suggesting that the engine had been catapulted from the car, as if by an explosion. The soles of Jamgon's feet were said to be scorched. On the day before the accident, the car had been serviced by mechanics who had been summoned from Delhi. Clearly, they had planted a bomb. Or they had tampered with the brakes. No, the mechanics had actually come from Bhutan, organized by Topga. More rumours: it wasn't Jamgon's driver who had been at the wheel at the time of the accident, but Jamgon himself. But this could not be announced publicly because it was a major infraction of protocol for rinpoches to drive.

But who stood to gain from Jamgon Kongtrul's death? He had been on his way to Tibet to fulfil the instructions of the prediction letter presented by Tai Situ. Only someone who wished to prevent that would benefit. The names of Topga and Shamar Rinpoche were whispered in corners. But there was no evidence of plot or sabotage. The police declined to launch an investigation into the incident. And so too did Jamgon Kongtrul's family.

Tai Situ was teaching at a convention of businessmen, the Young Presidents, in Taiwan at the time of Jamgon's death. He immediately cancelled his programme and hurried back to Rumtek, arriving some four days after the accident. The plan laid by the heart sons in March to send Jamgon Kongtrul to investigate the contents of the prediction letter would need to be redrawn. What to do? The logical thing would have been for the three surviving heart sons, all of whom had now gathered in Rumtek, to meet and decide what course of action to take. But such was the distrust and suspicion between Tai Situ and Shamar that no such meeting took place.

Following the death of Jamgon, and before Tai Situ's arrival, Shamar had joined in the funeral pujas. Then, he let it be known that following a dream which he had interpreted as 'a bad omen', he intended to retreat to his house, a short distance down the hill from the monastery, for a period of intensive meditation. Shamar's retreat apparently prevented him from meeting with either Tai Situ or Gyaltsab. He also had other plans. Rather than staying in Rumtek for the duration of the pujas, he had announced that he was shortly to leave for a conference in America.

On 9 May, he emerged from his retreat to attend a meeting with the Chief Minister of Sikkim, N.B. Bhandari, in Gangtok, to discuss the question of the prediction letter. According to Shamar, he explained to Bhandari that he was leaving for America, and requested the Minister to despatch a police guard to Rumtek as 'protection' for the letter. Bhandari agreed.

The Minister had also invited Tai Situ to the meeting. 'I suggested Gyaltsab should join us,' Tai Situ told me. 'But when we arrived Shamarpa was already with the Chief Minister. The secretary said he [Shamar] had come earlier than planned. So we waited. I had even prepared *khatas* for Shamarpa, because I hadn't seen him for months. And all of a sudden I heard a car door slam, and it was Shamarpa leaving.' At the meeting with the Chief Minister, Tai Situ requested an investigation into Jamgon Kongtrul's accident. 'We all felt a little uncomfortable and wanted to have it cleared up for us. And he said, there was a problem, because the accident had occurred in a different state and so on.' The two Rinpoches returned to Rumtek. 'And the next day Shamarpa left for America. I had not spoken to him one word.'

With Shamar having absented himself from Rumtek, Tai Situ and Gyaltsab now devised another plan. 'We got worried,' Tai Situ told me. 'We had told people we would make the announcement in October. And we were worried that if so many people heard these things in Tibet that unpredictable things could happen. The Karmapa's security could become a problem. So we thought we had to rush. Then we had a meeting with Gyaltsab and the other senior rinpoches left there, and we decided that Gyaltsab would send his general secretary Sherab, and I would send Akong, because he has much experience of Tibet, he has lots of projects there. Also Gyaltsab Rinpoche and I from the Palpung *labrang* wanted to sponsor lots of prayers for Jamgon Rinpoche, lighting the butter lamps in Jokhang, Lhasa, Drepung, Sera, all the different monasteries, because this also is necessary. So we gave a copy of the letter to Sherab and Akong and we sent them.'

On 9 May, Akong Rinpoche and Sherab Tharchin left Rumtek, carrying with them a copy of the 16th Karmapa's prediction letter. It would be three weeks before word finally came from Tibet. The new incarnation of the Karmapa had been found.

CHAPTER EIGHT

The Sound of the Conch Shell

Gyuto: August 2000.

His first memory, he said, was of horses. 'I was very young, but I have a feeling I was in a tent, and then some people are riding towards me. It isn't very clear, but the horses are covered with scarves. Later on, I understood that at that time one of my sisters got married, and according to the tradition of Tibet the people came there with their horses for the wedding party.' The Karmapa glanced up towards the back of the room, where the Indian security officer stood, eavesdropping on our conversation. His birth, his childhood, his upbringing . . . Every time I raised these subjects in conversation, a look of palpable indifference would flicker in the Karmapa's eyes, as if to say, what possible interest could these things be to anybody?

The Tibetan Buddhist teachings on death and rebirth are quite precise. At the moment of death, the senses shut down one by one, lights on a strand, flickering and darkening. Vision, touch, smell, recollection, discrimination, all cease. Deprived of its senses, the mind becomes aware of its own nature, without any projections or delusions, manifest as a clear, white light. For the ordinary mind, the light of the mind's own true nature is so piercing that the instinct is to turn away, desperately searching for the familiar. In this way the being enters into the *bardo*, where it remains for seven days, or seven multiples of seven, until once again being drawn by the inexorable forces of karma to seek rebirth in a new form. But for the yogi, who has trained his mind for just such a moment, the clear light represents the possibility of liberation, a

The 16th Karmapa performing the Vajra Crown ceremony. *Courtesy Rokpa Trust.*

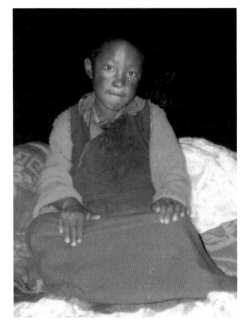

The first ever picture of Apo
Gaga – who would later be
recognized as the 17th Karmapa
– at home in Lhatok in 1992.
Courtesy Ward Holmes.

The 17th Karmapa's family at Tsurphu in 1993. *Courtesy Ward Holmes.*

The 17th Karmapa is carried from his car by his attendant Titi on his arrival at Tsurphu, 15 June 1992. *Courtesy Ward Holmes.*

The 17th Karmapa with Tai Situ Rinpoche at Tsurphu in 1993. *Courtesy Ward Holmes.*

The 17th Karmapa riding in the grounds of the Norbulingka Palace at Tsurphu monastery in 1993. *Courtesy Ward Holmes.*

The 3rd Jamgon Kongtrul Rinpoche. *Courtesy Diane Barker/Tibet Images.*

Old life, new life: the 17th Karmapa, in a ceremonial black hat, sits beneath a portrait of his predecessor in Tsurphu. *Courtesy Ward Holmes.*

Tsurphu monastery, the ancestral monastery of the Karmapas, photographed in 1992. *Courtesy Ward Holmes.*

Amdo Palden Rinpoche, abbot of Karlek *gompa* and the 17th Karmapa's first teacher. *Courtesy Norma Levine.*

The 17ᵗʰ Karmapa wearing (clockwise, from top left) the small, black 'activity' hat; the traditional travelling hat; the ceremonial Gampopa hat; and the *pandita*, or 'long-ears' hat, worn for initiations and empowerments. *All photographs courtesy Ward Holmes.*

The 17th Karmapa (right) and the 11th Pawo Rinpoche. Pawo Rinpoche was the first *tulku* to be formally recognized by the Karmapa. *Courtesy the Tsurphu Foundation, Holland.*

The 17ᵗʰ Karmapa lama dancing at Tsurphu, 1998. *Courtesy Ward Holmes.*

The 17th Karmapa meets the Chinese Premier Jiang Zemin, on his
first visit to Beijing in 1994. *Courtesy Ward Holmes.*

The 17th Karmapa with government officials on his second visit to China in 1999.
His attendant, Drupngak, who would later escape with him to India, is on the far
right. *Courtesy Ward Holmes.*

Gyuto monastery, near Dharamsala, where the 17th Karmapa was installed – ostensibly as a temporary measure – following his escape from Tibet, and where he has remained ever since. *Courtesy Hamish Dewar.*

Lama Tsewang, who planned and led the 17th Karmapa's escape from Tsurphu. *Courtesy Karen Davies.*

The 17th Karmapa and the Dalai Lama pose for pictures for the first time together in Dharamsala following the escape. *Photographer unknown.*

Thaye Dorje, Shamar Rinpoche's contestant to the Karmapa throne. *Courtesy H.H. Shamar Rinpoche.*

The 14th Kunzig Shamar Rinpoche. *Courtesy Karine Le Pajolec.*

The 17ᵗʰ Karmapa meets the world's media at his first press conference, at Gyuto monastery in April 2001. *Courtesy Karen Davies.*

The Dalai Lama and the 17ᵗʰ Karmapa with the 4ᵗʰ Jamgon Kongtrul Rinpoche, whose predecessor died in a car crash in April 1992, and whom the Karmapa recognized three years later. They are photographed at the Kagyu Monlam Chenmo ceremonies at Bodh Gaya in January 2002. *Courtesy Norma Levine.*

The 17th Karmapa, on the roof of Gyuto monastery, looking towards Tibet. *Courtesy Karen Davies.*

state in which he can rest in meditation for hours, or even weeks, and may even attain release from *samsara*.

The arithmetic of reincarnation puzzled me. The 16th Karmapa died in 1981. His reincarnation was born in 1985. Where did he spend the missing four years? Whenever I asked this question it would be greeted with an indulgent smile. The Pure Lands, people said; and even jokingly, 'He was taking a vacation in the Pure Lands.' According to the Mahayana teachings, the Pure Lands are a mental realm manifested by the compassion of Buddhas and bodhisattvas, a place devoid of poverty, suffering or hunger, where the conditions are conducive to progress along the path of the dharma. 'So with Karmapa,' Tai Situ told me, 'it can be Pure Land. Or maybe he stays in some meditative state. He could be reborn in another realm, another universe. Maybe only he knows that.'

If all this was true – if he was indeed the reincarnation of the 16th Karmapa, and if, as the histories said, the Karmapas were omniscient – then what memories did he have of his previous lives, and of the periods between lives? These, it seemed, were questions that were never asked, because they could never be answered; a thread in the veil of mystery, beyond words and common comprehension. It was a condition of taking Buddhist vows that one never talked of spiritual attainments; a condition of being enlightened, it seemed, that such questions should be deflected with a self-deprecating smile.

'Even in general, if you have the reincarnation of your previous life, still you will not remember things from your past, because there are lots of obscurations to that,' the Karmapa told me. 'Even if someone is a great enlightened one, like the 16th Karmapa, and now I'm the 17th . . . even despite the 16th Karmapa's wisdom there might be more obscurations, and then other causes and conditions might obscure the recollection of the past . . .' He paused. 'So frankly speaking, I don't remember. But reading the biographies of the 16th Karmapa and watching the videos I enjoy very much the activities of my predecessor . . .' He smiled.

And why – I struggled to formulate the question – why did he think the 16th Karmapa chose his parents as the vehicle for his birth?

If he thought the question odd, he showed nothing in his

expression. 'That is very much because of karma, and also because of the teachings of the Buddha – the manifestation of interdependent relations plays a very important role, I think; so maybe that is because of that.'

I could feel myself swimming further out of my depth. I had been told, I said, that as a child, his father had once met the 16th Karmapa, and that the Karmapa had named him. Did he think this meeting in any way significant in the circumstances of his own birth?

'It's true, the 16th Karmapa travelled all over Tibet, and he would give a name to any individuals according to requests. My father was one of them. And, as you say, I myself also have sometimes thought that maybe at that time the connection was made, like that.' His parents, he went on, were devout people, 'good practitioners', and growing up there would be many discussions about the dharma. 'So I believe that sometimes they would also talk about the 16th Karmapa. What I clearly remember is that in our family we had a small shrine, and on that shrine was a photograph of the 16th.'

Perhaps, I said, it was because they were such devoted practitioners that they were chosen.

'Well I can't say that is the real reason, because there are many other families who are as devoted as my parents – even more so, perhaps. But since His Holiness the 16th Karmapa made a decision to be born in my family, that means he definitely had certain aspirations to be there.'

You needed only to look at Ngödrup Pelzom and the Karmapa to know that they were brother and sister. Though she was seven years older, they might almost have been twins: the same broad, moon-like face, perfectly proportioned features, ruddy cheeks and almond-shaped eyes; the same sudden, dazzling smile lighting up an otherwise severe countenance. The same maroon, clerical robes: Ngödrup Pelzom was a nun. She had fled from Tibet, through Nepal, two months before her brother, and had stayed at Tai Situ's monastery Sherab Ling until word came of his escape. On the morning of his arrival in Dharamsala, she had been waiting at the Bhagsu Hotel to greet him. Now, she too was living in Gyuto.

We talked in one of the rooms in Gyuto. She was a shy girl, giggling behind her hand. She spoke no English, and a monk translated. When I switched on my tape recorder, she asked me to turn it off when she was speaking and record only his translation. She did not explain why.

She talked about her childhood. Her family, she told me, came from the village of Bakor, in the Lhatok district of Kham, eastern Tibet. Bakor was a nomadic community, made up of some seventy families, comprising around 430 people. In winter her family lived in a wooden house; in summer, in a tent, herding their animals to the good pastures for grazing. 'Our whole life was spent with animals and our living depended on animals.' The family had seven or eight horses, some 200 sheep and goats and fifty to sixty yaks. 'This,' she said, 'made us middle class.' There were nine children in the family. Life, she said, was very simple, 'but we were very happy. My duties were to take care of the younger sisters and brothers.' Such education as the children received was mostly related to religion. 'My parents would sit with books, and we'd study Tibetan scripture and pujas and prayers and memorize texts.'

There were three monasteries in the region of Lhatok. Traditionally, her family were most closely connected to Khampa Ga, the monastery of Khamtrul Rinpoche, who belonged to a sub-sect of the Kagyu called the Drukpa Kagyu. The other two monasteries were Karma Kagyu. Each year a lama would come from one or other to give teachings and blessings. It was the most important occasion of the year; there would be singing and dancing, and the men would drink *chang*, a particularly potent Tibetan beer.

Her family, like all those in the village, revered the Karmapas. A picture of the 16th stood on the family shrine. 'Our father used to tell us very much about Karmapa. And I remember in 1981 when His Holiness passed away, when that news came to Tibet, my father was very sad; he told everyone, "This is a sign that now is a time of dark age because His Holiness [has] passed away." So we respected him very much as one of the enlightened beings in this world.'

But nobody expected, I said, that Karmapa would be born into her family?

Her eyes widened with laughter. 'No, there was no such expectation.'

In accordance with local custom, the family's first son, her elder brother, was given up to the care of the local monastery, Khampa Ga, as a monk when he was seven years old. The next four children were daughters – she was the third. But her parents, Döndrub and Loga, longed for another son. They consulted a local yogi, Karma Norzang, who advised them to do the propitious acts of feeding beggars and fish in the rivers, to do a hundred thousand refuge prayers and to make a pilgrimage to Lhasa. They followed his instructions, but their next child was, again, a daughter. By the time they were ready to try for another child, Karma Norzang had died. Still yearning for a son, Döndrub and Loga now turned to another yogi, Thogden Amdo Palden Rinpoche, the abbot of Karlek, a *gompa* a day's ride from Bakor. Amdo Palden said that he would help, on the condition that when their son was born Döndrub and Loga would give him up to Amdo Palden as a monk. They agreed to his terms, and shortly afterwards, Loga fell pregnant.

In Tibet, great births come accompanied with great legends. Loga, it was said, dreamed of three white cranes offering her a bowl of yoghurt; of eight auspicious symbols wreathed in rainbow light.

Were these stories true, I asked?

Ngödrup Pelzom nodded her head. Yes, she said. All of this was true.

The child was born shortly before sunrise next morning, on 26 June 1985. 'There was a lot of excitement when he was born,' said Ngödrup Pelzom. There were many children in the family, so in a way there shouldn't have been excitement. But many things had happened before he was born. In that year, the weather was extraordinary. Because of that the flowers were blooming more than usual. And everybody in the area expressed that at that time they were somehow feeling very happy, without any particular reason. That feeling was there for everyone, not only our family. And then when His Holiness was born, he was a boy. In the family everybody had been expecting a boy, so everybody, especially my mother, was very happy about that. And my father, because of the signs that had happened for him, had confidence that this boy was somehow an extraordinary person.'

It is said that on the afternoon of the third day following his birth, the sound of a conch shell resonated through the valley for one hour, fulfilling the prophecy contained in the 16ᵗʰ Karmapa's prediction letter: '[With] the miraculous, far-reaching sound/ of the white one; [This] is the one known as Karmapa.'

Ngödrup Pelzom nodded. 'Yes, I heard that. Everybody heard it.' She giggled.

The young boy was taken to Amdo Palden, to be given a Buddhist name. But the yogi told the parents that their son was special and only a high lama could name him. Instead, the parents called him Apo Gaga, or 'happy child', a name that, his sister said, she had heard a magpie sing shortly after his birth. He was, she went on, a particularly pleasing, sweet-natured child. 'As a baby he behaved very well. And not just well behaved; he was very extraordinary. Normally, any child, whether a boy or a girl, they play and they kill insects and this and that; they don't know what is alive or not; they have a very wild way of playing. But even when he was very young His Holiness always cared for even the smallest insect, not to kill. And also, in his gesture of playing he would try to build a small house in sand or mud and call it a monastery. And then he would bring small pieces of wood and say, "That is my throne!" In this way he was a very extraordinary boy. Not only myself, but the whole family had confidence that he must be very special. Everybody in the village had that confidence, but nobody knew who he was exactly or that he was going to be a Karmapa.'

When Apo Gaga was four, his parents, honouring the promise they had made, gave him over to Amdo Palden, the abbot of Karlek *gompa*. Amdo Palden was a tall, gaunt figure with a long, wispy mandarin beard, his hair tied in a snake of plaits above his head. He had spent twenty-five years as a prisoner of the Chinese, and he had a reputation as a hard taskmaster. Karlek had been founded in the seventeenth century by the King of Lhatok, who was a disciple of the 9ᵗʰ Karmapa. There was no running water, no electricity. It was home to 100 monks. Both the miraculous signs that had accompanied Apo Gaga's birth and Amdo Palden's own instincts suggested that the young boy was certainly a *tulku*, although at this stage he had not been identified. As such, he was accorded some privileges. He had his own attendant, and his own small throne to one side of the shrine room, set below the

level of the abbot's throne. His days followed a strict regime. He would rise at five each morning for prayers. After a simple ~~of~~ breakfast
of *tsampa* (roasted barley), powdered and mixed with butter and cheese, and strong tea, there would be lessons in reading; then after lunch, lessons in writing. In the evenings he would revise what he had learned during the day. He was taught the life of the Buddha, and the basic principles of his teachings; how to perform various rites with drum, *dorje* and bell. Because of his age, he was often allowed to return home to his family, or they would visit him.

And so the years passed. In the summer of 1991, a ripple of excitement passed through the small community at Karlek. Tai Situ would be visiting Palpung to give empowerments. Monks from monasteries throughout Kham would be making the pilgrimage to Palpung, and the monastic community of Karlek would be joining them. In late October, the party of monks and laypeople (the young Apo Gaga's parents among them) set off from Karlek in a ragged caravan of horses and pack animals, laden with food and provisions. The journey took four days. Snow lay thick on the ground, the horses scrabbling to navigate the icy escarpments, the party stopping each night to make camp around a blazing fire. Apo Gaga's parents travelled in a state of high expectation. They had been told by Amdo Palden that their son was certainly a great rinpoche, even if Amdo Palden himself had declined to specify exactly whom he might be. Surely Tai Situ would be able to provide the answer.

The monastery of Palpung is set high on the mountain known as Gosela, or 'grey hat'. According to local legend, someone might stand at the bottom of the mountain with black hair, but by the time they have arrived at Palpung it will surely have turned grey, so hazardous is the climb. The monastery was *en fête*. Some 3,000 monks and nuns, and more than 100 rinpoches from all over Kham had come for the ceremonies. Every room in the monastery was filled to bursting point, and the grounds around had become a sprawling encampment of tents, pavilions and improvised shelters.

Over the next six weeks, Tai Situ presided over the empowerment ceremonies, made his decrees on the recognition of new *tulkus*, and performed the hair-cutting ceremony on the legion of monks who processed before him. It was here that Tai Situ and the boy whom he would subsequently recognize as the reincarnation of the 16th Karmapa were to meet for the first time. The exact details of this meeting are unclear. Tai Situ would certainly have seen the young monk Apo Gaga, and would certainly have performed his hair-cutting ceremony, as he did with dozens of young monks. It is likely that he would have been made aware of the remarkable circumstances that had surrounded Apo Gaga's birth. In the course of his stay at Palpung, Tai Situ would recognize more than 100 new *tulkus*. Could he possibly have failed to recognize his former guru, the most powerful figure in the Karma Kagyu hierarchy? But Tai Situ would insist that he had no inkling that the young boy passing in front of him was the Karmapa. 'Now His Holiness is giving me a very hard time, saying, why didn't I recognize him!' he told me.

At the conclusion of the empowerments, the young Apo Gaga and his family set off on the arduous journey back to Lhatok, his parents doing their best to disguise their disappointment that their son had not been recognized as a great rinpoche. If Apo Gaga was indeed special, Tai Situ had said nothing of it to his parents.

And yet, it seems that the young boy had made an impression. In November, Tai Situ left Palpung to return to India. His journey took him through Beijing. There, in his hotel room, he prepared gifts to be sent to the young monk from Karlek: a large silk *khata*, on which he wrote a four-line verse of praise to the boy, invoking the name of Guru Rinpoche, and a coral *mala* which had belonged to a previous Tai Situ. His accompanying letter, however, made no mention of any suspicions he might have had that Apo Gaga was the Karmapa. If Tai Situ had made up his mind that he had at last found the object of his search, he kept this information to himself.

The young boy returned to Karlek, where he remained for some months. In the spring of 1992, he was given leave by Amdo Palden to see his parents. The family were preparing to leave their winter home for the summer pastures at Bakor, where Apo Gaga had been born. The young boy told them they must make haste. There were monks, he said, coming from his monastery to collect him.

Not from Karlek, but from *his* monastery. Three days later, the search party from Tsurphu arrived.

According to the official records of Tsurphu monastery, the search party had left Tsurphu on 12 May 1992. A week earlier, on 5 May, the *labrang* at Tsurphu had met with representatives from the government of the TAR, shown them a copy of the prediction letter, and received formal permission to mount the search for the new Karmapa. The letter had been sent from Rumtek by Tai Situ and Gyaltsab Rinpoche. The party that set out from the monastery was comprised of four monks, led by Drupön Dechen's right-hand man Lama Tomo, and two drivers, travelling in two vehicles that had been provided by the government. The instructions in the letter had specified that the reincarnate would be found in the district of Lhatok, in the old province of Kham – a journey of some three days by car and a further one or two days by horseback from Tsurphu.

'The first stop for the search party was the monastery of Khampa Ga,' Ngödrup Pelzom told me. 'They said they were pilgrims and that they had a letter from their friends to give to a certain family. They mentioned the name of His Holiness's mother, Loga. That monastery directed them to go to the Karlek monastery. When the search party came there, they asked if there was a lady called Loga who lived in this region. The manager of the monastery told them that there was a lady called Loga, whose son was a rinpoche in Karlek, and that his father's name was Döndrub. So then the search party asked to be directed to the family, and in that way they came to our home.'

The search party arrived at Bakor on 21 May. And then they waited for twenty-four hours. The date was deemed to be not propitious for such an important event as greeting the new Karmapa. The following day, the party presented themselves at the tent of Apo Gaga's family. 'At that time His Holiness was with the family,' said Ngödrup Pelzom. 'On that first day when the search party arrived they didn't tell us that he was Karmapa. After checking thoroughly, they told us only that he was a rinpoche in their monastery. And also on the first day they didn't meet His Holiness. It was only on the second day that they met His Holiness and spent some time with him. It was then that they told the family that he might be Karmapa.' Ngödrup Pelzom's eyes widened at the memory. 'So when we learned this, there was an extraordinary feeling. Nobody had ever imagined this.'

Apo Gaga's parents were told to say nothing about the possibility of their son being the Karmapa, but to look after the young boy and take him back to Karlek as soon as they could. Two monks from the search party remained with the family, while the rest of the party returned to Tsurphu, to report their findings to Drupön Dechen.

At the end of May, a second, larger 'welcoming' party set out from Tsurphu to collect the young boy. Once again, Lama Tomo led the party, but this time it also included officials from the Chinese government's religious department and a representative of the United Front. The recognition of the new Karmapa had now become official government business. Akong Rinpoche and Sherab Tharchin had left Rumtek on 9 May, bound for Tibet. The plan was for the two lamas to travel to Chamdo, where they would rendezvous with the party that had been sent from Tsurphu, before proceeding on to Lhatok. But in Kathmandu, Akong and Sherab were delayed, waiting for visas to enter Tibet. The delay was undoubtedly political. For the Chinese authorities it was imperative that the first group to formally meet the new Karmapa should be lamas from within Tibet, accompanied by government officials, rather than lamas who were in exile. By the time Akong and Sherab finally reached Chamdo, news had already filtered through that the search party had located the reincarnate. The young boy, they were told, was now back at Karlek. The two lamas made their way there as quickly as they could. The small *gompa* was doing its best to accommodate the fact that Apo Gaga, the young monk who had been living there for the past three years, had now been recognized as the Karmapa. He was installed in the abbot's quarters, attended by the monastery's senior monks and members of the party from Tsurphu.

Akong Rinpoche had his own duties to perform. As Tai Situ's representative, he told me, it was necessary for him to confirm to his own satisfaction that the boy was indeed the Karmapa. He was ushered into the boy's rooms, where he met the new Karmapa for the first time. 'Then I knew . . .' Akong paused. 'The reason I have no doubts is that the 16th Karmapa gave me many, many

relics – he always gave me whatever I asked him for. But one thing
I asked him was, can I have one of his teeth after he died. And he
promised me that I could. When he passed away and was
cremated in Rumtek, it was too much for me to face. I didn't
go. I had been looking after him in Chicago, and grown very close
to him at that time. So I asked people, I'm sure there is a tooth that
did not burn in the fire, and if there is one, please take care [of it]
and may I have that. When they opened the stupa after the
cremation, they said there were some teeth that did not burn,
but somehow I was never given one. I was very upset. So when I
first saw Karmapa, I said to him, before you died you promised me
something, so where is it? He had a small carpet, and under the
carpet there was one of his milk teeth. And he gave it to me. So
that solved my problem.'

Akong had one more duty to perform. According to tradition, it
was necessary formally to request the family to give up their son
for training as a rinpoche, and to offer gifts as recompense. At the
family's home, Akong presented money, food and bolts of cloth.
'Then the father and mother requested that since their son is
something very precious for them, that he is their heart, that they
should be given something precious in return.' Akong presented
them with a precious statue of the Buddha which he had carried
with him from Sikkim. 'And then they were very happy, but in
another way they were very sad too.'

In the first week of June, preparations began at Tsurphu for the
arrival of Apo Gaga. Prayer flags were erected beside the newly
levelled road leading to the monastery, along with small stone
pyres for burning juniper incense sticks. In the monastery itself,
the huge mast from which the Karmapa's ensign traditionally
flew, and which had lain on the ground since the death of the 16th,
was hauled upright, bound like a maypole in multicoloured prayer
flags.

On the morning of 15 June, a convoy of vehicles comprising
half a dozen jeeps and two trucks wound its way up the dirt track
to the gates of Tsurphu's summer palace. Behind them came a
large party of Khampas on horseback, dressed in their finest
clothes. The third jeep, a Chinese government vehicle, was
swathed in white *khatas*. Seated next to the driver was the young
Karmapa, dressed in a tunic of handsome yellow brocade. In the

vehicles behind were members of his family. With the sound of *gyalings* blowing mournfully in the wind, and amid clouds of incense, the young child was lifted out of the car by his new attendant Didi, and carried through the gate into the summer garden. A large crowd had amassed for his arrival, among them a Chinese television crew. A marquee had been erected in the summer garden, where the Karmapa and his family took refreshment, while people gathered around. The party then got back into the cars for the short drive to the monastery. By now there was a crowd of several hundred people to greet the boy. There followed a round of ceremonies, during which the boy fidgeted, casting his quick, curious eyes around him, absorbing the strange new surroundings. In the main shrine hall, the Karmapa sat on the high throne as, for an hour, hundreds of people filed past to gaze at the incarnate and to take his blessing. The young boy's life had changed for ever.

CHAPTER NINE

The Fox Cries

Throughout the weeks of May and early June, with the Shamarpa in America and the search party already on their way to Lhatok, events at Rumtek had gathered an irresistible momentum. On 17 May, Tai Situ and Gyaltsab gave a talk to the monastic community, stating that since they had been unable to meet Shamar Rinpoche to discuss the matter of the search with him, they had decided to act alone in fulfilling the plan that had been laid in March. Akong and Sherab Tharchin had left Rumtek a week earlier. Tai Situ and Gyaltsab waited. On 3 June, the two Rinpoches left Rumtek for Dharamsala, carrying with them a copy of the prediction letter. Word had now come from Tibet about the discovery of the boy from Lhatok. It was necessary to inform the Dalai Lama of developments.

The Dalai Lama was shortly to leave for Brazil, where he was scheduled to attend the first Earth Summit. On 5 June, Tai Situ and Gyaltsab arrived in Delhi. From there, Tai Situ telephoned Tibet. There was no phone at Tsurphu. A contact in Lhasa was obliged to go back and forth to the monastery to carry messages. Over the telephone, the contact recounted the findings of the search party, how the names of the mother and father matched the letter, and the auspicious signs that were said to have surrounded the young boy's birth. The welcoming party were with the Karmapa now, Tai Situ was told, ready to bring him back to Tsurphu. 'We told them, please don't do anything more,' said Tai Situ. 'We will go to the Dalai Lama and talk to him, and if His Holiness approves then we will do the right thing; and if he doesn't approve, we must look elsewhere. This is what we told them.' From Delhi, Tai Situ and Gyaltsab drove north to Dharamsala to see the Dalai Lama. But they had miscalculated: the spiritual leader had left for Brazil three days earlier. Tai Situ contacted the Dalai Lama in Brazil by phone from his private office. The prediction letter and a report on the candidate and his family were sent by fax. Later that same day the Dalai Lama called back Tai Situ to tell him that after studying the documents, and bearing in mind his own divinations, he approved the recognition of the boy from Lhatok as the 17th Karmapa.

The next morning Tai Situ and Gyaltsab left Dharamsala with a letter confirming the Dalai Lama's recognition, signed by his private secretary Tendzin Chonyi Tara. This, it would later be explained, was merely a 'holding document', to serve as proof of the recognition until the Dalai Lama returned from Brazil and issued the formal Seal of Approval, the Buktham Rinpoche. The letter summarized the details of the Karmapa's birth and discovery, before going on to state: 'The Tulkus, lamas and sangha residing both inside and outside Tibet, from Gangtok's Rumtek's place of Dharma, Tsurphu monastery and from all the Karmapa's monasteries requested with one-pointed devotion and aspiration, the compassionate advice for whether it would be appropriate or not to recognize this boy . . .' Was the Dalai Lama aware of Shamar Rinpoche's dissent over the matter of the prediction letter, and of the row that was now brewing among the Kagyu Regents? If he was, he had chosen to overlook it. From the post office in Dharamsala, Tai Situ telephoned his contact in Lhasa. 'I told the Tsurphu lamas that His Holiness the Dalai Lama had finally confirmed the recognition; now do everything properly. And that's how it happened.'

On 7 June, Shamar Rinpoche arrived back in Rumtek from his sojourn in America. The forty-nine-day pujas for Jamgon Kongtrul were now entering their final stages, and the monastery was still crowded with monks, Kagyu dignitaries and overseas visitors. Shamar's American trip had not, it seemed, been altogether successful. He would later claim that he had taken with him a photocopy of the prediction letter, hoping to find someone to examine the handwriting to establish whether or not the letter was a forgery. But his search had been fruitless. Now the situation was quickly slipping out of his control. Passing through Delhi, he learned that a search party, following the instructions contained in the letter, had already made contact with the young boy, and that he would soon be on his way to Tsurphu. Now, arriving in Rumtek, Shamar discovered that Tai Situ and Gyaltsab were in Dharamsala, seeking the official approval from the Dalai Lama for their candidate.

Shamar had been written out of the script. Nor, at this most critical juncture, could he rely on the support of his cousin and principal mainstay, the general secretary Topga. Shamar arrived at Rumtek to discover that, mysteriously, Topga had decided that his presence was no longer required for the pujas for Jamgon Kongtrul and that he had more pressing affairs to attend to at his home in Bhutan. For years, the four Rinpoches had been able to maintain a veneer of unity, throughout the cloistered meetings in hotel rooms, the numerous false dawns of announcements that the incarnation would soon be found. Now that illusion of harmony was about to be smashed apart.

On the day after his return, Shamar convened a meeting in the Nalanda Institute with the monks of Rumtek. Westerners were not admitted. As everybody was now aware, Shamar began, at the meeting between the four Rinpoches in March it had been agreed that Jamgon Kongtrul would go to Tibet to investigate the contents of the letter that had been presented by Tai Situ. It had also been agreed that there would be no further announcement until October. But now, said Shamar, the situation had 'turned around completely'. As the old Tibetan proverb had it, 'the fox must cry because the ghost is slapping its cheek', and it was his responsibility, he said, 'to speak my part'.

Apparently referring to the non-existent letter which the Regents had claimed to have put in the *gau* box in 1986, Shamar declared that there was an 'unmistaken instruction' from the 16th Karmapa, but that its meaning was not easy to understand. However, he went on, there was another instruction which acted like 'a key' for deciphering the meaning of the Karmapa's letter. He, the Shamar, knew who held this letter, 'but the person who has this instruction does not say anything precisely.' However, when the time was right, he went on, 'this person' would reveal what he knew. Jamgon Kongtrul Rinpoche, Shamar claimed, had also been aware of this 'key' letter, held by the unnamed person. But whether or not Situ Rinpoche and Gyaltsab Rinpoche were aware of it, Shamar declared, he was unable to say. He then went on to give his version of what had occurred in the meeting in the Karmapa's sitting room on 19 March: how Tai Situ had produced the envelope, saying it was the true prediction letter of the Karmapa and how he, Shamar, had expressed doubts about its authenticity and called for the letter to be forensically tested. If the prediction letter presented by Tai Situ was proved to have been written by the 16th Karmapa, then he would accept it '100 per cent', Shamar said. 'Otherwise I cannot accept it.' In the meantime, he went on, he had 'full confidence' that, eventually, the meaning of 'the first letter' would become clear. 'If the final result of the instruction is not positive, I will renounce my function as the Shamar Rinpoche.'

It was a baffling proclamation. Though his audience at this stage were unaware of the fact, there had been no 'first letter', only the verse which Gyaltsab had recalled from memory, which Jamgon Kongtrul had written down and which had then been placed in the *gau* box. If there had been no first letter, how could there be a 'key' letter that would explain it? So who then was this person who could explain an instruction that had never existed in the first place? Perhaps, as Shamar Rinpoche claimed, Jamgon Kongtrul could explain. But Jamgon Kongtrul was dead. However confusing Shamar's explanation may have been, however, one thing was clear. The illusion of harmony between the four heart sons, which had been so carefully maintained since the death of the 16th Karmapa, was now being blown apart.

To the senior lamas gathered at Rumtek the implications of this were clear. So far, Shamar had confined his accusations to an audience of monks. It was an appeal to his authority in the lineage; a political gambit. For most Tibetans the politics of religion were nothing new; they harboured none of the idealistic ideas about the immaculate perfection of high lamas that many of the Western students did. But the prospect of a public row between Shamar and the other heart sons would not only do irreparable harm to the good name of the Karma Kagyu; it threatened to shake the faith of devotees in the very dharma itself.

A deputation of young *tulkus* approached Shamar, begging him not to make any more statements until all three regents had found the opportunity to meet together and resolve the matter privately. Among them was Ponlop Rinpoche. 'The Shamarpa showed us a photocopy of the original prediction letter, alongside a photocopy of another letter from the 16th Karmapa, and a letter written by Situ Rinpoche,' he remembered. 'He said, "look at these three . . ." I grew up with the Karmapa, attending his Holiness. I could clearly see the prediction letter was authentic. But Shamar Rinpoche then said, "If you look at this letter thinking it is Karmapa's handwriting, you will see it as Karmapa's handwriting; if you look at it thinking it's a forged letter you will see it is that." He was saying we were looking at the letter with prejudiced eyes. But he agreed not to call the meeting. Then he called the meeting the next day.'

On 9 June, Shamar addressed the Westerners who had gathered at Rumtek, repeating the allegations he had made to the Tibetans two days earlier, sparing no detail. He described how when Tai Situ had first presented his prediction letter, he, the Shamarpa, had immediately doubted its authenticity. While Gyaltsab had accepted it unquestioningly, Jamgon Rinpoche, Shamar claimed, had also expressed doubts. Together, he went on, all four Rinpoches had agreed to say nothing publicly until October, when Jamgon Kongtrul had returned from Tibet. But now Jamgon Rinpoche was dead, and Tai Situ and Gyaltsab had broken the agreement. They had gone behind his back by spreading news of the contents of the letter to Nepal and Tibet. Now, Shamar went on, this letter, which he could not accept, had been confirmed by everybody. He had been told that Situ and Gyaltsab had been to Dharamsala to see the Dalai Lama, and that the Chinese government was providing full support for the new incarnation, 'So therefore I had to make noise now.' He had also been told, he said, that Akong Rinpoche had spread word that the boy would soon be enthroned and then brought to every centre in Europe. 'If that boy is not the true one, and they enthrone him and do everything and three million people in Tibet follow that . . . And if the two Rinpoches [Situ and Gyaltsab] are supporting it and everybody is following like that, then if this is not the true one – since so much doubt is there – and if they bring this up, then one day we cannot clarify things any more. Then if there is maybe only me left, how can I run to each of you saying, "This is not true, this is not true"?'

It was an exposition of his worst fears. He then went on to tell the meeting what he had told the Tibetans the previous day; that there had been an original letter in the *gau* box, written in Karmapa's hand, but nobody had been able to understand it. However, he claimed, both he and Jamgon were aware of a 'very trustworthy person' to whom the 16th Karmapa had given instructions on how to interpret the letter – the 'key'. 'Maybe the full instruction is with him,' Shamar Rinpoche said. 'I don't know. He must have been told by Karmapa to hint [to the] two of us that he is the one who has it. If you asked me who it is, whether he is a monk or not, whether he is a rinpoche or not, I will not say anything.' But if this 'trustworthy person' proved to be false, he repeated, then he, the Shamar Rinpoche, would resign.

Among his audience there was a stunned silence, and then an audible intake of breath. It was the sound of illusions shattering. Could the Shamarpa possibly be accusing another high rinpoche of lies, forgery, a massive act of deception?

Then came a barrage of questions. People were drawn to Buddhism by the possibilities of transformation: why then wasn't politics transformed in Buddhism? How was it possible for a high rinpoche not to tell the truth? Weren't bodhisattvas supposed to be fully realized beings? This, replied Shamar, depends on their *bhumis*, or levels of realization. 'Sometimes they are realized, sometimes not. Some, they always realize, some they don't realize. But the cause is making them bodhisattva. Many are there.'

How, someone asked, would they know if Tai Situ's letter was not authentic? Would it be sent for forensic testing?

'Should be soon, yes,' replied Shamarpa. 'We will discuss that. The sooner the better.'

And where, somebody else asked, was Topga? What could possibly have taken the general secretary away from Rumtek at such an important time?

Shamar replied that he had been told Topga was busy in Bhutan, solving 'family problems'. But there were other issues involved, he went on. In America and Germany rumours were being spread that the general secretary had been responsible for the death of Jamgon Rinpoche. 'So many stories, really!' Perhaps,

Shamar suggested, this had something to do with Topga's absence. 'Who knows? Maybe his wife is nervous, "Maybe my
husband will be killed by somebody." Who knows . . .?'

The meeting broke up in confusion and disarray. Events at the
monastery were now unfolding at a bewildering speed. Two days
after his speech, Shamar issued a formal statement questioning
the authenticity of the prediction letter. On that same day Tai
Situ and Gyaltsab returned from Dharamsala, bringing with
them the letter of confirmation that had been sent out by the
Dalai Lama's office. An announcement was made: on the following day there would be an important meeting which all should
attend, Tibetans and visitors. The rumour crackled through
Rumtek like a bush fire. The reincarnation of the Karmapa
had been found.

The next morning, 12 June, some 400 people assembled in
the quadrangle in front of Rumtek's main shrine hall. The two
dormitory blocks flanking the courtyard were under reconstruction. Piles of sand and gravel littered the courtyard. On the
porch in front of the door to the shrine hall, three chairs had
been set out: Tai Situ and Gyaltsab occupied two of them. The
third was empty. Shamar was not present. Behind the two heart
sons stood some of the most senior lamas of the Kagyu lineage,
among them Ponlop Rinpoche, Thrangu Rinpoche and Bokar
Rinpoche. His words crackling through an antique public
address system, Tai Situ spoke to the group in Tibetan. Then
Gyaltsab spoke, also in Tibetan. Then Tai Situ began to speak
again, this time in English. He explained how following the
death of the 16th the four Rinpoches had searched everywhere
for the prediction letter but had been unable to find it. Then
they had met in Rumtek. In the absence of a letter, Gyaltsab had
recited the four-line poem of the Karmapa, which had then been
put in the *gau* box. 'Then we had a long discussion about what
to say to people. We made a decision, wrote it down, everybody
signed it, and a public announcement was made.' He paused.
'That is a true story.'

His words began to sink in among the astonished audience.
There had been no 'first' prediction letter. Tai Situ then went on to
explain how in 1981, in his suite in the Oberoi Grand Hotel in
Calcutta, the 16th Karmapa had given him the protection pouch,

and how he had worn it, first around his neck and then his waist before finally opening it in his room at Sherab Ling. He had then informed the other heart sons that he had news 'similar to the joyful cries of peacocks'. He explained how, after many delays, the heart sons had finally gathered in Rumtek, and he had presented the letter to them – 'Our late Jamgon Kongtrul Rinpoche and Gyaltsab Rinpoche were very happy, their eyes were full of tears, and I myself felt that way' – and how they had then removed from the *gau* box the four-line verse that had been recited by Gyaltsab and written by Jamgon, and replaced it with the prediction letter that he, Tai Situ, had found. The four-line verse, he said, was now in Gyaltsab's possession. He explained how the Dalai Lama had told him about his own sacred vision pertaining to Karmapa's rebirth, and how, following the tragic death of Jamgon Kongtrul, neither he nor Gyaltsab had been able to meet with Shamar Rinpoche in Rumtek, and had therefore taken the decision to despatch Akong Rinpoche and Sherab Tharchin to Tibet to search for the new incarnation. Tai Situ had then written to Drupön Dechen at Tsurphu, informing him about the discussions in Rumtek and instructing him that the incarnation of Karmapa, once found, should be brought to Tsurphu and remain there until arrangements had been made to bring to him to Rumtek for his enthronement. After some weeks, Tai Situ went on, he and Gyaltsab had proceeded to Dharamsala, only to discover that the Dalai Lama was in Brazil. He had contacted the Dalai Lama, who had confirmed the recognition according to the details of his own sacred vision. The next day the Dalai Lama's secretary handed him a letter, confirming the Dalai Lama's decision.

Tai Situ waved the letter in his hand, and was about to read it when there was a sudden commotion at the back of the courtyard, 'a sound', as one onlooker remembers, 'that didn't belong'. An army jeep was edging through the crowd, sounding its horn, before finally pulling up at the foot of the steps leading to the shrine room. An Indian soldier was driving; sitting in the back seat were two more soldiers brandishing carbines. Riding shotgun in the front was Shamar Rinpoche. Behind the jeep was a truck, also loaded with soldiers. Shamar jumped from the jeep and strode up the steps, his armed escort following behind. Situ Rinpoche and

Gyaltsab rose from their chairs. Situ arranged the folds on his robe and extended his hands to Shamar in greeting. 'Go inside', said Shamar. Brushing past the two Rinpoches, he strode into the shrine room, beckoning to his escorts to follow.

Inside the shrine room, Shamar jumped on to a wooden table and shouted, 'Soldiers and rinpoches to stay. Everybody else, leave!' An alarmed Gyaltsab turned to Situ Rinpoche and whispered, 'Do you suppose they intend to kill us?' Outside, scuffles had broken out, as monks attempted to prevent the armed soldiers entering the shrine room. 'The old monks were saying, "This is why we came out of Tibet," ' remembers one onlooker, ' "this is exactly what happened in 1959." '

In the ensuing confusion, Tai Situ and Gyaltsab Rinpoche were hurried upstairs by their attendants into a living room, the door firmly shut and locked. Shamar followed, making his way to the 16th Karmapa's private apartment, from where he sent a message demanding that Tai Situ and Gyaltsab come immediately. The two Rinpoches refused his request. Eventually, Shamar had no option but to go back downstairs. He emerged from the shrine room and strode back to his jeep through the crowd, people staring in disbelief.

Quite what Shamar was hoping to achieve, or how he had come to have an Indian army escort was never properly explained. He would later claim that on arriving in Gangtok from America he had been alerted by the 'military department of Sikkim' that two bus-loads of Khampas had left Kathmandhu *en route* for Rumtek, intending to attack him and the monastery if he insisted on having the prediction letter forensically tested, and that he had been given a military escort for his protection. On the afternoon of 12 June, he said, he had been informed by the monastery office that Tai Situ and Gyaltsab were giving an important speech in the monastery yard and he had been requested to join them. 'At first I was reluctant to go,' he said, 'but they insisted . . . I sent a message up to the monastery saying that I would come and join them. The soldiers had orders not to let me go anywhere alone, so I had no choice but to be escorted by them.'

In a subsequent report by the *Sunday Times* of India, Sikkimese Chief Minister N.B. Bhandari suggested an alternative reason for the military escort. He claimed that it had been provided to

Shamar following an approach from the Bhutanese royal family to the Indian Ministry of External Affairs. The state administration, Bhandari went on, had 'not received any complaint about a law and order problem in and around the Rumtek monastery' prior to the incident. There were no 'bus-loads of Khampas' at Rumtek.

Was all of this borne of a genuine fear on Shamar's part for his own safety? Or was it a clumsy attempt by him to disrupt Tai Situ's announcement about the discovery of Karmapa? A desperate bid to impose his fading authority over Rumtek? Whatever Shamar's motives, the presence of armed Indian soldiers in the monastery provoked fury in Sikkim. The following day, the State government called a two-day public strike in protest against troops being deployed by central government without their knowledge or permission.

On 14 June the forty-nine-day pujas for Jamgon Kongtrul officially came to an end. Jamgon's mummified body was brought in solemn procession from the monastery to the main hall in the Nalanda Institute – Jamgon's first major project – where it was to remain in state for a further week while more offerings were made. The procession was led by Tai Situ and Gyaltsab Rinpoche. Shamar Rinpoche was nowhere to be seen. The following day, during pujas, a petition was circulated among all the senior lamas, asking them to affirm their support for the recognition of the boy from Lhatok as Karmapa. Virtually every senior lama in the order added his signature. In terms of tradition, the endorsement of this lama or that rinpoche meant nothing in formally authenticating the identity of the Karmapa, but the symbolic significance was obvious. Tai Situ's judgement had been validated. Shamar was being increasingly marginalized.

Among the monastic community at Rumtek, divisions began to appear between those monks loyal to Tai Situ and those loyal to Shamar. Both men, as one observer put it, 'began fishing for monks. Because some are good at meditation, some are good at prayers, ritual and so on. Situ got most of them. But Shamar got two or three good fish.'

On 15 June came word that the new Karmapa had arrived at Tsurphu. Tai Situ announced that horns should be sounded next morning from the balcony of Rumtek. Shamar, in a show of defiance, instructed the senior monks not to comply. Torn between the conflicting orders, that evening three chant-masters, a Dorje Lopon and a discipline master quietly slipped away from the monastery. The ceremonies went on without them.

The next day, another visitor arrived at Rumtek. Tulku Urgyen Rinpoche had been a close friend of the 16th Karmapa, and a teacher of both Tai Situ and Shamar during their early years in Rumtek. He was a universally respected figure. Now, as the crisis escalated, he had hurried from his monastery in Nepal to mediate in the dispute between his two former pupils. On his first day, Tulku Urgyen, along with his son Choekyi Nyima Rinpoche, met Shamar at his house. Tulku Urgyen tried to reason with the Shamarpa. Shamar's refusal to give his agreement would cause many problems, he said. There were people in Tibet who would exploit the disagreement between the two heart sons; the Karma Kagyu school would be split in two. Furthermore, the new incarnation had already been recognised by the Dalai Lama and accepted by the Chinese, and there was nothing Shamar could do to alter that. 'Tulku Urgyen pleaded with me to give my agreement, tearfully prostrating to me,' Shamar would later recall. 'I could not refuse him. He is a senior lama to me and my main Nyingma teacher. I realized at this point that everything was already decided regarding the boy.'

On 17 June, Shamar drafted a letter acknowledging his acceptance of the prediction letter. An English translation, provided by Michele Martin, who had also translated the prediction letter, was issued the next day. It read:

> On March 19, 1992, Tai Situ Rinpoche, Jamgon Kongtrul Rinpoche, Gyaltsab Rinpoche and I held a meeting in which Tai Situ presented us with His Holiness' hand-written letter of prophesy, the sacred testament, which was found in Situ Rinpoche's protection talisman. At that time, a little doubt arose in my mind, but now I have attained complete confidence in Situ Rinpoche, and the contents of this letter, according to which the reincarnation has definitely been discovered and further confirmed by His Holiness the Dalai Lama as the incarnation of His Holiness the Gyalwang Karmapa. I offer my willing acceptance and henceforth, I will no longer pursue the matter of examining the sacred testament, etc.

The translation was made and the letter distributed around Rumtek. Four weeks later, after consultations with Topga, who had now returned to Rumtek, Shamar issued another statement. His letter, he now claimed, had been translated incorrectly. He offered a revised translation:

On March 19th, 1992 at a meeting with Jamgon Rinpoche, Gyaltsab Rinpoche and myself, Situ Rinpoche presented a hand-written prediction letter from his protection pouch, claiming it was the written instructions of H.H. 16th Karmapa. I had some doubts. At this point, I rely on Situ Rinpoche (giving me correct information about H.H. the Dalai Lama's decision). Relying on our confidential discussion, I go along with the decision made by H.H. the Dalai Lama that a reincarnation has certainly been found as reincarnation of H.H. the Gyalwa Karmapa. Hence I *suspend* my demands such as having the handwritten prediction letter being subjected to a (forensic) test. [my italics]

The truce was over as soon as it had begun.

While, to Western minds, the Shamar's call for a forensic test might have seemed perfectly logical and the rational solution, to Tibetan minds it contained an inherent paradox, demanding the sort of empirical proof which is nowhere to be found in Tibetan Buddhism. In the first place, it would have been difficult, if not impossible, to conduct such a test. While there was no shortage of witnesses from either side – former students or functionaries of the 16th, allies of Tai Situ and Shamar respectively, who were pre-pared to state that in their opinion, the letter was, or was not, in the Karmapa's handwriting – their testimony could hardly have been said to be impartial, or conclusive. It would have been necessary to find a forensic expert intimately acquainted with Tibetan handwriting. No easy task in itself. Furthermore, under the normal criteria of forensic testing, an expert would require a comparable sample not only of the subject's handwriting, but also of a document written under similar conditions, taking into consideration such factors as the health or state of mind of the subject at the time the document was written. If Tai Situ's account was to be believed, the prediction letter had been written by a man who was most likely in his late fifties, in the grip of a terminal illness, and presumably in a meditative state. In this document he was purporting to predict the exact circumstances of his rebirth some years later. There was no comparable document. As evidence in itself, the document would fail on all counts in a court of law. What forensic scientist, even one expert in Tibetan script, would argue that a dying man could predict his own rebirth some four years hence? What court of law would even accept the idea of rebirth? By the criteria of Western rationalism, the letter could not be what it was purported to be.

But more critically, the demand for the letter to be forensically tested flew in the face of the most fundamental tenets of Tibetan Buddhism, the entire edifice of which is constructed on a nebulous architecture of prophecy, divination, and supernatural processes which, by definition, preclude empirical proof. For example, many of the primary texts in Tibetan Buddhism are *terma* – or 'treasures' – ostensibly 'revealed' centuries after they were written, either through dreams or divinations, or in the form of statues and texts discovered, supposedly hidden in rocks and trees. The 'proof' of the authenticity of these teachings lies not in determining their factual or material origin, but in the authority and reputation of the *terton*, or treasure seeker, who has discovered them.

A further claim of verification for the choice of the boy from Lhatok as the authentic reincarnation of Karmapa, and for Tai Situ's role in his discovery, would come in the form of a prophecy by the venerated nineteenth-century *terton* Chogyur Dechen Lingpa, who was supposedly gifted with a vision in which Guru Rinpoche, or Padmasambhava, appeared, surrounded by twenty-one manifestations of the Karmapa – the fourteen who had been born up to that time, and seven who would follow. Chogyur Dechen Lingpa described this vision to a master painter, who rendered it as a *thanka*. In this, the 17th Karmapa is shown seated under a leafy tree with Tai Situ. Chogyur Dechen Lingpa's commentary describes the scene: 'Under a verdant tree, on a rocky mountain is the seventeenth incarnation with Khentin Tai Situpa [Tai Situ]'. The surroundings in the picture bear no resemblance to the rocky moonscape around Tsurphu, but they do evoke the landscape of the Himalayan foothills around Dharamsala, to where the Karmapa would eventually escape. (While acknowledging the authenticity of Chogyur Dechen Lingpa's vision, the Shamarpa would dispute the interpretation. Between the 14th and 15th Karmapas, he maintained, another incarnation had been born who had died at a very young age. While this incarnation was not formally acknowledged in the lineage, the 15th could, therefore, be counted as the 16th, the 16th as the 17th and so on. Chogyur Dechen Lingpa's prophecy, the Shamar argued, could therefore be taken to refer to the close relationship between the previous Karmapa and the previous Tai Situ.)

The entire hierarchy of Tibetan Buddhism is dependent on similarly 'magical', and ambiguous, principles. Selecting *tulkus* is not a scientific or for that matter democratic process, open to public scrutiny or rational debate. The authenticity of the sixteen previous Karmapas rested either in letters of prediction, or in the equally unscientific criterion of self-declaration, confirmed by the divinations of other high lamas. Indeed, the authority of Shamar Rinpoche himself, as of all the other high *tulkus* in the order, depended on just such 'magical' procedures. There could be no scientific evidence to 'prove' that he was the 14th incarnation of his line, any more than to 'prove' that Tai Situ was the 12th incarnation of his. For more than 800 years, the entire *tulku* system had been constructed on a sleight of hand between politics and the supernatural in which the weight of belief was infinitely greater than the weight of reason.

By this criterion, the 'proof' of the Karmapa's authenticity would only emerge gradually over the years, in his conduct, his self-discipline and the wisdom of his teachings. 'Why did Shamar say the prediction letter should be analysed?' says Ngödrup Burkhar. 'This is a point in his favour to the modern Western audience, who will think, why not? There's no harm. It's an appeal to rationalism; not blind faith. But the second thing is that he knew this test could never be done, and that would again be in his favour. He could say, "Look, I am asking for something very straight, very plain, something the whole world acknowledges, and they're not going to do it!" But he knew that nobody would plunge themselves into hell by desecrating the letter.'

But whatever Shamar said was anyway, by now, irrelevant. On 27 June the official New China News Agency reported that Apo

Gaga had become 'the first reincarnated Living Buddha approved by the Chinese government since the Tibetan democratic reform in 1959'.

The statement added, 'According to conventional practice, the choice of any Living Buddha must be approved by the central government.'

Two days later, on the morning of 29 June, Tai Situ and Gyaltsab Rinpoche met with the Dalai Lama in Dharamsala to discuss the release of the Dalai Lama's formal Seal of Approval for the recognition. That same afternoon the Dalai Lama had a separate meeting with Shamar. Shamar made a desperate plea to the Dalai Lama to reverse his recognition and repeated his claim about the 'trustworthy person' who, he claimed, alone knew the 16th Karmapa's true instructions. When the Dalai Lama asked for this person's name, Shamar said he was not at liberty to disclose it. The following day, the Dalai Lama issued his Buktham Rinpoche, conferring his official recognition of Apo Gaga, the boy from Lhatok as the 17th Karmapa. The matter was settled.

The Chinese government's approval of the new Karmapa was heralded as an historic event: the first time that Beijing had formally approved the recognition of an incarnate since the Chinese had assumed absolute control of Tibet. How had the lamas of the Karma Kagyu managed to negotiate such an unprecedented occurrence with their Chinese overlords – and to whose advantage?

For the Chinese, there were clear political benefits to be gained. The atrocities of the Cultural Revolution had failed in their purpose of extinguishing the 'poison' of Tibetan Buddhism; faith had proved defiantly impervious to the twin weapons of persecution and ridicule. The 'hearts and minds' policy initiated under Deng Xiaoping in the late seventies and early eighties had been born of a dawning recognition that Tibet could not be effectively governed by suppression, and that co-option, not least of Tibetan Buddhism, might prove a more effective course. Controlling Buddhism meant taking control of the monasteries; by controlling the monastic administrative councils, in some cases by placing lamas on the state payroll, and, above all, by controlling the recognition of the *tulkus* who were at the very heart of the monastic system. The recognition of reincarnates – 'Living Buddhas', or the even more bizarre and grotesquely inappropriate 'soul boys' as the Chinese referred to them – was, of course, completely contradictory to the atheist beliefs underpinning communism, but it was politically expedient.

Since 1959, there had been no major recognitions of *tulkus* born in Tibet. The Chinese policy was to acknowledge as Living Buddhas reincarnates who had been recognized before 1959, as it suited their purposes, but to refuse to accept any born since then and particularly any recognized by the Dalai Lama or exiles outside Tibet. As a consequence, such reincarnates that had been located within Tibet were usually smuggled out of the country to India or Nepal as quickly as possible by the exile community. By the mid 1980s, however, the Chinese had adopted a tacit policy of allowing recognitions to take place within Tibet, but without involving themselves in the critical procedures of identifying or searching for the candidates. For the most part such recognitions had been of minor *tulkus* in the old provinces of Kham and Amdo, not in the heartland of the TAR, and none had ever received the official imprimatur of the central government in Beijing.

But the Karmapa provided a case where it would be politically advantageous for Beijing to become actively involved in the discovery and enthronement of the new incarnate. As head of the Karma Kagyu school, the Karmapa was the single most important lama to have been born in Tibet since Chinese occupation. For the Chinese, formal approval of his recognition would send out powerful signals to the Tibetan people, and to the world at large, about Beijing's new 'tolerance' of religious practice. As a Karma Kagyu lama, the Karmapa's recognition had the further advantage of not depending on the Dalai Lama. While it was true that the exiled Tibetan leader would later confirm the recognition through his own divinations, the critical part of the discovery process rested on the Karmapa's own prediction letter, and the deliberations of the Kagyu hierarchy.

The Chinese could also point to the strong historical connections between the Karmapas and successive Chinese emperors. The official announcement from Beijing on 27 June laid stress on the fact that previous Karmapas had 'constantly paid tribute to Emperors of the Yuan (1271–1368) and Qing (1644–1911) dynasties and received imperial titles many times'. Implicit in this was the suggestion that anyone who had received titles from the Emperor was, by definition, the subject of the Emperor; in other words, that Tibet always was, and continued to be, a part of China.

Furthermore, the lamas of the Karma Kagyu had proved themselves to be people who were prepared to work with the Chinese in a conditional way, and whom the Chinese felt they could trust. Tai Situ, Jamgon Kongtrul and Akong Rinpoche, among others, had all been back and forth to Tibet in previous years, developing religious and educational projects without causing undue problems. The development of Tsurphu monastery was a model of the liberal policy of religious tolerance. The formal approval of the Karmapa, then, provided an opportunity for the Chinese not only to demonstrate their tolerance of Buddhist practice, but also to assert what they claimed as their 'sovereign right' over the choice of *tulkus* and, by implication, of their rule over Tibet.

Establishing this principle was important to the Chinese not only in the case of the Karmapa but also in the recognition of another, even more politically significant reincarnate: the Panchen Lama. Following his release from prison in 1978, the Panchen Lama continued to live in Beijing. In January 1989 he was allowed to return to his ancestral seat at Tashilhunpo, to restore relics of past Panchens to their rightful resting place. A week earlier, he had spoken out once more in criticism of the Chinese government, declaring publicly that Tibet had suffered more than it had gained from Chinese rule over the previous thirty years. On the night of 27 January he was taken ill in his room at Tashilhunpo. By the following morning he was dead. He was fifty-three years old. Rumours quickly spread that he had been poisoned by his Chinese doctors, although there was no evidence of this.

The Panchen's death left a vacancy that the Chinese were anxious to see filled to their satisfaction. The Panchen Lama was not only a figure of reverence in Tibet. As the second-most important figure in the Gelugpa hierarchy, the Panchen Lamas have historically been closely involved in the recognition of the Dalai Lamas. Taking the long view, a compliant Panchen would be a valuable asset to the Chinese in the interregnum following the

Dalai Lama's death and before the recognition of his successor. By 1992 when the seventeenth incarnation of the Karmapa had been discovered – and three years after the Panchen Lama's death – no reincarnation of the Panchen had yet been found; but for the Chinese, putting the seal of government approval on the recognition of the Karmapa was a way of testing the waters, and of establishing a formal precedent for the future.

But if there were clear political benefits for the Chinese in allowing the recognition of the Karmapa, what were the benefits for the Tibetans? The process of seeking Chinese approval had not been a casual one. The exact details are not known, but it is clear that soundings had been made long before the boy's discovery in Lhatok – a series of conversations at local level between the lamas of Tsurphu and officials in Lhasa, perhaps; word filtering back to the department of religious affairs in Beijing; informal discussions, perhaps, between the exiled lamas on their journeys in and out of Tibet: what would be the official government position if . . .? For the Kagyu lamas, the time could not have seemed more favourable to risk pressing for the recognition of such a high-profile reincarnate as the Karmapa. Since 1985, the Chinese had allowed the development of his traditional seat at Tsurphu; the new breath of liberalism coursing through Chinese policy suggested that Beijing would be amenable. Conditions in Tibet were difficult, but not impossible.

One option would have been quietly to smuggle the boy out to India, Nepal or Bhutan, as had happened with other reincarnates; but for the Karmapa to resume his ancestral seat at Tsurphu would clearly infer that Buddhism was flourishing in Tibet in the face of all attempts to quell and control it, and it would give faith to the Tibetan people themselves, fanning the flame of Buddhist dharma. It was a high-risk strategy, calculating on the plausibility of the Chinese 'freedom to believe' policy, and calculating too that the character of the child, and the efficacy of his upbringing and education would be sufficient to resist any attempts at coercion by the Chinese.

But there was another compelling reason for leaving the Karmapa in Tibet, steeped not in *realpolitik* but in faith. By this argument, the Karmapa's reincarnation in Tibet was a matter of design, not accident; and whatever followed would inevitably be of benefit – even if that benefit were not immediately apparent. From this, one could unfold a whole tapestry of intention, woven from the moment of the death of the 16th Karmapa in the hospital in Mount Zion, Illinois, in November 1981: the prolonged search for the prediction letter; the disputes which had arisen between the heart sons; the years of waiting, and the eventual discovery of the new incarnation in 1992, at precisely the time when the Chinese were most accommodating to the idea of recognition. Ponlop Rinpoche expounded this argument to me. 'The common sense in our spiritual belief is that the Karmapa took birth deliberately in a place where he had a mission to accomplish. We respected his decision. And we can see his purpose. It was the first recognition of a reincarnate lama in the history of Chinese communism. He completed the rebuilding of Tsurphu, which had been completely destroyed in the Cultural Revolution. It was important in keeping alive the flame of Buddhism. He really has done a great deal for spiritual practice in Tibet.'

'For us it was Karmapa's miracle,' Tai Situ told me, seated in his office at Sherab Ling. 'It's not the kind of miracle where water is turned into milk. But for me the things that worked for Karmapa were more of a miracle than turning water into milk. The People's Republic of China said we accept the reincarnation! This is unbelievable! The Chinese don't believe in people dying and being reborn. They don't believe in anything! Of course, politically people calculate that they must have had other reasons; how important Karmapa is; how many devotees he has and all of that. But maybe the Chinese thought that respecting him was more beneficial than stopping him. They can do only two things, right? One is to say, you're not allowed; the other is to say, OK. And they chose to say OK.'

It would be only a matter of time, however, before it became apparent that the Chinese were not to be trusted. In July, Tai Situ gave an interview (which was published the following month) to the *Tibetan Review*, a journal published in Dharamsala, in which he stated that while the young boy was presently in Tsurphu, he expected the enthronement to take place in Rumtek, 'though we can't say at the moment when. We have informed the government of Sikkim of these developments and they have promised to do all they can to expedite the process of welcoming the 17th Karmapa to Rumtek. I am confident there won't be any problem regarding this.' Tai Situ's confidence was to prove misplaced.

On 12 July, Tai Situ and Gyaltsab Rinpoche arrived at Tsurphu to formally prostrate themselves in front of the new Karmapa and make offerings to him for the first time. Over the next few weeks the young boy and his two Regents were to be almost inseparable. On 2 August, in the Jokhang temple in Lhasa, Tai Situ and Gyaltsab performed the traditional hair-cutting ceremony. The ceremony signifies taking the first step on the path of the dharma, and follows the tradition of the Buddha Shakyamuni, who cut his hair on the banks of the Nairanja River before attaining enlightenment at Bodh Gaya. The 2 August was the anniversary of the Buddha's first teaching at Sarnath. In the Jokhang temple, the young Karmapa made prostrations in front of the great Jowo Buddha statue, then Tai Situ and Gyaltsab cut a few strands of his hair, to mark his ordination and offered him his new monastic name: Pal Khyabdak Ogyen Gyalwe Nyugu Drodol Trinley Dorje Tsal Chokle Nampar Gyalwe De (Glorious Master Ogyen, the Emerging Victorious One, the One Whose Activity Tames Beings, the Vajra's Creative Play, Victorious in All Directions). He would be known as Ogyen Trinley Dorje, or more simply still, Ogyen Trinley.

Gradually, the young boy began to acclimatize to his new surroundings and status. The German film-maker Clemens Kuby was among the first Western visitors allowed access to the Karmapa, filming him at play in the grounds of Tsurphu and poring over the growing mound of toys brought by devotees. He was also shown a film of his predecessor, the 16th, visiting America in 1974. The moment is captured in Clemens Kuby's film. At the sight of the 16th, the young Karmapa is visibly galvanized, his eyes widening in an expression, it seems, almost of shocked recognition.

But by the beginning of September it was apparent that the original plan to enthrone the Karmapa at Rumtek had faltered. Not only did the Chinese have no intention of allowing their most prized religious asset to leave the country, but the Indian government were proving no more keen to allow him into Sikkim. Instead, preparations began for the enthronement ceremony to take place at Tsurphu on 27 September. In the days before the ceremony, pilgrims began to arrive at Tsurphu from all over Tibet, in convoys of trucks and on horseback, bearing gifts: ritualistic objects; rolls of silk and brocade; bags of food; musical instruments. A small city of tents and pavilions began to grow in the valley below the monastery as some 20,000 pilgrims jostled for space and amused themselves with music and dancing. On the night before the ceremony a heavy snow fell on the mountains behind the monastery. It was taken as a propitious omen.

The next day, the young boy was brought into the Great Shrine Hall. Communist party officials from Lhasa and Beijing were waiting to greet him. In a showcase ceremony designed to demonstrate China's authority over the recognition, the Director of the Commission for Nationality and Religious Affairs announced the government's official acknowledgement of the Karmapa, and read a statement assuring the government's support of religious freedoms. In a flagrant contradiction of religious protocol, the Director had insisted that the Karmapa should not be given a seat higher than his own. Having stamped their political authority, the Chinese then left, and the enthronement ceremony proper began.

Dressed in an ornate brocaded cloak and wearing the small, black 'activity' crown [signifying his lineage], the Karmapa was led to his throne. Tai Situpa moved forward, prostrating himself, and presented the Karmapa with a copy of the prediction letter and a letter of formal confirmation from the Dalai Lama. The young boy was then presented with objects symbolizing the enlightened body, speech and mind: an image of the Buddha, a longevity sutra and a stupa. For the next two hours a procession of eminent rinpoches and high lamas gave teachings and discourses, while the young boy sat impassively on his throne. Outside the temple, thousands listened intently as the ceremony was transmitted by a public address system. Among the crowd were the Karmapa's parents, shown no special privilege or favour. At the conclusion of the ceremony, a great cheer went up. From the rear of the crowd, white and gold ceremonial scarves were thrown forward, gathering momentum until the sky was thick with silk, floating towards the monastery to finally break, like a huge multicoloured wave, against its walls. Inside, dignitaries passed in front of the Karmapa's throne, making offerings and receiving his blessing. Unable to contain themselves any longer, the weight of the crowd pressed against the doors of the Shrine Hall. The doors burst open and the crowd flooded in. The people had voted. Two days later the Karmapa's parents left Tsurphu. They assembled in his room for their farewell. The boy, one eyewitness remembers, showed 'not one flicker of sadness'. He gave *khatas* and blessings to his parents. They posed for pictures. And then they were gone. Ogyen Trinley Dorje, the 17th Karmapa, was about to begin his new life.

CHAPTER TEN

Difficult, but Possible

Gyuto: November 2000.

I felt sorry for the monks at Gyuto. The conditions were overcrowded, inefficient, absurd. There was only one telephone line into the monastery, which often rang unanswered. If somebody happened to pick it up, the chances are they would not speak English. There was one computer, but no Internet connection. It seemed inconceivable that the administration of one of the most important figures in Tibetan Buddhism should be so haphazard, so chaotic; a miracle that anything was done at all.

In the months since his escape the Karmapa had become an international celebrity, and people clamoured to see him: devotees, journalists, movie stars, wealthy supporters from America and Singapore; everybody wanted a piece of him. It was Lama Phuntsok's responsibility to organize all of his audiences, to liaise with the media (which meant refusing all requests; the Karmapa was still forbidden by the Indian government to give interviews), to juggle appointments and requests for private meetings. These responsibilities had taken their toll. Steadfast and loyal, Phuntsok wore a perpetually beleaguered expression. He was the only monk I had ever heard utter the words 'I need a holiday'. Did monks take holidays?

Lama Phuntsok had escaped from Tibet with the 16th Karmapa's party in 1959, when he was one year old. He had grown up in Rumtek, and become a monk at the age of nine. 'To be honest,' he told me, one evening, as we sat having dinner in a small restaurant in Dharamsala, 'it was not my choice.' He had fallen dangerously ill, he said, and neither Western nor Tibetan medicine could help. In desperation, his mother consulted the Karmapa. 'He told her that I must change clothes,' said Phuntsok, 'and then I would survive. In Tibet that means only one thing; that you must change from lay clothes to monk's robes.' And so he had become a monk.

And was he happy with this, I asked?

'There could be no greater honour than to serve His Holiness,' he said.

As we ate Phuntsok talked about the motivation of the bodhisattva, the need for mindfulness in all thoughts, all actions. 'For example, we are eating this meal.' He pointed to the plates, brimming with food. 'Normally, some will be thrown away. But think of what has been necessary to bring us this meal. There is the person who has grown the bell pepper, the person who has chafed the wheat. Perhaps some pesticides have been used and sentient beings have died for us to eat this. All of this is part of our karma and we must remember this.'

Something had been preoccupying me since my arrival in Dharamsala. On my frequent journeys from Delhi I had tried every available method of travel. I had travelled by taxi and by train. On one occasion I had even flown, a nerve-wracking ninety-minute flight in an antiquated nine-seater German aircraft which had been blown around the sky like a scrap of paper in the updraughts from the mountains. (By chance, I found myself sitting next to the Dalai Lama's younger brother, Tenzin Choedrak. I had taken this to be talismanic, but he passed the flight apparently even more apprehensive than me, muttering under his breath, 'Perhaps we are all going to die.') On this occasion, I had taken the overnight bus. At Delhi, the driver's mate had thrown my bag into the trunk of the bus and then demanded a fee of twenty rupees – next to nothing, but still a liberty, one of the minor tests that India exacts on the patience of the traveller. Reluctantly, I fished in my pocket, handed him a 100-rupee note and waited for my change. He turned away and busied himself collecting money from other passengers. At length, I tapped him on the shoulder and asked for my change. He brushed me aside and continued loading the bags on to the bus. The money was irrelevant. This had become a matter of principle. My anger rising, I grabbed his arm and shouted, 'Rupees! Rupees!' With a look of utter contempt he threw a handful of coins in my hand and again turned away. What to do? To have wrestled the money out of his pocket would have been a pyrrhic victory. Not only would it have meant a complete collapse of dignity and self-control; it would also have certainly jeopardized the chances of my bag arriving in Dharamsala. It would have been flung off or traded at some stop in the journey while I was dozing in my seat on the bus. But simply to walk away, cheated of my money, would mean defeat. Doing my best to compose myself, I shrugged and climbed on board. For the next two hours, as we bumped and rocked through the sprawling suburbs of Delhi and north towards Chandigarh, I brooded over the incident, re-examining from every angle my behaviour, my overheated feelings, my motivation. The driver's mate, I was sure, had forgotten all about it, and about me, the moment he turned his back on me. But I had allowed the incident to weigh on my mind, carrying it with me as the bus sped on through the darkness. There was surely a moral here.

Carefully spooning more rice on to his plate, Lama Phuntsok listened patiently to my story. So what, I asked him, would have been the correct Buddhist response to the problem?

'Actually, what I would have done is gone to a shop and ask them for change, because if you give this man 100 rupees you know he will keep it! Then I would have given him twenty rupees and got on the bus.' He laughed. 'This has nothing to do with Buddhism. This is what happens when you are in India!' Phuntsok gave me a sweet, understanding smile, and motioned to the waiter to put all the food that was left on the table in a bag, for him to take back to the monastery.

At the door to the monastery, the ritual was always the same. The prolonged examination at the desk of my passport (as if they had never seen it, or me, before); the laborious copying of its details into the log; the body search; the bag search; no tape recorder, no cameras, no batteries. The mustachioed Indian security man raised an eyebrow at my notebook – 'Ah, the writer': word had evidently got around – and allowed me to carry it through. Along the corridors, past the kitchen, the pungent smell of cooking, the day's supply of vegetables piled on a large trestle table, and up the stairs. Outside the interview room, the white cockatoo paced fretfully back and forth along its perch. The security man had followed me upstairs and idled outside the door as I waited, watching me watching the bird. 'Its name is Nikki,' he said.

It's a pity for it to be chained to its perch like that, I said. Wouldn't it be kinder to let it fly?

He understood the metaphor as well as I did. 'Too dangerous to fly,' he said with a smile. 'The other birds will attack it and do it harm . . .'

I had now met the Karmapa on four or five occasions, but still I felt that, as a person, I hardly knew him at all. My hopes that I would be allowed to become a fly on the wall – be given access to his daily activities; share lunch with him; play chess or computer games; lend a hand, perhaps, in his English lessons – had proved utterly fanciful. My meetings with him would be restricted to tantalizingly brief windows in his regular audiences – ten minutes here, twenty minutes there. I would walk in the door, we would talk, and I would then be ushered out again, while he retreated to his private rooms. Requests to spend time with him informally were politely evaded or ignored, if never actually refused. I couldn't decide whether this was a question of security, or something else. A bit of both perhaps. But then who was I? An outsider, a usurper. My concerns were not theirs. I sensed that there was no interest in demystification, in tearing down the curtain of protocol and formality; that to do so would only detract from his spiritual authority. The Karmapa was a spiritual figure, not a Western pop star. To those around him, the personal detail of his life was important only inasmuch as it served to maintain this spiritual role. His 'celebrity', in the Western meaning of the word, was irrelevant. And so were most of my questions.

This much I knew. His daily routine was unbending. He studied. He meditated. He conducted private audiences on most days, and public ones twice a week. He was writing poetry, spontaneous songs of the dharma, long-life poems for Tai Situ and his tutor Thrangu Rinpoche and 'mind *terma*' – poems that are said to arise from some deeper level of mind. He was also painting. One day he brought a portfolio of his work to show me: exquisite sketches in Chinese ink; a few graceful lines conjuring a procession of seven lamas, wreathed in smoke; the morning sun

rising behind trees. And watercolours of oriental characters, a
bearded man with flashing eyes, dressed in a billowing tunic, like a
figure from *The Arabian Nights*, bursting with life and humour.
Each picture was stamped with the seal of the Karmapas. He
showed them with a look of tentative self-deprecation, a schoolboy being judged in an art contest – his face lighting up when I
complimented him on his skill, his eye for colour. Do you have a
teacher, I asked? 'No, no, I teach myself. It's spontaneous.' He
gave a shy smile. There was also, I was told, another painting, of
his visions and dreams, which he would describe to a master
painter who had come from Kathmandu, and who was rendering
them on a large *thanka*. I asked to see it. The request was met with
a polite smile, but nothing came of it.

I asked one of his attendants, what did the Karmapa talk about?
What was he like as a person?

The question appeared to unsettle him. His Holiness, he said, at
length, enjoys talking about religion. 'If somebody is asking
questions about the scriptures or philosophy, no matter how
tough, he enjoys answering them. But actually His Holiness is
very comfortable socially. Whether the talk is of serious subjects,
or light subjects, or just telling stories, or chit-chat he always puts
people at their ease. He has great maturity. It doesn't matter who
is with him, he knows how to talk to them and make them
comfortable.'

And what relationship did he have with the Karmapa?

The veil of protocol descended. 'Honestly, for me, because of
his status I cannot talk to him like I talk to my friends. If he's very
quiet then I can feel uncomfortable. You know, sometimes his
look is so powerful I can hardly look in his eyes.' He thought
better of this. 'But he makes it very easy to be with him . . .'

But the private Karmapa, of course, was not the point. His true
measure lay not in his casual pastimes, nor the conversations that
passed back and forth between him and his attendants, but in his
teachings at his public audiences on the requirement for compassion, diligence and devotion, the words of encouragement and
consolation to the devotees who prostrated themselves in front of
him, their upturned faces seeking some flicker of recognition and
inspiration in his own. Here his authority was palpable, his
manner effortless and assured; it was here that one best under-

stood his purpose, the tradition that underpinned him, the years of training, all turned to honing him as a focal point for inspiration, a living example of the teaching of the possibility of perfection. Elaborations on the teachings, guidance on practice, practical advice on how I too could be a better, happier, person . . . these are the things, perhaps, I should have been asking in our private meetings, as I sat cross-legged in front of him, notebook on my lap. But I had more prosaic questions.

And so I asked about his discovery and his recognition, and being taken from the family home to Lhasa to assume his throne. It must have been painful, I said, to have left Lhatok and your family.

A slight tilt of the head as he considered the question; the same implacable half-smile. 'Not so painful.'

You didn't feel sad.

'Perhaps a little bit . . .'

But at the same time, perhaps, knowing that this is how things had to be.

'Yes.'

What can you remember of the search party coming to find you?

'To be honest, not so much. Maybe because I was so young at that time. But I understood a little of what it meant.'

And when did you begin to understand what it meant to be Karmapa?

'When I started the journey from my home to Tsurphu. From that moment I started to understand little by little what they were going to decide regarding me . . .'

To come from a remote village as you did, and to be thrust into the tumult and ceremony of Tsurphu must have been exciting and confusing.

'Yes, I felt excitement when I arrived at the city. Seeing so many cars and vehicles for the first time.' He gave a boyish smile, remembering something. 'The shape of the cars looked just like small houses.'

And your enthronement . . . did you understand what was going on?

'Not very much. Most of the important parts I understood, because I'd been told what it meant . . .'

You have grown up not being able to play with other children;

have there been moments when you have wished you could
behave just like any other normal boy, leave your studies and
play?

'Sometimes. But when I have that thought or feeling that I want
to go out, like a normal boy, at the same time I remember and
understand that there is benefit for the spiritual reasons in the way
I have been brought up, and a very important responsibility for me
to benefit all beings.'

Outside the audience room, the cockatoo stretched and preened
its feathers. I made my way back downstairs. At the monastery
door, the mustachioed security guard rose from his chair and
whispered something as I passed.

'I have something to tell you . . .' What did *this* mean? He
glanced around and beckoned me to follow him outside.

'The bird's name,' he said, 'I got it wrong. It's not Nikki, it's
Kiki . . .'

Ah . . .

He gestured for me to take out my notebook, and watched as I
dutifully wrote down this valuable new piece of information. Kiki.

I left him, strolled down the monastery steps and along the
rutted path to the road. On the roadside was a small general
provisions shop, and beside it a phone booth. I stopped to make a
telephone call. When I came out of the booth, the security guard
was standing outside the shop, drinking a Coke. He had followed
me. He smiled, a pantomime gesture of surprise – fancy seeing you
here! – and struck up a conversation.

So, how is the book going? This Karmapa, he's an interesting
boy, yes? You ask many questions. What does he have to say for
himself? And what will this book say, and will I be able to buy it in
India?

If this was an interrogation, it was a particularly clumsy one. At
length, I walked away. A hundred yards down the road I could
still feel his stare, burning on the back of my neck.

Drupngak was the Karmapa's chamberlain. He was sixty-three, a
skeletal figure, with a wispy mandarin moustache and beard, and
huge, rheumy eyes staring out from above sunken cheeks. Drupngak had been among those who had escaped with the Karmapa
from Tsurphu; a refugee, then. I had noticed him, sitting on a chair

on the veranda outside the interview room, prayer-beads clicking between his fingers, watching the line of supplicants who stood expectantly at the door, clutching their *khatas* and offerings, waiting to be ushered inside. He spoke no English, but through an interpreter he agreed to talk to me.

As a young monk, he said, he had been an attendant of the 16th Karmapa at Tsurphu. When the 16th Karmapa escaped in 1959 Drupngak remained behind. 'Then the Chinese came and destroyed the monastery. There was nothing, no monks, it was lifeless. And so I went back to my family. Then, much later, Drupön Dechen Rinpoche was asked by the Karmapa to go back to Tsurphu. And he said, well if you think dharma is going to spread in Tibet then I will go back there, otherwise it's worthless. And the Karmapa assured him that dharma would be there and that he should go back and rebuild Tsurphu, which is what he did. Then Drupön Dechen said I should come back and serve the Karmapa. He said to me, you knew the previous Karmapa, you know exactly how he liked things, what he ate, how to do things for him, so you must do it exactly for this Karmapa as you did for the previous Karmapa.'

Drupngak folded his hands in front of him. 'If you want to know what I did, just look at the Karmapa's day. When he got up in the morning I would bring him water to wash. I would take the clothes he slept in and bring him fresh clothes. I would take care of his bedding, serve him his food. Everything. I've been with the Karmapa from the moment he arrived at Tsurphu until now, from morning till night, and I love serving His Holiness. And I think His Holiness is very fond of me as well.' The Karmapa was just seven years old when he arrived at Tsurphu, he said. 'I think it was all very strange for him. For the first couple of months he was just getting used to it, being with people from central Tibet. There were lots of ceremonies for him, and then the enthronement in September. And after that things settled down into a routine.'

This routine, of prayer, ritual and study, was essentially the same as previous Karmapas had observed for hundreds of years. The Karmapa would rise each morning at six, said Drupngak. He would wash, then he would meditate before eating breakfast, and then his studies began. He had two tutors. For an hour he would study texts with Umze Thupten Zangpo. Then Ashang Lodro would teach him writing. He would have a short break, then lunch. In the afternoon he would conduct private meetings in his small audience room downstairs, and then public audiences in the temple. Then he would study writing again. At five o'clock there would be the Mahakala puja, lasting some forty-five minutes, which he always attended. Afterwards there would be more study, going over what he had been taught earlier in the day. He would then eat his evening meal, followed by more study, then sleep. These primary lessons would be complemented later by teachings in dialectics and philosophy from Lama Nyima, a monk who had studied at the great monastic university of Sera, and was thus well trained in Gelug logic, and who arrived at Tsurphu in 1994.

'There weren't many hours of play because the study was so important,' said Drupngak. 'But he wasn't attracted to playing anyway. He liked studying a lot. And there was a lot to do.' Much of his study consisted of memorizing texts, not least the twelve main rituals of the Karma Kamtsang tradition. Drupngak listed them. 'For example, the Chakrasamvara practice is 100 double-sided pages; Dorje Phagmo is sixty sides; Mahakala is over 200 sides; Chopa is also more than 200 sides. These weren't just short texts. The texts were this long and this wide.' He held out his hand to indicate a block about one foot long and four inches deep. 'Not only did he memorize these texts, but he studied many of the major treatises of the Buddhist tradition as well: the Bodhichar-yavatara, *The Guide to the Bodhisattva's Path*; a text of Mai-treya's, *The Supreme Continuum*. He studied *pramana* texts, all the texts dealing with the reasonings. And he studied many of the texts and collections on poetry. He loves poetry, and there was a *khenpo* in Tsurphu who taught him all the poetry he could find. He also studied a text by the 3rd Karmapa called *The Profound Inner Meaning*; and a text by Patrul Rinpoche, *The Words of My Perfect Teacher* . . .'

Drupngak paused in his recitation, pulled a handkerchief from the folds of his robe, blew his nose volubly, then carefully tucked the handkerchief back in his robe and continued. 'The Karmapa has also learned different styles of calligraphy and writes beauti-fully. He has a very good intellect, very sharp, and he likes to study.' (His tutor, Umze Thupten Zangpo had once offered a more critical appraisal. The young child was 'not a particularly attentive student to start with,' he said, but some texts he needed to read only once before committing them to memory, 'as if he was not learning them at all, but simply reminding himself.')

Would Drupngak also play with the Karmapa, I wondered.

He laughed. 'I'm too old for that! He had a younger attendant named Titi whom he was very fond of, and they used to play together a lot. In the summer he would go out to the parks, but even then he would never miss the eight hours' study a day. At Losa [Tibetan New Year] he got three days of holidays.'

And did he ever misbehave, like all young boys sometimes do?

Drupngak shook his head. 'That could never happen! His teachers were very, very strict with him. And he was a little bit fearful of his teachers, so he followed what they said. He was a good boy.' The old attendant was being diplomatic. Other stories of the Karmapa arriving at Tsurphu tell of a child who could be wilful, boisterous, given to flashes of temper (devotees attributed this to the 'wrathful' aspects of Karmapa): a Khampa nomad boy who needed the rough edges knocking off. One visitor recalls the young boy pelting him with the heavy wooden pieces of a chess set which he had been given as a gift.

Locked in Tsurphu, the Karmapa was insulated within layer upon layer of security. At the entrance to the monastery was a post manned by Chinese police. There was an internal security department, ostensibly set up to protect the young lama, but which actually served to watch for any signs of dissent from within the monastic population itself. The monastery's activities were overseen by the Democratic Management Committee, responsible both for the day-to-day running of the monastery's affairs, and for checking the teaching and activities of the monks. The Democratic Management Committee was answerable to the local Tölung County authorities, which in turn fell within the jurisdiction of the Lhasa city authorities, which in turn was answerable to the Religious Affairs Bureau of the TAR. Which in turn was answerable to Beijing.

Within this wall of security, the young Karmapa enjoyed a relative degree of freedom. There was no interference in his religious teachings. He held public audiences and was free to receive visitors. His family had taken up residence in Lhasa, and would occasionally visit him in Tsurphu. But even they were not exempt from protocol; like any other devotees, they would be expected to prostrate themselves before him and offer *khatas*. Throughout their meetings, the Karmapa would always be sitting on a higher seat. Nor was it allowed for the family to be photographed together. The toys from devotees piled up in his private apartments, to amuse him in his spare time: electric cars; Gameboys; board games; a huge Lego set which Tai Situ had brought from India. It was a curious paradox that a boy who was supposed to embody the philosophy of transcending attachment lacked for nothing (although most of his toys would be given away). His favourite toy was a remote controlled car, which he would chase around the roof of the monastery. 'He was a bundle of energy,' remembers one visitor.

It had by now become apparent that the Chinese had no intention of honouring their agreement to allow the Karmapa to travel to India. In 1992, following the enthronement at Tsurphu, Tai Situ and Gyaltsab travelled to Beijing for talks with Chinese government officials. 'We asked them for travel documents for Karmapa, and they said everything would be fine,' Tai Situ remembered, 'that at the proper time he could go. Then they were asking us security questions: would he be OK, or would Shamarpa do anything. This kind of thing. Actually, I don't think they were really concerned. They were just playing games.' The following year, the Karmapa was formally denied an exit visa, prompting diplomatic protests, including one from the US Secretary of State for Human Rights, John Shattuck. At the same time, the Dalai Lama wrote to the Indian Prime Minister Narasimha Rao asking for his help to facilitate a visit by the Karmapa to India. Nothing happened. The Indian government, it seemed, were no more inclined to press for the Karmapa, who would have been travelling on a Chinese passport, to visit monasteries in India and Sikkim, than the Chinese were to give him permission to leave Tibet.

Over the next three years, Akong Rinpoche, as Tai Situ's representative, would make three trips to Beijing for talks with members of the United Front, the department charged with decision-making about Tibetan issues, to plead for the Karmapa to be given permission to travel. The meetings, he recalls, were always 'very friendly', and totally fruitless. 'There was never any conclusion other than the Chinese saying that they would think about it,' says Akong. 'They would say he was too young to travel, you must wait until he's older, or the time is not quite right. There were different reasons each time. They would never say outright that he could not travel, but nor would they ever say that he could.'

'The Chinese could see the advantage of having the Karmapa there,' says Lama Yeshe. 'Of course, they had their own motivation, but if you look into it, even then the Karmapa had a mind of his own. When he was less than eight years old, my brother [Akong Rinpoche] and I were at Tsurphu having lunch with Karmapa, and some Chinese and high Tibetan officials came to pay him a visit. They brought many presents. And they were saying, can we take [our] picture with him? And he just got up and walked to the window; he wouldn't have his picture taken with them. He didn't want to know! Even then the Chinese were telling officials, you people be careful; this boy is going in the wrong direction.'

In 1994, after two years in Tsurphu, the authorities deemed that the young Karmapa was ready to be paraded in public, and in September an entourage including his teachers, attendants and the head of the Democratic Management Committee of the monastery set out for a tour of the major monasteries in Tibet, and several cities in China. To mark the occasion the Chinese government issued a statement trumpeting their supposedly distinguished history of supporting Buddhism in Tibet, and reiterating the 'freedom to believe' policy, under which, it was claimed, religious activities continued to be 'well protected and conducted in accordance with the law and relevant policies'. Between 1980 and 1993, it was claimed, the 'central and Tibetan governments' had earmarked 200m yuan for repairing 1,600 monasteries and temples throughout Tibet. The Tibetan Buddhism Institute had trained 3,000 monks and nuns, and the government had printed 1,000 copies of the Tengyur.

The Karmapa's progress was dutifully recorded by the Chinese government press agency, Xinhua. In Lhasa, on the first stop of his tour, he was reported to have met with officials of the TAR, thanking the regional party committee and government for 'the constant concern and support for [Tsurphu] monastery,' and pledging that he would 'study well and always follow the

Communist Party of China.' In the Jokhang temple, he prostrated himself in front of the giant Shakyamuni statue and 'in high spirits' visited the newly renovated Potala Palace. 'Having thrown a piece of snow-white silk "hada" [*khata*] on to a five-metre stupa housing the remains of the 5th Dalai Lama, he clapped his hands and jumped with joy,' Xinhua reported. One of the Karmapa's tutors was quoted as saying that the young lama was 'obsessed in Buddhism and able to recite 500 pages of sutras like an eighteen-year-old lama.'

The party moved on to Sera and Ganden monasteries, to Tashilhunpo, the ancestral seat of the Panchen Lamas, and then to Beijing, where the nine-year-old boy was paraded before Chinese dignitaries at a series of official functions. He visited the Forbidden City, the Great Wall and the Memorial Hall of Mao Zedong, where it was reported that he had 'chanted for Mao's soul' (notwithstanding the fact that Buddhists do not believe in souls). At Yonghegong, the largest Buddhist monastery in Beijing, he was reportedly received by one hundred lamas, 'dressed in their holy best', and prostrated himself before a statue of Tsongkhapa. At a reception to mark the forty-fifth anniversary of the founding of the People's Republic of China, hosted at the Great Hall of the People, he was fêted by Li Peng, the Premier of the State Council.

A few days later, on 1 October, he joined President Jiang Zemin on the rostrum in Tiananmen Square, in front of 100,000 people, for the National Day celebrations. The meeting was not, to use a favourite Buddhist term, auspicious. On being presented to the President, the young Karmapa asked, 'Who is this man?' Officials studiously ignored the question, as did the Chinese media who instead reported that the Karmapa had put his hands together and said, 'Long live the Republic of China.'

By the end of the month-long tour, the Karmapa had visited Beijing, Nanjing, Suzhou and Shanghai. He returned to Tsurphu burdened down with the fruits of official largess: plaques, scrolls, incense-burners, a colour TV, and more picture albums of historic sites, factories and economic development zones than any nine-year-old should decently be expected to feign interest in. China's promotion of him continued apace. In October 1994, Xinhua announced that Tsurphu monastery had won an award for its 'outstanding patriotic and law-abiding performance'.

But behind the scenes the mood had begun to sour. In January 1995, dissent flared at Tsurphu when news spread among the monastic community that in a meeting with the Karmapa, Chinese officials had made derogatory remarks about the Dalai Lama. Five monks fled from the monastery after putting up dissident posters accusing the Chinese of manipulating the Karmapa. One managed to escape. The remaining four, including the monastery's *umze*, or chant-master, and the *geyok*, or deputy disciplinarian, were arrested. Such dissent was kept well away from the public eye.

Just two months later, Xinhua were reporting that the '17th Living Buddha' had been presented with a 'horizontal inscribed board' from the Bureau of Religious Affairs, inscribed with the words 'Our Solemn Land' in Chinese and Tibetan characters. In September came another gift – a new Toyota 4500, presented on behalf of the Communist Party Central Committee, and apparently intended 'to inspire preaching by the young Buddha, who is the first person in China to acquire such a gift'.

There were other, more magical, stories from this time. In April 1993, while walking past Tsurphu's newly constructed temple, the Karmapa had pressed his fingers into the solid rock of the foundations, leaving indentations clearly visible in the rock. On a different occasion he draped a red robe over a rock and traced the words 'Karmapa Chenno', leaving an indelible impression in red on the rock.

A monk told me another story. Shortly after the Karmapa's arrival at Tsurphu, he was talking with the attendant of Gyaltsab Rinpoche, who was visiting from Rumtek. The attendant had originally come from the same area in Kham as the Karmapa, and the two were talking about the nomadic life, when the Karmapa suddenly declared that on the previous night he had 'travelled through space' to Rumtek. The young boy, of course, had never been to Rumtek, yet, according to the attendant, he described it perfectly – the placement of the buildings, which was Tai Situ's room and which Gyaltsab's. But, he went on, there were no monks in the monastery itself, they were all in a building on the hill, and 'I don't know why.' What the Karmapa would not have known was that at that time the monks' quarters were being rebuilt, and the monks had been temporarily billeted in the *shedra* on the hill.

If life for the Karmapa in Tsurphu was, in some senses, difficult, it was also, as one lama put it, 'possible', his continuing presence a demonstration of 'using skilful means to re-plant the seeds of dharma in Tibet'. Of course, the Chinese had approved his recognition for their own purposes, to bring religious practice more firmly under government control and to assert their 'sovereign right' over the *tulku* system. But as compromised as his activities may have been, his presence in Tsurphu was a Buddhist Trojan Horse – a way of keeping the teachings alive and flourishing, and of fanning the flame of popular devotion even in the face of official attempts to control it.

Crucially, the official approval of his recognition also set the precedent for the further recognitions of other *tulkus*. This process was now enshrined in a five-point government ruling. Under this, lamas could proceed as tradition demanded – looking for signs of a rebirth, despatching a search party and identifying a candidate. But they would then have to inform the government of their choice, and the government would confer official approval. Both sides could claim some satisfaction in this delicate compromise between Church and State: the lamas could be assured that the chosen child was the right one, while the government could claim sovereignty over the recognition. The religious belief and the politics could coexist – at least for the moment.

In 1995, at the age of ten, the Karmapa made his first recognition of a new reincarnate, the Pawo Rinpoche – one of the most senior figures in the Kagyu hierarchy. The Pawo Rinpoche's ancestral monastery was at Nyenang monastery, some twenty-five kilometres from Lhasa. Historically, Nyenang and Tsurphu had close religious and social as well as geographical ties. The Pawo lineage extended back to the seventeenth century and successive Pawo Rinpoches had been both pupils and teachers of the Karmapas. The 10th Pawo Rinpoche fled from Tibet in 1959. For fifteen years he lived in the Dordogne in France, close to the centre that Bernard Benson had donated to the 16th Karmapa. He then moved to Nepal, establishing a teaching centre in Baudhanath, where he died in 1991.

In June 1995, a deputation of monks from Nyenang approached the young Karmapa at Tsurphu, to formally request his guidance on whether the reincarnation of the Pawo Rinpoche had been born, and where he might be found. The deputation was led by one of the monastery's senior monks, Lama Tsewang. I had noticed Lama Tsewang among the monks at Gyuto. He was one of the party who had fled with the Karmapa from Tibet, and, I was told, the principal architect of the escape. He was a stocky, bullish-looking man in his late thirties, with a black moustache and goatee beard. His heavily lidded, coal-black eyes and poker-faced expression lent him a curiously intimidating air. We could talk, I was told, in his room.

He was seated on the bed when I arrived, practising Tibetan calligraphy in a notebook. He rose to shake my hand, gestured for me to take a seat and then resumed his calligraphy, clearly wishing to finish one thing before starting on another. I immediately realized I had misjudged him. I had taken him as a rough and ready type, but his touch on the paper was astonishingly light, his line graceful and assured. At length, he put his pen and notebook to one side, and began to tell his story.

For generations, he said, his family, had been associated with Nyenang monastery. Like Tsurphu, Nyenang had been virtually destroyed during the Cultural Revolution. When, in 1984, Drupön Dechen arrived from Ladakh to begin the rebuilding of Tsurphu, Lama Tsewang joined him there as one of his monks. He remained at Tsurphu for four years, until Drupön Dechen instructed him to begin the restoration of Nyenang. He had rebuilt the monastery from nothing, and founded a school in the village nearby. By the time the Karmapa arrived at Tsurphu, Nyenang too was ready for the return of its spiritual figurehead, the Pawo Rinpoche. The Pawo Rinpoches, said Tsewang, had traditionally been recognized by the Karmapas, and so it was that in June 1995, Tsewang had approached the Karmapa, requesting his guidance in the matter of the Pawo Rinpoche's reincarnation. The Karmapa told them that in order to remove the obstacles to finding the reincarnation, and to make the situation auspicious for inviting the new Pawo Rinpoche to his monastery, certain rituals must be performed – namely a recitation of the Kangyur and Tengyur (the complete corpus of Buddhist texts) in their entirety, and 100,000 repetitions of the concise ritual of the protector deity Mahakala. After a few months, Tsewang returned to Tsurphu to inform Karmapa that the rituals had been completed.

'His Holiness told us then that the incarnation of Pawo Rinpoche was already born and we had to make the search now, and if we found him easily then we must invite him immediately to the monastery, otherwise there could be some obstacles. During that conversation, His Holiness stayed in meditation for a while. And right after that he asked us to bring a pen and paper and he started to write the instructions for the search. In that letter he wrote, "From Tsurphu monastery it is on the north-eastern direction, in the town of Nakchu. And from Nakchu itself it is to the north." It said, "There are ten family members in that family, but not all of them are present there. The main door of the house is facing north." It said, "There is a shrine outside to the spirit Tsen" – traditionally these shrines have a red roof; they are called Tsenkhar [Tsen houses]. He said, "Nearby there is a heap of *mani* stones [stones inscribed with prayers]." Also he said, "The family come from Kham; the name of the mother begins with the syllable Da; the name of the father begins with the syllable, Lha, and the child himself was born in the Year of the Dog." '

After he had finished writing the letter, the Karmapa gave it to Tsewang. 'I went to Drupön Dechen Rinpoche, to discuss how to carry out the search. He advised me, "You'd better not go yourself, because everyone knows you're from Nyenang monastery. Pawo Rinpoche is a very high rinpoche, so this should be kept secret or there could be lots of obstacles." ' Instead, said Tsewang, it was decided that Lama Nyima, a *khenpo* at Tsurphu and one of Karmapa's teachers, together with another Tsurphu lama, should conduct the search. Their journey would be kept secret from the authorities.

The next day the two lamas left for Nakchu, a 300-kilometre drive from Lhasa. Arriving in the city, they searched its northern precincts. There, true to the Karmapa's instructions, they found the remains of a Tsenkhar, its red roof clearly visible among the rubble. 'They went a little further,' said Tsewang, 'and they reached a place where there was a huge heap of *mani* stones. So now two things are exactly as described. And then they found a house with a door facing north. An old woman was coming out of the house. They pretended to be businessmen, to find out more information. And the old woman said exactly what was in the letter: we have ten family members, but two are not present in the

house at the moment – one person has gone for pilgrimage, and a
child is at school. When the lamas asked, what is the name of the
mother in the house, it began with the syllable Da. And the father
was called Lhapa. The lamas said, and do they have a young
child? And the woman said, yes; and that child was born in the
Dog Year. And then the two lamas had no doubt.' Saying nothing
more to the old woman, Lama Nyima and his companion hurried
back to Tsurphu. With Drupön Dechen and Tsewang, they went
once more to see the Karmapa, to make their report.

'His Holiness said, "This is the true, unquestioned incarnation
of Pawo Rinpoche." So His Holiness made the final decision at
that time.' Shortly afterwards, Lama Tsewang himself, along with
Wongdu, the steward at Nyenang, set off for Nakchu, to break the
news to the family. 'We explained everything to them. We showed
them the letter that His Holiness had written. The family were
astonished, because everything was so clear. Then I said, "This is
the real and true incarnation of Pawo Rinpoche. I am from
Rinpoche's monastery. Will you let me take the child to the
monastery?" They said, "Of course. How can we say no? Because
he has been recognized by His Holiness, and Pawo Rinpoche is
one of the very high lamas. If we can serve the teachings of Buddha
and all sentient beings then we must do that. So you can take him
any time you like to his monastery." This is what they said.' Then
Lama Tsewang performed purification rituals with water that had
already been blessed by the Karmapa – 'I'm not qualified to do
such a ceremony for such a high rinpoche' – and offered the child
his first monk's robes.

Tsewang paused. He rose from the bed, took a thermos flask
from the table and poured two cups of thick green tea. He
gestured for me to take one, then resumed his story. 'You might
ask, what did I feel meeting the reincarnation of Pawo Rinpoche
for the first time? I had never met the previous Pawo Rinpoche,
but as soon as I met this child I could see that he was very special.
Although he was only fifteen months old, it seemed to me that he
was older – more than two years old. He looked a very mature
child, and very special. Usually, little children in Tibet, they like to
play in the dust, and things like that. But what he liked to do was
go to the shrine and make prostrations. So this child had very
special qualities from the very beginning. The other reason I had a

very strong conviction that this was the right boy was that everything was exactly as it had been written in the letter. Even if there had been nothing special with the child I would have been very happy. But on top of that there were very miraculous things about the child.

'Wongdu had been a monk when the previous Pawo Rinpoche was alive, and he had visited him where he was living in France. At that time Pawo Rinpoche had told him, I will see you in Tibet. The previous Pawo Rinpoche never returned to Tibet; he passed away in Nepal. But when Wongdu saw his reincarnation for the first time, it seemed as if the child recognized him. He pulled Wongdu to him and touched foreheads, a very special greeting in Tibet. We offered the child some *torma* and some rice, and he took some *torma* from the cup and put it in Wongdu's mouth. Then Wongdu was very moved, and tears rolled down his cheeks.' Lama Tsewang and Wongdu left the family then, he said, telling them that a time would be arranged when the boy would be brought to Nyenang, and that in the meantime they must take good care of him.

As Tsewang had been talking, others had joined us in the room, pausing while engaged on some errand or another, or perhaps curious to know what was keeping Tsewang preoccupied for so long with a Westerner. A young monk with an excitable, almost girlish demeanour who spoke fractured English had drawn up a chair and was helping with translation. A second monk, tall and shy, stood, arms folded, by the door. Now a woman entered. She was in her fifties, dressed in the traditional *chuba* and striped apron, her face strong-boned and etched with deep lines, pieces of turquoise braided in her greying hair. She settled herself on the end of the bed, listening intently. Everybody loves a good story.

Now that the Pawo Rinpoche had been found, Tsewang continued, it was necessary to inform the authorities in Lhasa. 'The Lhasa government told me that because the Pawo Rinpoche was a very high incarnation in Tibet, and because he had been recognized by His Holiness Karmapa who has been approved by our government, then I could invite him to his monastery. But they said at that moment they could not give permission; they would have to talk to Beijing.' Tsewang was advised that he could collect the young Pawo Rinpoche on 'an unofficial basis', but that he should be kept quietly in the monastery until the Chinese government had given their approval for the enthronement.

At length, an 'inviting party' of eighteen monks made the journey back to Nakchu, to collect the young Rinpoche, and accompany him in procession back to Nyenang. For a long time, remembered Tsewang, and for a long time there had been no rain. 'All the farmers were very worried about their crops. But on that day the weather became pleasant, and at the same time it started raining. All the villagers became very devoted, generally to the dharma and especially to the Rinpoche.' Approaching Nyenang, a welcome party greeted the young child. Monks had come from Tsurphu as well as Nyenang itself. Tents had been erected on the road to the monastery, and people had come from miles around on horseback, dressed in their finest costumes. 'All came with these traditional things,' said Tsewang, 'bells and banners and drums. That is a custom in Tibet to welcome the high rinpoches.'

The woman who had joined us vigorously nodded her agreement, 'Yes, yes . . .' – apparently an authority on matters of religious etiquette – and repeated after him, 'Bells, banners, drums . . .'

Two thrones had been placed in the main tent, Tsewang continued, a higher one for the Pawo Rinpoche, a lower one for Drupön Dechen Rinpoche. 'Pawo Rinpoche was not able to speak, but he could show his feelings very clearly. And very unexpectedly, he jumped from his throne into Drupön Rinpoche's lap, just like a baby jumping into its mother's lap!' Tsewang laughed.

A few days later the young boy was taken to meet Karmapa for the first time. 'He was showing much veneration to His Holiness. When the older lamas made prostrations, Pawo Rinpoche also tried to make prostrations. Then he went to His Holiness and without anyone's help he bowed down his head to take a blessing. He looked very happy.' There were pujas in the main temple with monks from both monasteries. Then Karmapa performed the hair-cutting ceremony on the child, and named him Palden Pawo Tsuglak Drayang.

Lama Tsewang had been speaking for almost an hour. The room had grown uncomfortably warm, and the tall, shy-looking monk opened the window to let in some air. But nobody seemed inclined to break up the gathering. Tsewang said there was another story he wished to tell me, to illustrate the greatness of the Pawo Rinpoche.

The previous Pawo Rinpoche had been a great meditator; he enjoyed solitude. Perhaps it was his previous life memory, said Tsewang, but even when he was very young the present Pawo Rinpoche also enjoyed solitude, and liked to walk in secluded places. One day the Pawo Rinpoche and a small party of monks walked into the hills above Nyenang for a picnic.

'Pawo Rinpoche went off on his own, climbing further up into the mountain. One of the monks was a little concerned and he went after him. Eventually, he caught up with him, and Pawo Rinpoche said to the monk, "Do you need a *zi* stone?" A *zi* stone is a very precious stone. He said, "If you need one, you should dig here." The monk said, "I don't think we'll find one here." And Pawo Rinpoche said, "Yes, yes, you'll find one." So they took a stick and marked the place, then came back down to where the other monks were. The main attendant, the *tsimpon*, said, "Is there really a *zi* stone there?" And Pawo Rinpoche said again, "Yes, yes." And the *tsimpon* said, "If there's no *zi* stone there and you say there is this will be a big embarrassment for you; you are Pawo Rinpoche. If you say it and it's not true, then you will be red in the face." So they walked back to the place and found the stick. They dug for about a metre and they hadn't found anything. But then they saw something gleaming black. They dug down a little further and it turned out to be two black stones, one of which looked like a bird. They left it like that. The next day they went back on horseback, and there, where they had dug, was a *zi* stone sticking out of the earth, and there was coral and turquoise and gold, that had just appeared in their absence. There was one large *zi* stone and a smaller one, a whole variety of things. So they picked them up and took them back to the monastery. Then Pawo Rinpoche said, "We have to do Mahakala puja." So they did that. And all the stones were wrapped in silk, then placed inside the glass cabinet where the statue of Mahakala is, and the cabinet was sealed. And it was said that the black stone was a self-arisen Buddha, and the bird was his emanation. They also found a white conch shell, and that was a self-arisen emanation of Guru Rinpoche.'

Lama Tsewang paused, gave a theatrical cough – a master story-teller – and pulled his robe around him. 'I was in Lhasa at the time. I came back and I heard this story, and I asked Pawo Rinpoche directly, "How did you know to look there? And who buried these things?" And he said, "The one who had buried this was the 8th Pawo Rinpoche." So this is almost 200 years ago.'

I glanced around the room. Every pair of eyes was fixed on Lama Tsewang, rapt at the power and wonder of his story.

'You might ask,' he went on, 'what's the purpose of burying these things? They are not anything special, not very useful. Much later, Bokar Rinpoche was asked this question, and he said the point was, there would come a time when trust and belief in the lamas had diminished, and there would be a need for something to inspire people in their faith.'

And that, I said, is why the 8th Pawo Rinpoche had buried them?

'Yes', said Lama Tsewang. 'So that they could be found.'

I turned the story of the discovery of the Pawo Rinpoche over and over in my mind. Like all the stories of recognitions it left me feeling confounded, asking the question, how could it be? Lamas tended not to talk about such things, to offer explanations. These supernatural phenomena, prophecies, divinations, existed beyond the scope of rational explanation. They were held as self-evident proof of the realization of a great lama. Extraordinary, but not miraculous in the sense that we in the West would understand the word.

One day I asked the Karmapa to explain the process to me. I did not expect him to answer, but after some moments' consideration he nodded and began.

Traditionally, he said, it was necessary for a lama to be requested to make a recognition. The lama would then go into meditation. 'In that quietness there is not too much going in the way of discursive thoughts. So in that moment they remain very clear and calm, and in that moment certain visions come. And how clear that vision is depends on the individual's level of attainment. All lamas are not at the same level of enlightenment or attainment in the inner sense. If someone is highly attained in the inner way, then at that moment they might see a very clear vision. But even if the individual lama is not too advanced he might still get a certain vision, but not so clear. And then according to that he also makes some description.'

He paused, to make sure I was following this. 'So what I'm telling you right now is very much based on what I do and how I recognize *tulkus* and rinpoches. It doesn't mean that it is the only method. But I don't know how other rinpoches do it. I can't generalize. This is not something that's taught by someone. Somehow, when one does the meditation it comes like that, spontaneously.'

Is this facility a sign of purity of mind, or is it based on some previous karmic connection, or both?

He pondered the question. 'It can be from both sides, from your practice and also to do with the individuals you have to recognize. But the most powerful or most important thing is the individual who is trying to recognize the other one – it is through his power and through his meditation and wisdom. For example, some rinpoches you have to recognize, maybe there is no connection in the past, so it does not depend on that. It purely depends on the clarity of your wisdom.'

So is this vision omniscience?

'You cannot say there is no limitation. For example, you might ask me a question that is related to daily life, something you want to fulfil. I might give you an answer. But the cause and conditions of what you want to do might change, for different reasons. So while I might see very clearly at that moment, your karmic causes and conditions could change many things, so it doesn't stay as I predicted. Recognizing rinpoches or *tulkus* is quite different. Because of their own attainment they are making a decision to come into this world again, to be of benefit. And because of the clarity in their mind and in their decision, once they have decided they will not change their decision. So when I or another lama recognize rinpoches what we are seeing is a clear intention that will not change.'

So it is two clear minds, apprehending each other?

He nodded. 'Yes, both sides.'

And at what age, I asked, did you first become aware that you had this facility?

He smiled at the question. 'I don't how old, but when I first recognized a *tulku*, that was when I got this feeling.'

The Pawo Rinpoche?

'Yes, the Pawo Rinpoche. But the clearest, I think, was Jamgon Kongtrul Rinpoche . . .'

I had read an account of this, published by Jamgon Kongtrul's *labrang* in Nepal. In 1994, two years after Jamgon's death in the car crash at Siliguri, a delegation from his monastic seat in Nepal had approached the Karmapa to make the preliminary supplications about the Karmapa locating his reincarnation. The search and confirmation procedures had taken almost a year before the Karmapa finally bestowed his seal of recognition on a two-year-old child living in the Tibetan village of Karak Shang. The details of the Karmapa's divinations and instructions conformed in every particular to tradition, with one notable exception. In order to better describe the house where the young boy would be found, the Karmapa had constructed a replica with his Lego set.

CHAPTER ELEVEN

A Rival Candidate

The enthronement of the new Karmapa at Tsurphu left the Shamar Rinpoche increasingly marginalized. Shamar claimed he was the victim of a plot. Not only had Tai Situ forged the prediction letter, Shamar maintained, but he had also misled the Dalai Lama. In submitting the original documents to the Dalai Lama when he was in Brazil, Tai Situ had deliberately given the impression that all the Kagyu Rinpoches were in accord over the authenticity of the letter and the validity of the choice, when in fact he, the Shamar, was vehemently opposed to it. It was on the basis of this misinformation that the Dalai Lama had given his formal confirmation. The Dalai Lama had been deceived.

But the Dalai Lama himself appeared to deny this version of events. In July 1992 his office issued a letter of clarification, stating that while 'certain controversy' had arisen over the Sacred Letter, 'there had never been any traditional lapse or impropriety from His Holiness the Dalai Lama in having given his approval to the recognition of the 17th Karmapa.' The Dalai Lama, the statement went on, had studied all of the documents pertaining to the recognition – a copy of the Sacred Letter, interpretations of its contents, a precise report of the consistent findings of the search party and other supplementary materials – before making his decision. On 29 June, he had met, first, with Tai Situ Rinpoche and Gyaltsab Rinpoche and, later in the day, with Shamar Rinpoche, to discuss the matter before finally granting his formal Seal of Approval and recognition on the following day. 'Thus,' the statement concluded, 'His Holiness the Dalai Lama granted his final Seal of Approval and recognition to the 17th Karmapa, not randomly or hastily for any reason, but after satisfying himself by means of hearing a series of reports from all those concerned; studying and paying due consideration to the overall matter; and reconfirming the final indications with exclusive traditional examinations.'

Shamar Rinpoche changed tack. The Dalai Lama and the Tibetan government-in-exile, he now suggested, had been party to the conspiracy from the very beginning. Seated in the lounge of the Hyatt Regency Hotel in Delhi, Shamar called for more coffee, and then carefully outlined his case. I should understand, he said, that this dispute was not about religion, it was about politics, the settling of old scores, and it was about ambitious people who would stop at nothing to secure power.

His accusation was this: Tai Situ had joined forces with the Dalai Lama and the government-in-exile and carefully orchestrated the 'discovery' and recognition of Ogyen Trinley, in order to wrest control of the Karma Kagyu school from its rightful leader – he, the Shamarpa. This plot could be traced back to the 1960s, and the 16th Karmapa's resistance to the attempts by the Dalai Lama and the Tibetan government-in-exile to unify all the different schools of Tibetan Buddhism. Together with the government-in-exile, he alleged, Tai Situ had conspired with the Chinese to identify a reincarnated Karmapa in Tibet. In this way, the new Karmapa would be under Chinese control and hence pose no possible challenge to the Tibetan government-in-exile, while at the same time allowing Tai Situ to assume the dominant role in the Karma Kagyu school outside Tibet. The intention, he claimed, was to deprive the Buddhist communities of the Himalayas of access to the true Karmapa, and to undermine the Karmapa's administration in Rumtek, Sikkim.

'So . . .' Shamar leaned forward, fixing me with his gaze. 'Exile government play divide and conquer. They found the one who would go with them; the one who said, "OK, I will destroy my school for your favour." And this is Tai Situ and Gyaltsab Rinpoche also. These are the ones who joined with the Dalai Lama. Tai Situ's aim,' he said, 'was to close Rumtek. He wanted his own monastery, Sherab Ling, as the head of the Kagyu. The exile government also wanted to close Rumtek, because otherwise all power goes to Karmapa and again he is competing with Dharamsala. Each have their own reasons, so they co-operated.'

The recognition of Ogyen Trinley as the Karmapa, he went on, was in flagrant defiance of the Kagyu tradition. As the senior Regent within the Kagyu school Shamar, and he alone, had the right to recognize the Karmapa. Furthermore, he maintained, the Dalai Lama's official confirmation was, effectively, meaningless: 'by tradition and history' the Dalai Lamas had never played a role in recognizing Karmapas; it was strictly a Kagyu affair.

In fact, this was only partly true. While the Dalai Lama had traditionally played no part in the magical processes of recognition of the Karmapas, from the seventeenth century onwards and the ascendancy of the Gelug school the Dalai Lama, as the temporal head of Tibet, had traditionally conferred his seal of confirmation after the Karmapa had been recognized and before enthronement. The 16th Karmapa, for example, had received the imprimatur of the 13th Dalai Lama. Indeed, the 14th and present Dalai Lama had officially ratified the reinstatement of the Shamarpa's own lineage in the 1960s, at the request of the 16th Karmapa. Nor was it the case that historically the Shamarpas had sole responsibility for identifying and recognizing Karmapa incarnations. By tradition, the Karmapas had identified themselves, either by means of a prediction letter, or by self-declaration at an early age, and a variety of different lineage-holders had been involved in recognizing and enthroning Karmapas at different times. The Shamarpas were not involved at all until the time of the 5th Karmapa in the fifteenth century. And while subsequent Shamarpas had been instrumental in confirming the recognition of Karmapas, and served as their lineage holders and teachers over the course of the next 300 years, they had played no part in the process after 1792, following the banishing of the Shamarpa line.

But it was the echo of that fateful event which could now be heard again, some 200 years on. For in his allegations against the Dalai Lama, the Shamarpa was once again invoking the old spectre of the annihilation of the Red Hat by the Yellow Hat, and casting himself as the true defender of the Kagyu faith. The politics of the eighteenth century were being played out once more. Just as the 10th Shamarpa had been framed by the Gelugpa for daring to stand up for the Kagyu teachings, so the present Shamar maintained he too was the victim of a Gelugpa plot.

Shamar's voice rose in indignation, his gestures grew more animated. From the very beginning he said he had acted with the best of intentions. He had not concurred with the plan, he said, to put the verse of the 16th Karmapa in the *gau* box. 'Jamgon and Gyaltsab were the two people who said we should maybe use this as the authentic letter. I didn't agree, and nor did Tai Situ.' He said he had been the victim of slander and falsehood. 'Many, many blames were put on me . . .' He had been blamed for trying to bring forward the son of the King of Bhutan as the Karmapa's reincarnation. He had been blamed for the death of Jamgon Kongtrul. 'They said that I was the person who planted the bomb in Jamgon Rinpoche's car and killed him! These rumours were spread everywhere. I said, "I didn't kill!" But everywhere people say this, because the rumour spread. There was no place to go for me!'

He sighed deeply and shrugged his shoulders. The rumours, the stories, the aspersions that had been cast on his character. 'It's so cruel. This is very ruthless politicians' behaviour, not at all Buddhist teachers' behaviour. Not even a good politician's behaviour! But then gradually I realized, perhaps they are somehow possessed. Sometimes in Buddhist doctrine there is a belief in *mara*, that when the evil wish is strong sometimes some bodhisattvas also can be possessed by their greed. Something like that can happen . . .'

He paused. I should understand, he said again, that this was not just about religion and practice; it was also about culture, politics, fault lines and affiliations that would not be apparent to Westerners. 'People who support His Holiness the Dalai Lama know clearly they have to do that for the political reason. They don't care who is the right or wrong Karmapa. Among the [Kagyu] followers maybe some are blindly believing, others are openly understanding. But then there is the social question: "Ah, Situ Rinpoche is doing wrong, but since he is my mother or father's guru I must support him," or, "Shamar Rinpoche is my grandfather's guru so I must follow him." ' He gave a rueful smile. 'Actually, there is more of that for Situ than for me, because

Shamar has only been reinstated after 200 years, so Shamar has less followers . . .'

In this, at least, he was correct. His resistance to Ogyen Trinley's recognition as the Karmapa, and his defiance of the Dalai Lama's authority, left Shamar an increasingly isolated figure not only within the Karma Kagyu school, but also within the Tibetan Buddhist community at large. Virtually all of the senior figures in the Kagyu school had accepted the validity of the prediction letter and accepted Ogyen Trinley as the authentic reincarnation of the 16th. The major Kagyu centres in Britain and America – Samye Ling in Scotland and the 16th Karmapa's American seat at Woodstock – had immediately welcomed the recognition, as had the majority of centres throughout Asia and the Far East. For most Tibetans, the Dalai Lama's ruling had settled the question once and for all. Whatever Shamar's arguments about the Dalai Lama having no role in Kagyu politics, his imprimatur as the spiritual leader of Tibetan Buddhism was paramount, his integrity held to be beyond question. For most Tibetans – and, for that matter, most Westerners – when it came to matters of Tibetan Buddhism the word of the Dalai Lama was law. Shamar's supporters were relatively few. He could count on the loyality of his brother Jigme, who was in charge of the 16th Karmapa's centre in the Dordogne; he had the support of a number of Kagyu lamas and rinpoches in India and Nepal, and devotees in Malaysia and Taiwan. He also had one significant ally.

Ole Nydahl had come a long way since opening his first centre in Denmark in 1973. Blessed with a seemingly indefatigable energy, abundant charisma and a messianic zeal, Nydahl had founded centres throughout Europe, in Australia, America and South America. He opened the first Buddhist centre behind the Iron Curtain, in Poland, followed by centres in Hungary, Czechoslovakia and Russia. By the early 1990s he had established more than 150 centres around the world under the aegis of his 'Diamond Way' organization. No longer plain Ole Nydahl, he had now become 'Lama Ole', another title to add to his credential as 'Buddhist Master', which had been given to him by Shamar Rinpoche in 1983.

Nydahl rejoiced in a lust for life. He liked skydiving, driving fast cars and motorbikes. In his autobiographies he depicted himself as half Viking, half Tibetan warrior, a sort of Buddhist Jean-Claude Van Damme, ceaselessly travelling the world, an evangelist and protector of the Vajrayana teachings. The books were liberally laced with photographs of Nydahl, frequently stripped to the waist, the better to display his boxer's physique, posing, Zelig-like, with senior Tibetan lamas. Like the best-selling books of 'Lobsang Rampa', Nydahl's accounts of his life demonstrated an enthusiasm for the more fantastical aspects of Tibetan Buddhism. Nydahl hinted at past-life experiences as a Tibetan warrior-king, and claimed a particular connection to the principal Karma Kagyu protector-deity Mahakala, or as Nydahl called him, 'Black Coat'. According to Nydahl, the 16th Karmapa himself had anointed Nydahl as 'Dharma General' of the Karma Kagyu and on one occasion had turned to him among a group of people and declared, 'This is the Bearer of the Black Coat.' Everywhere Nydahl went, it seemed, extraordinary things happened. Arriving in Iceland in 1984 his presence apparently prompts strange meteorological disturbances. 'This was nothing new. It often happens when I introduce the power field of Karmapa and Black Coat to a new place. Every quarter hour there was a new combination of rain, snow, wind, sun and hail.' Visiting Tibet two years later he is besieged outside the Jokhang temple by 'thousands of people who all wanted a blessing'.

Lama Ole's barnstorming, Elmer Gantry style, did not endear him to everyone. In 1984 an order went out from Osel Tendzin, the head of Dharmadhatu, the organization that had been founded by Chögyam Trungpa, warning American centres not to entertain Nydahl as a teacher. Alleging that the Danish teacher 'blesses people with a reliquary amulet which he claims holds a single hair from each of the sixteen Karmapas, along with other relics', the order accused him of provoking 'considerable confusion' among the centres' students in the Bay Area in California.

According to all reports, his teaching style, more than the content, runs contrary to everything we have been taught and have come to recognise as genuine. Our students' basic perception of his approach is one of self-aggrandisement accompanied by a so-called 'spiritual zap' which he seemingly transfers to other people . . . There have been instances in the past where students, out of confusion, have misused these precious [Vajrayana] teachings to create a personal fortress of charlatanism and egohood. This appears to be the case with Mr Nydahl.

Ole laughed off the criticism, publishing the prohibition order in his book as evidence of Dharmadhatu's narrow-minded and reactionary attitude.

According to one former student, Nydahl's public appearances often seemed to bear more resemblance to a rock concert than traditional Buddhist teachings, 'with Ole as the star'. The centrepiece of his teachings was the Phowa practice, an esoteric Vajrayana practice, designed as a preparation for death. This involves the student learning a particular visualization that raises power through the body, and sometimes results in the opening of a small hole at the crown of the head from which blood seeps. It is generally held that it requires eight or nine days of intensive instruction from an experienced lama for a student to achieve this remarkable effect. But Nydahl, who first gave the practice in 1987, could apparently achieve it in half the time. His account of a visit to Russia in 1990 displayed typical industriousness: 'Never have I worked harder,' Nydahl wrote. 'The job was to give seventy chronically disillusioned people their first introduction to Buddhism, [to give them] Refuge, a trustful contact to Karmapa as the Buddha of Limitless Light and a hole in their heads – all in five days. During the third afternoon, the change happened and we gained Russia.'

For many people, particularly in Eastern Europe, Nydahl had provided their first introduction to Buddhism. Initially, lamas from all four Tibetan Buddhist schools were welcomed to teach in his centres. But Nydahl began to display a growing disenchantment with Tibetan teachers, criticizing them in his books and newsletters as reactionary, hypocritical and obscurantist, peddling a hidebound Buddhism still stuck in feudal times. 'At first his group was the only place for Tibetan teachers to come,' remembered one former Polish student. 'But then it became more sectarian, and he was opposed to inviting teachers from the Gelug, Sayka and Nyingma. It was, "Karma Kagyu is the best." Then it became not all the Kagyu teachers are so good. And then it became there's only one teacher who is any good . . . An early criticism of his teaching was that it was too much Shangri-La – deifying and glorifying Tibetan teachers in a completely unrealistic way. Later on it became the complete opposite. It became like some people were followers of Tibetan Buddhism, and others were followers of Ole Nydahl. And in the end it appeared that only the people that followed Ole Nydahl were welcome.'

One lama enjoyed special exemption from Nydahl's increasing castigation of Tibetan teachers. Throughout the 1970s and 1980s, Shamar Rinpoche was a regular visitor to Ole's centres, and Shamar's blessing had done much to give Nydahl a stamp of institutional authority. Ole's wife Hannah had also become close to Shamar, accompanying him in his travels around Europe, America and Asia, acting as his translator, confidante and adviser. Following the events at Rumtek in 1992, and the discovery and enthronement of Ogyen Trinley, Nydahl threw his weight behind the Shamarpa, echoing his demands for the prediction letter to be forensically tested and supporting Shamar's claim that as 'the senior Regent' he, and he alone, was entitled to recognize the Karmapa reincarnation.

Nydahl spelt out his views in an open letter to his centres:

When [such] blatantly egotistical traits surface as during the recent search for the official Karmapa candidate. When the examination of the letter is refused which all intelligent beings must insist upon . . . When so many and distasteful rumours are spread . . . Where, then, can we place our trust? Who is still up to the standards of Western idealism? . . . Kunzig Shamarpa is not an orator to the masses, a victorious general nor a sly politician . . . His Bodhisattva qualities, however, have recently come to impress Hannah and me more than ever. He has manifested a balance and endurance which are worthy of a saint.

Henceforth, Nydahl wrote, he would place all his centres around the world under the Shamarpa's guidance.

On 17 November 1992 Shamar issued a formal statement, in which he declared that he would not object to the Chinese government's decision 'in recognizing a child as Karmapa as I have no right and jurisdiction in China and am completely unable to stop it.' However, henceforth, he went on, he would continue to devote his energies to following the 'genuine instructions' of the 16th Karmapa, 'whenever the time was right'. In order to do this, he declared, he would give up his commitments at Rumtek, and the monastery would be left exclusively in the custody of its monks and the Karmapa Charitable Trust. Shamar announced that he would be relocating to the centre in the Dordogne, administered by his brother Jigme. Topga had already left Rumtek and returned to his home in Bhutan.

With Shamar and Topga having absented themselves from Rumtek, on 30 November 1992 a meeting of delegates under the name of the Kagyu International Assembly convened at the monastery. Among them were representatives from KTD at Woodstock, from Samye Ling, Australia, Tibet, India, Nepal and Bhutan. Also present were representatives of the five Kagyu monasteries, six Buddhist organizations and eight Tibetan organizations in Sikkim. Conspicuous by their absence were Shamar Rinpoche, or any representatives from Ole Nydahl's numerous groups throughout Europe, America and Australia. In his opening address Tai Situ proposed that the present board of Directors of the Karmapa Charitable Trust be dissolved and a new board appointed in their place.

The KCT had been set up in 1961 by the 16th Karmapa. Following the death of the 16th, it was the Trust that had the responsibility for managing affairs at Rumtek, until such time as his reincarnation was found. The original board had been made up of a mixture of members of the Karmapa's inner circle, including the general secretary Damchoe Yongdu and local patrons and supporters. In the years since the death of the 16th, the make-up of the Trust had changed as original trustees died or retired, to be replaced by new nominees. Following the death of Damchoe Yongdu, Topga had become chairman. Shamar Rinpoche had also been inducted on to the board, as had Tai Situ. But the board was weighted in Shamar's favour in the dispute. Theoretically, only the trustees or the Karmapa himself, having attained the age of majority, could change the composition of the board. Nonetheless, Tai Situ's resolution was passed by the delegates.

At the same time, Topga was relieved of his duties as general secretary. A resolution spelled out the case against him. Topga, it stated, had refused to accept the evidence of the prediction letter and the confirmation of the Dalai Lama in recognizing Ogyen Trinley as the reincarnation of the 16th Karmapa. He had 're-peatedly' attempted to establish Shamar Rinpoche as the owner of Rumtek, and had himself made attempts to take over the proper-ties of the 16th Karmapa, and 'sold for a price' the Tashui Choeling monastery of the 16th Karmapa in Bumthang, Bhutan. His actions, the resolution went on, had persistently created 'disruptions' between dharma teachers and their disciples. In short, it concluded, since the death of the 16th Karmapa, Topga had been guilty of causing 'destruction of the dharma' and was no longer fit to hold office as treasurer and general secretary of the Karma Kagyu institutions. Tenzin Namgyal was appointed in his place.

On the final day of the conference another resolution was passed, declaring 'the complete faith of all the followers of the Kagyu order' in His Holiness the 17th Karmapa, Ogyen Trinley, and pledging 'never to acknowledge any other person who may be falsely given the title'.

An uneasy peace settled over Rumtek. Topga was now pro-hibited from coming to the monastery, and subject to a State government order denying him entry to the eastern regions of Sikkim. The old administration had gone. But the divisions in the monastic community which had become apparent during the pujas for Jamgon Kongtrul, when the two factions had been 'fishing for monks', continued to fester. While Shamar had left the monastery, a significant body of monks loyal to him remained. Tai Situ's support meanwhile had been swollen by the arrival of new students who had enrolled at the Nalanda Institute. The tension between the two factions grew. On 27 June 1993, cele-brations were held to mark Ogyen Trinley's birthday. Tai Situ and Gyaltsab Rinpoche offered long-life prayers for the new Karmapa in the main prayer hall. A rainbow was seen to appear over the monastery – a portent, it was believed, of good fortune. Four weeks later, Rumtek exploded into violence.

The Yarney, or six-week summer retreat, dated back to the time of the Buddha, and had been observed at Rumtek since the monastery's inception. It was traditionally marked by a ceremony to announce its beginning. On 12 July Shamar Rinpoche sent word to the students at the Nalanda Institute that the Institute would be closed for holidays from 1 August to 1 September. This, Shamar's letter maintained, was because the period marked the summer holidays in Europe and staff from the Institute were being sent there to teach. At the end of July, Shamar himself departed for a lecture tour of Ole Nydahl's centres in Europe. The closure of the Institute meant that the traditional Yarney pujas would not be performed at the monastery after all. Tai Situ, however, decreed that in accordance with convention, the ceremonies should go ahead. Bowing to Shamar's instructions, on the night of 1 August monks loyal to him locked the doors of the main shrine hall. The next morning Tai Situ and Gyaltsab presented themselves in front of the locked doors. A crowd began to gather, quickly joined by a contingent of police. The monks were ordered to hand over the keys to the shrine room, and fighting broke out. Windows were smashed; monks from the rival factions, joined by the agitated crowd, exchanged punches and threw bottles and stones. Finally, the police quelled the disturbance, the keys were handed over and the ceremony went ahead. Bloodied and indignant, the monks loyal to Shamar, more than 150 in number, retreated from Rumtek, taking sanctuary in his residence a mile away. They would remain there, bivouacked in the grounds, for years to come.

Now, under the guidance of Gyaltsab Rinpoche, peace at last settled on Rumtek. But within five months, there would be a new, and even more dramatic twist in the saga. Shamar was about to play his trump card.

The news that Shamar had found a candidate whom he claimed to be the 17th Karmapa came in a brief statement on 26 January 1994. 'I hereby announce,' it read, 'that the authentic reincarnation of the 16th Karmapa Rangjung Rigpe Dorje, has been found. H.H. Karmapa is presently in India. Details regarding the traditional procedures of his installation will be made known in the near future.' The young boy in question, it seemed, had arrived in India from Tibet some two weeks earlier and was being kept at a secret location under Shamar's protection. Word quickly began to spread among Shamar's followers. Ole Nydahl's wife, Hannah, was in Delhi at the time of the boy's arrival. Nydahl himself was in

Russia, but Hannah notified him that she had seen 'Karmapa' and had no doubt he was authentic. She had shown him photographs of Ole and he had apparently remarked on how Ole's hairstyle had changed over the years.

At the end of February, students at KIBI were invited to meet the young boy. Two bus-loads of students were driven to a park outside Delhi. In a curious ceremony, he sat on a plastic chair while students were invited to come forward for a blessing. Two Western students who were present at the ceremony wrote a letter describing the scene that was subsequently photocopied and circulated around Kagyu circles. The boy, they wrote, was 'pale and trembling. He was perplexed.' The young boy's name was Tenzin Khyentse; Shamar Rinpoche would subsequently give him the monastic name Thinlay Thaye Dorje (Thinlay meaning 'Buddha activity'; Thaye, 'limitless'; and Dorje, 'unchanging').

But who exactly was Tenzin Khyentse, and where had he come from? Shamar would offer a lengthy explanation of his discovery of the boy he claimed was Karmapa at a conference of his supporters at KIBI, in March 1996. According to Shamar's account, Tenzin Khyentse's mother was Dechen Wangmo, the daughter of a noble family, said to be descended from the legendary King Gaesar of Ling – Tibet's version of King Arthur. His father, Shamar claimed, was the 3rd Mipham Rinpoche. This was curious. The 1st Mipham Rinpoche, who was born in 1846, was a distinguished Nyingma practitioner who immediately before his death in 1912 is said to have stated on at least two occasions that he had no intention of reincarnating ('Now I will definitely not stay, nor will I take rebirth. I have to go to Shambalah in the north'). But spiritual status apparently abhors a vacuum, and the Mipham's proclamation did not prevent the emergence of a succession of people claiming to be his reincarnation.

Shamar said that he had first heard about Tenzin Khyentse in 1986, when he was visited in Delhi by an eminent Sakya lama named Chobgye Tri Rinpoche. Shortly before the 16th Karmapa passed away, Chobgye Tri Rinpoche told him, he had dreamed of the Karmapa circumambulating the steps at Baudhanath, in Nepal. He appeared to be sad. Then, just recently Chobgye had again dreamed of Karmapa, again walking around a stupa.

This time, he recounted, Karmapa's mood was cheerful. That same day, a relative of Chobgye's arrived from Lhasa, bringing with him a photograph of a child who was said to have declared that he was the Karmapa. So important was this news, Chobgye said, that he had hastened to Delhi to inform the Shamarpa. Acting on this information, Shamar went on, he had asked his friend Lopon Tsechu Rinpoche, who was visiting Lhasa, to make further enquiries. Lopon Tsechu, Shamar claimed, had discovered that the boy's father possessed religious objects and letters belonging to the previous Mipham Rinpoche, among them a letter stating that in the Mipham's next incarnation he would have a son, Rigpe Yeshe Dorje. Shamar had taken the words 'Rigpe Dorje' to refer to the 16th Karmapa's name, Rangjung Rigpe Dorje. A handwritten copy of this letter, he went on, was now in his possession. Shamar had then despatched to Tibet another emissary (whom he declined to name) to pursue the investigation. Arriving in Lhasa, this person had contacted the family on the pretext of requesting spiritual advice, and on entering their home the boy in question had immediately told him, 'You've come to look for me.' This, said Shamar, was a clear sign of 'a high spiritual capacity'.

Shamar had then begun his own spiritual investigations. In the course of a meditative retreat, he said, the late Karmapa had appeared to him, sitting on a seat performing a ritual to free a deceased person from the suffering of the world. In the dream, Shamar said, the Karmapa had told him, 'I've liberated the person I set out to liberate. Now I can come to wherever you want.' Convinced by these signs that the boy in Lhasa was the reincarnation, Shamar went on, he had travelled to Lhasa himself incognito, but on discovering the family's home he had realized it would be impossible to approach them without being recognized and that any contact could have 'undesirable consequences. I had learned that the authorities knew I was in the country and that they were probably watching my movements.' Instead, 'in order to divert the authorities' attention from my real purpose', he had travelled to a tourist area called Namtso before returning to Lhasa and leaving the country. Following this visit, he had instructed yet another lama, Tsultrim Dawa to travel to Parphing, near Kathmandu, where a spontaneously arisen image of Tara serves as a place of worship. There, Tsultrim Dawa had used a form of divination employing dough balls that declared that Tenzin Khyentse was the reincarnation of the Karmapa. The same exercise repeated at three other holy sites had produced the same result. All of this, said Shamar, had led to his belief that his candidate was the right one.

This story begged numerous questions. If Shamar had been first told about Tenzin Khyentse in 1986 – at a time when all the heart sons were supposedly working in unison to find the prediction letter – why had he not mentioned this crucial information to the others? And why had he continued to keep secret his numerous investigations after that? Shamar's explanation was that the various meetings between the four heart sons to discuss the reincarnation 'had become increasingly political' and he felt unable to share the information he had. 'I wasn't convinced that I could trust the others with it. This was not because I lacked respect for them.'

But what then of his earlier declaration in his public speech at Rumtek, in June 1992, when he had not only appeared to perpetuate the untrue statement about the 'first' prediction letter in the *gau* box, but declared that he knew of an unnamed person who supposedly held a 'key' letter which would explain the (non-existent) instructions? There was, Shamar acknowledged, a 'contradiction' between the account he had given at Rumtek in 1992 and the account he was giving now, but in 1992, he explained, he had still felt it necessary to maintain 'a facade of goodwill' with the other heart sons. 'I felt at the time that I couldn't disclose the truth about our resolution in the meeting. I felt that I couldn't break my promise to the others.'

So what, then, of the unnamed person who held the 'key' letter? Shamar now offered an explanation. In 1987, he claimed, he had been approached by a person who was a devotee of the late Karmapa, 'and who is well respected by many'. This person told him that he had been left instructions by the Karmapa indicating who the next reincarnation would be. Throughout the course of his – the Shamar's – own investigations into Tenzin Khyentse he had frequently consulted with this unnamed person 'to see if he had any objections. He always answered that he didn't,' Shamar went on, 'but that he couldn't reveal the information he'd been given until the time he was instructed to do so had come.' In 1992,

following Tai Situ's disclosure of the letter in the protection
pouch, Shamar had again contacted this unnamed person and
asked whether the letter was authentic. 'He answered that it is not
authentic, but as nothing could be done I should let the others do
whatever they had set out to do.' He had waited for a year,
Shamar went on, before deciding that the time had come to invite
Tenzin Khyentse to India. The unnamed person, Shamar told his
audience, had raised no objection to this. 'He said, "You are the
Shamar incarnation; I can't see anything improper in your course
of action." ' But when Shamar once more asked this person to
reveal the details of the instructions entrusted to him by the 16th
Karmapa, he had, again, replied that he was unable to do so until
the specified time. 'He insisted on doing things exactly as he had
been instructed.' The late Karmapa, Shamar went on, 'had definite
intentions in leaving his instructions in this way. His intentions
and purposes cannot be fathomed by ordinary people . . .'

But who was this person who was apparently so critical to
authenticating the Karmapa's reincarnation? It was the question
Shamar still declined to answer. But, he told his audience, 'If you,
individually or [as] a group, feel that it would be beneficial to
reveal his identity, I could introduce him to you. But first you must
know whether this would be beneficial or not.' Remarkably,
nobody seemed to feel that it would be beneficial. Shamar was
not called upon to name his mysterious contact.

In fact, there may be some evidence to suggest that Tenzin
Khyentse was familiar to the other heart sons long before his
arrival in Delhi in 1994. Sometime in the 1980s, it seems, a letter
was delivered to Tai Situ, Jamgon Kongtrul and Gyaltsab Rinpoche by a monk named Gendun Gyatso, written on behalf of
Tenzin Khyentse's father and requesting an investigation into
whether or not his son was the Karmapa. According to this letter,
at the age of three Tenzin Khyentse had declared that, 'My
teachers are Marpa and Milarepa, my monastery is Tsurphu,'
and that on seeing the Potala Palace in Lhasa for the first time his
words were: 'Today is good. I have two birds and they have flown
to Tsurphu.' Local people, the letter said, had 'said this was
wondrous and that he was the reincarnation of Karmapa and
had great reverence for him'. When the 16th Karmapa was alive,
the letter went on, he had told a relative, Dorje Khandro, that even

though she was old, she would see him again. 'He said this, but no opportunity arose to meet him again. She said that the incredible things being said by the great son of Ju Mipham meant that he must be the reincarnation of the Gyalwang Karmapa. And in accordance with what he had said, before she died she was able to see him again. She then borrowed a house from within the Mipham Institute in order to serve him. This old relative Dorje Khandro has since died.'

Could this be the same letter that had been delivered to Chobgye Tri Rinpoche? 'All of us sat down and discussed it,' Tai Situ told me, 'I'm not sure if we discussed it with Shamarpa, but possible. But we dismissed it. Anybody who says their son is Karmapa, it's quite obvious they're not.'

CHAPTER TWELVE

The Twisted Knife

Delhi: November 2000.

On 17 March 1994, an enthronement ceremony was conducted for Thaye Dorje in the temple of KIBI in New Delhi. The majority of people inside were Westerners from various Ole Nydahl groups. Outside, a large group of monks and laypeople from a number of Buddhist associations who had gathered to protest against the enthronement waved banners and maintained a steady chorus of catcalls and boos. As the demonstrators surged around the monastery gates, some began throwing stones and bottles over the wall into the Institute, smashing windows and injuring several people inside. The young Thaye Dorje was swiftly ushered to the upper enclaves of the shrine room, and police reinforcements eventually arrived to break up the disturbance

Following his enthronement, Thaye Dorje moved to a house in Kalimpong provided by the Shamarpa, to begin his education. In 1997 he made a pilgrimage to Bodh Gaya, the place where the Buddha had attained enlightenment, and in the same year he travelled to Bhutan to attend the cremation of Rumtek's old general secretary Topga.

Topga's banishment from Sikkim in 1992 had lasted almost three years. In December 1994, N.B. Bhandari lost the elections and his place as Chief Minister. The ban against Topga was revoked. In August 1995, he led 100 of the monks who had been bivouacked in Shamar's home, together with a number of other supporters, on a march to Rumtek monastery. They were denied entry by the Rumtek administration and monks and were finally dispersed by police. It was Topga's last throw of the dice. In September 1997, he died of cancer in Delhi, reportedly in a state of meditation. The erstwhile monk and smuggler was cremated in full state in a ceremony attended by the Bhutanese royal family.

In 1999, Thaye Dorje was deemed ready to conduct his first teachings, and he embarked on an extensive tour of European countries, including France, Austria, Hungary, Germany, Poland, Denmark and Switzerland. Many of these teachings were organized under the aegis of Ole Nydahl, who featured prominently in Thaye Dorje's appearances. By the end of 2000, Thaye Dorje had returned to India, and was ensconced in KIBI, continuing his religious education. KIBI was located, somewhat incongruously, on a commercial estate on the southern fringes of New Delhi; a large building in the traditional Tibetan style, set behind a high brick wall, flanked by purpose-built office blocks, housing corporations and institutions.

The front gate was locked. I stated my business to the guard at the sentry box, and waited while this information was processed back and forth until eventually I was allowed to pass. Broad steps led up to the main shrine hall, which was flanked on either side by three-storey blocks containing dormitories and classrooms. Students could be seen sitting out on the balconies; all appeared to be European. There seemed to be few monks in residence.

The Director of Studies at KIBI, and Thaye Dorje's principal tutor, was Khenpo Choedrak Tenphel Rinpoche. A cousin of Shamar Rinpoche, Choedrak had been the *khenpo* at Rumtek until the climactic events of 1993, when he had left the monastery for good. He occupied a first-floor room that served as his bedroom, office and sitting room. A wooden bed was pushed against one wall. There were shelves, lined with textbooks, a photograph of the 16th Karmapa and a picture of the Shamar Rinpoche as a young boy. In the centre of the room a sofa and chairs were arranged around a low table. A curtain was pulled across an open doorway leading to an adjacent room, from which drifted the smell of cooking and the chatter of women's voices. As we talked a succession of people came and went: Western students, dropping off papers; Khenpo's two nieces, ferrying food and tea. A tall, dark-haired and angelically faced Western boy in his early twenties lounged on a chair with an air of sulky languor.

This, I was told, was Trinley Tulku, who had been recognized by the 16th as a *tulku*; one of the first Westerners to have been recognized as the reincarnation of a Tibetan lama.

Khenpo Choedrak was a short, stocky man in his forties with a bullish, purposeful manner. His translator was an intense Swedish woman of similar age, who appeared to enjoy a familiar relationship with him, teasing, clucking and ticking him off in fluent Tibetan like an indulgent wife. Choedrak seemed to take this all in good grace. There appeared to be a preponderance of Western women of a certain age in Tibetan Buddhist circles, acting as translators or secretaries, particularly in Shamar's circle; a legacy, I assumed, of his close relationship with Ole Nydahl's organization.

We talked about politics, Khenpo Choedrak extemporizing at some length about the historical struggles between the Kagyu and the Gelugpa, and emphasizing the authority of his cousin, the Shamarpa, in the Kagyu hierarchy. When the 16th Karmapa enthroned Shamar in 1964, Choedrak said, he announced that Shamar would be the next lineage holder, and to commemorate the event he had written a prayer of auspiciousness for the Shamarpa. 'It says, "I empower you as the absolute owner of the doctrine of this lineage of *mahasiddhas*." ' This, Choedrak said, was proof of the 16th's wish for Shamar to lead the order. 'I grew up with the Karmapa. He made other announcements to the same effect many times. This is one of my reasons for following Shamar Rinpoche.'

I should understand this, Choedrak went on: the dispute was 'a power game. It's an issue that has arisen out of politics. It has nothing to do with religion, the Karma Kagyu lineage. It's a creation of people who are politically minded and power hungry.' What this was really about, he said, was an attempt by the Gelugpa to take control of the Kagyu; the old argument that had been raging for 500 years. Tai Situ and Gyaltsab Rinpoche had sold out the Kagyu to the Gelugpa establishment to further their own ends. 'Situ Rinpoche and I were childhood friends,' said Choedrak. 'He knew about my ancestral loyalties, and he knew I would never give them up. I grew up under the guidance of the 16th Karmapa. That's where my loyalties were. I would only follow a course of action that maintained the independence of the

Karma Kagyu school with the Karmapa as its head. Situ Rinpoche knew I would never go along with making this a Gelug affair – the Dalai Lama recognizing the Karmapa.'

Our talk turned to Ogyen Trinley. Had I read the report, Choedrak's interpreter wanted to know, that revealed that he was not a boy at all but a fully-grown man? I had read it. It was a news story that had allegedly appeared in a Hindi newspaper, *Amar Ujala*, and which I had read in translation on the web site of Ole Nydahl's Diamond Way organization. In April 2000, four months after his arrival in India, the Karmapa had been taken to a hospital in Chandigarh for a series of routine medical tests. That much was fact. However, the report went on to allege that a specialist who had examined the Karmapa had concluded that 'according to the measurement data prescribed in medical text and the vein, thymus, thyroid and the whole structure of his body' it had been determined that the Karmapa was not a fourteen-year-old boy but 'a fully grown-up man' who had 'crossed twenty-one years old'. I had checked with the Chief Administrator of the hospital in Chandigarh and been told that the story was completely untrue.

But the interpreter had an even more fantastic twist to offer. Khenpo Choedrak's father, she said, had been a minister of the King of Derge. Through his connections, he had learned that shortly after his enthronement as Karmapa in 1992 the young Ogyen Trinley had suffered a serious stroke. Half paralysed and unable to speak he had been kept away from visitors in the hope that his condition would improve. 'They let people see him,' she said, 'but he would only bless them with a stick. We were told that the monks who were in charge tried various medical treatments, having been told that one can train a person who has had a stroke so they regain certain faculties. They tried everything, and then they thought, this isn't working.' In 1997, she went on, Ogyen Trinley went into a year-long retreat. 'And when he came out he had changed. He was this very tall young man. And the fact that he had changed so much was attributed to some sort of mystical powers because of his meditations and so on. But according to Khenpo's sources, it is rumoured that it is his older brother – that Ogyen Trinley was substituted.'

I had no idea what to say to this. I had spoken to countless people who had been with the Karmapa since 1992. Nobody had ever mentioned a stroke. Surely the story was preposterous. Instead, I asked about Thaye Dorje. How, I asked, had he been brought from Tibet into India?

Shamar Rinpoche, Choedrak replied, had kept the details to himself, to protect those involved. 'I can't reveal his point of exit. It would endanger too many people.'

But he had arrived in Delhi by plane?

'Yes! He landed at Indira Gandhi airport.'

And where, I asked, did the plane come from?

Choedrak slapped me on the knee and roared with laughter.

What then, I asked, had convinced Choedrak himself that Thaye Dorje was the Karmapa? He had known the 16th well: could he see any similarities between them?

'In terms of his mannerisms and so on, no,' he said, 'I can see no particular similarities.' However, he added, there was one notable thing that gave him conviction. In 1977, the 16th Karmapa, using Choedrak as his secretary, had narrated a series of accounts of his previous incarnations. Choedrak had written them down. At the time, he said, it seemed that the Karmapa intended to publish these accounts, but he later changed his mind. 'He said that the majority of people will not believe these accounts; they will have no purpose and no one will benefit. His Holiness told me to burn the manuscript. I had to do it in his presence.' Choedrak laughed. 'He knew I wanted to keep it. In one of these accounts,' he went on, 'the Karmapa told me that he had been born in Africa – this was before what we call civilization, at a time when written language didn't exist. And in that rebirth he had collected herbs from the forest and initiated a system of herbal remedies as medication for various ailments. Anyway, in 1995 I was giving Karmapa Thaye Dorje some teachings, and he did a drawing of a landscape and he told me, this is Africa, a place where I was born a very long time ago, and then he told me that same story.'

Choedrak watched me with a smile as this was translated, anticipating my look of astonishment. 'How would he have known this?' he went on. 'I was the only one who knew this story. So I'm convinced.'

There were other signs, he said. Tibetan lamas perform divinations using a variety of methods, sometimes by rosary, sometimes by dice. But the late Karmapa never used such means. 'He would be asked a question, and just give the answer. And this one does the same. And just like the previous one, I've never known this Karmapa to be wrong, ever.'

Had Thaye Dorje, I wondered, been doing recognitions of other *tulkus?*

Choedrak nodded. 'One or two. He has recognized a reincarnation of a Drugpa Kagyu master; and a reincarnation from a border area in Nepal.'

As we were talking, another monk had entered and sat down quietly at the back of the room. This was Choedrak's brother, Tsultrim Namgyal. He had been the attendant of the 16th Karmapa, I was told. Following the Karmapa's death he had remained at Rumtek, leaving with Choedrak and Shamar after the tempestuous events of 1993. He was now the attendant of Thaye Dorje.

Tsultrim reached into his robe and produced a hunting knife, its eight-inch blade bent double on itself. Karmapa Thaye Dorje, the interpreter said, had given this knife to Tsultrim Namgyal. Karmapa had then taken the knife and bent it like that with his bare hand. 'And he told Tsultrim Namgyal, "It's a gift, for your devotion." Later a gentleman from Sikkim examined it carefully, and according to him you cannot bend metal like that because it would snap.' Tsultrim put the knife back into his robe with a smile.

If I wanted to meet Thaye Dorje, said Khenpo Choedrak, I should come tomorrow.

I returned to KIBI next day. Shamar Rinpoche's Austrian interpreter was waiting to greet me. She led the way through a door beside the main temple, and up two flights of stairs to a deserted corridor, where she left me to wait. Karmapa, she said, would be along shortly. The air of casual informality was disconcerting. I had not expected to have to negotiate the same cordon of security that surrounded the Karmapa in Gyuto, but I had anticipated at least some degree of ceremony. At Gyuto, there was no question that Ogyen Trinley was the centre of gravity in the monastery. But the casual visitor to KIBI might not even have known that Thaye

Dorje was here. My meeting felt strangely like a business appointment.

After a few minutes, a tall boy, dressed in a brown *chuba* and brown linen shirt came along the corridor. This was Thaye Dorje. Tsultrim Namgyal followed a few steps behind him. Thaye Dorje tentatively offered an outstretched hand. His eyes blinked shyly behind wire-rimmed spectacles; there was a dusting of teenage acne across his upper lip. I offered a *khata*. He took it, perfunctorily draped it back around my neck, and then led me into a room. There were four chairs set around a table, and a bookshelf against the wall with a handful of slim volumes. No shrine; no hangings; no decoration of any sort. This, Thaye Dorje explained, was where he took his classes. The windows looked out on to a veranda, an extension of the corridor where he had greeted me. I could see Tsultrim Namgyal standing there, waiting patiently.

'Before we start,' Thaye Dorje said, 'you will understand that I am not able to talk about any matters to do with politics. I'm sure you'll understand this.' His English was surprisingly fluent, but his manner hesitant, almost apologetic. There was little sense of the authority so apparent in Ogyen Trinley; rather Thaye Dorje had the shy, polite air of a Tibetan English-language student.

Our conversation proceeded at a faltering pace; through his education, his responsibilities, his current timetable. At the moment, he said, he was in the midst of retreat: for ninety minutes each morning and two hours each afternoon.

I asked about his interests. In his free time, he enjoyed travelling, he said, and reading 'Tibetan books, computer magazines, *Newsweek* or *National Geographic*. I don't have a computer now. It's not so good when you're doing retreat. But I have played computer games – strategy games.'

But not violent games, I said.

He smiled. 'Violent games are OK, I think. Not real.'

He enjoyed playing cricket and listening to music – 'classical, or normal; jazz or techno. Devotees bring me a lot of things.' He smiled. 'Sometimes too much . . .' And he liked taking pictures, particularly of wildlife. 'I take pictures a lot and try to be a photographer for the *National Geographic*! The pictures in there are really wonderful.'

I had also been told, I said, that he was especially interested in medicine.

'I would like to learn, yes . . .'

At a Western university, perhaps?

'That would be a possibility. If it was needed in the future, I could do that. But my main purpose is to teach, so for that I have to know all the answers.' For the next four years, he said, he would be studying in earnest.

And then, I joked, he would be free.

'I won't be free actually.' He gave a shy smile. 'During the time I'm studying actually I think I'm more free. But I'd like to learn more and study more.'

I felt a surge of sympathy for Thaye Dorje. I liked his quiet, self-deprecating manner, his enthusiasm for cricket and pop music. He seemed like a normal, adolescent boy with normal, adolescent enthusiasms; intelligent, likeable. But his situation, of course, was far from normal. I could not begin to fathom the twists of destiny that had led to him becoming embroiled in all this, nor to divine his true feelings about it all. I was impressed that he had met me alone, without an interpreter or anybody to monitor my questions and his replies. Was that his decision, I wondered, or somebody else's?

I asked about his childhood. I had read, I said, that he had declared himself to be Karmapa at an early age.

'That's what people say. I don't remember exactly. I think I was too small.'

What about leaving Tibet? Was that difficult?

He looked at me for a moment, distrusting the question. 'Not really difficult. As I said before, I like travelling so it was exciting. But I'd like to visit Tibet if I can.'

Being declared as Karmapa, I went on, must have placed a great responsibility on him.

'At that moment I felt quite surprised to find myself like that. But later on I felt, yes, this is my responsibility and it felt quite natural.'

I presume he had seen photographs and film of the 16th Karmapa; what did he feel when he saw those?

He shrugged. 'I can't really tell how I really feel when I look at that. I can't explain.'

A particular connection, perhaps?

'I don't know whether to say connection or anything like that. I just feel very natural. Quite normal.'

My mind went back to my conversation with Khenpo Choedrak, and his story about the 16th Karmapa's previous lives. Was it true, I asked, that Karmapas traditionally had insights into the past and the future?

'Most of the great lamas have written prophecies and so on, but they haven't done it so openly. It's not the tradition to do it openly, for the *samaya* of the practice. It is not proper to talk about these things, because otherwise it will be lost. But if something is appropriate to the moment, they will say.'

And did he have memories of previous lives?

He nodded. 'Sometimes I remember things, but I'm not really allowed to explain.'

And had he been recognizing other incarnates?

'No, not yet.'

What feelings, I wondered, did he have about Ogyen Trinley? Again, the look. Did this count as a 'political' question? It probably did.

'Actually,' he said at length, 'I don't feel anything special. What I would really wish, and what I would expect, would be for him to do the same thing as me. Since he's a Karmapa also his duties should be to help all sentient beings through teaching the dharma. That's the main duty for the Karmapas, I think. So he should continue that; that's what I'd expect.'

His choice of words – 'since he's a Karmapa also' – surprised me. Wasn't that, I wondered, what this whole dispute was about? Was he saying that Ogyen Trinley was Karmapa?

'For myself I really can't say that, if he is or not. I think it really depends on the people, who they want to think. Otherwise, saying I am and he's not is quite stupid, I think. In a way that would be quite selfish. So it's depending on the people, whom they choose to see in this way.'

I was struck by the lightness of his answer, as if he, at least, regarded the dispute as something not to be taken too seriously. Would he like to meet Ogyen Trinley, I asked?

'Hmm . . .' He thought about this. 'I don't mind. No problem at all. It would be interesting.'

Perhaps, I ventured, you should both sit down and talk and the politics would disappear.

'Sure! I wish we could do that actually. I think that would be one of the best ways.'

With his new protégé installed in Kalimpong, Shamar Rinpoche and his followers opened a new front to the battle, in the courts. Between 1993 and 1998, a series of suits were filed in various Indian courts, by various claimants, challenging the 17th Karmapa's recognition by the Dalai Lama and Tai Situ, and the take-over of Rumtek in August 1993.

The most assiduous petitioner was one Shri Narayan Singh, a former Rumtek monk who in 1998 filed a criminal complaint in the office of the Chief Metropolitan Magistrate in Delhi, charging, among other things, that Tai Situ, Gyaltsab Rinpoche and others had 'hatched a conspiracy to bring about the dis-integration of India by bringing about the amalgamation of the State of Sikkim with the Tibetan Autonomous region of the People's Republic of China.' An outline of this conspiracy, Singh maintained, was contained in a confidential report, dated 24 May 1997, which had allegedly been written by Sri Sridhar Rao, an official in the government of Sikkim, and submitted to the Cabinet Secretary of the government of India, Sri T.S.R. Subrahmanyam. This report purported to offer a summary of the events surrounding the recognition of Ogyen Trinley as the Karmapa, and the true reasons behind it. It paralleled the allegations that Shamar Rinpoche had laid out to me at my meeting with him in the Hyatt Regency Hotel.

'The Tai Situ Rimpoche (sic) group', the report alleged, had 'managed to get their candidate approved by the Dalai Lama as well as the PRC [People's Republic of China] in spite of the fact that there were fundamental doubts about the correctness of the so-called instructions left behind by the sixteenth Gyalwa Karmapa.' Since then, it went on, 'the Tai Situ Rimpoche group has been influencing local opinion in Sikkim to continuously pressurize the authorities for bringing the Karmapa reincarnate to Rumtek and formally install him in the monastery.' This, the report implied, was all part of larger Chinese ambitions to influence the process of recognizing senior reincarnates, and to influence Tibetan Buddhism through controlling monasteries along the entire Himalayan belt. 'It is reported that the Chinese have been making efforts to penetrate into these monasteries and as of now no less than eleven monasteries are headed by Lamas who can be considered as protégés of China.' The report declined to name these lamas or their monasteries. 'Given the fact that Sikkim occupies a strategic position,' the report went on, 'it would be most undesirable to have a situation where a Tibetan incarnation that is basically a Chinese national, recognised by the Chinese, formally occupies a position in a monastery in Sikkim.' Such an event, it went on could 'lead to consequences quite unpredictable and may affect the security interests of the country very substantially.' It concluded by speculating 'a) Whether Dalai Lama can be influenced to recognise the reincarnation [of Thaye Dorje] and b) Whether steps can be taken to restore the trustees their legitimate control over [Rumtek] monastery'.

It subsequently emerged that while this document had been written on official notepaper it did not have the formal backing of the Sikkimese government. In November 1997, Sonam Wangdi, the Chief Secretary of the government of Sikkim, wrote to the Cabinet Secretary of the government of India stating that there was no record of the letter having being written in the files of the office of the Chief Secretary. Sonam Wangdi disassociated the Sikkim government from the report, and reaffirmed the government's support for Ogyen Trinley as the Karmapa. After an enquiry by the Criminal Bureau of Investigation, Singh's case was dismissed in 1999.

But the gist of Singh's allegations, and of Sri Sridhar Rao's report would apparently find some support within the Indian intelligence community. The suggestion that the 17th Karmapa was a possible agent of Chinese ambitions in Sikkim would figure highly in the Indian government's appraisal of the situation when he escaped from Tibet at the end of 1999, and in the decision not to allow him immediately to assume his ancestral seat at Rumtek.

For Tai Situ, the damage had already been done. Following a series of newspaper articles in Indian newspapers rehearsing the allegation that he was an agent of the Chinese, in August 1994 the Indian Ministry of Home Affairs issued an order banning his entry into the country on the grounds of 'anti-India activities'. Tai Situ was in Taiwan when he learned of the ban. He was given no explanation. 'Somebody told me it was because the Indian government thought I was a Chinese spy,' he told me. 'But that's ridiculous.' Unable to return to India, he flew to London to make enquiries at the Indian High Commission. 'They were very nice. But they didn't know the reason either.' For the next three years he led a peripatetic life, travelling in America, Canada, Britain, France, Germany, Scandinavia, Taiwan and Malaysia. In each country, he would apply for an entry visa to India. It was always refused. The ban was finally lifted in July 1998, allowing Tai Situ to visit areas other than the north-east of India and Sikkim, and on the condition that he did not involve himself either in the affairs of Rumtek monastery or in the issue of the Karmapa succession.

In May of that same year, Shamar Rinpoche himself launched the case that would have the most long-lasting implications in the Karmapa dispute. The suit, filed in the High Court of Sikkim, pitted Shamar and the Karmapa Charitable Trust against the State government of Sikkim, its Ecclesiastical Department and Gyaltsab Rinpoche. It arose from the violent confrontation at Rumtek during the Yarney celebrations in August 1993, and the Kagyu International Assembly when the original trustees of the KTC had been replaced, and Topga replaced as general secretary. The suit alleged that the State government had colluded with Gyaltsab to take unlawful possession of Rumtek, preventing the legally elected members of the KCT from entering the premises and discharging their duties as trustees. It called for the eviction of Gyaltsab Rinpoche, for the return of the main key to the principal shrine hall of the monastery and for a decree that Shamar and his co-trustees were alone entitled to possess and administer the property until the 17th Karmapa attained the age of twenty-one. At issue in this was not only who controlled Rumtek, but by implication who would hold the key to the treasures locked in the monastery's vault – among them the priceless Vajra Crown. The case would rumble on for the next six years, and prove a further obstacle to the Karmapa being allowed to go to Rumtek, following his escape from Tibet.

The lawsuit was the culmination of Shamar's endeavours to consolidate the position of his candidate Thaye Dorje. Three years earlier, in 1995, in a meeting with Sikkimese ministers, he had proposed what he described as 'a compromise solution' to the Karmapa issue. Since the Chinese government had authorized Ogyen Trinley – 'the Chinese Karmapa', in Shamar's words – to take over Tsurphu, the logical solution would be to allow his nominee, Thaye Dorje, 'the Indian Karmapa', to take Rumtek monastery. Under the rules of the Karmapa Charitable Trust; Shamar went on, the Trust must hand over its assets to the Karmapa when he reaches the age of twenty-one. 'Therefore the Trust must hand over its assets to both the Indian and Chinese Karmapas when they reach twenty-one. At that point, the Karmapas themselves must decide who owns what properties. Of course, I added the caveat that the Chinese Karmapa must be an Indian citizen to own property in India.' He might also have added a further caveat: that his candidate, Thaye Dorje, would reach the age of twenty-one some two years before Ogyen Trinley.

At the same time, and notwithstanding his argument that the Dalai Lama had no role to play in Kagyu affairs, Shamar turned his attention to seeking the Dalai Lama's approval of his candidate. In January 1997, at a meeting in Dharamsala, Shamar recounted his story about his discovery of Thaye Dorje, and requested the Dalai Lama to meet with and give the novice-vows of ordination to the young boy. At the same time he restated his proposal that Ogyen Trinley should be the throne-holder of Tsurphu and Thaye Dorje the throne-holder of Rumtek.

There was some doubt, it seems, about whether Shamar's 'solution' was based on political or metaphysical grounds. Tibetan Buddhism provides innumerable precedents of great practitioners being reborn in different 'emanations' of the aspects of body, speech and mind. This theory of multiple reincarnations had been used to solve disputes over recognitions in the past – a testament not only to the efficacy of the bodhisattva teachings and the accomplishments of great yogis, but also to the Tibetan skill in religious politics. Was Shamar then trying to suggest that both Ogyen Trinley and Thaye Dorje were emanations of the 16th Karmapa? The Dalai Lama apparently thought so.

On 3 February, his office stated his position in a lengthy letter. This said that at a meeting in late January with a delegation of senior Kagyu representatives, including Tai Situ and Gyaltsab Rinpoche, the Dalai Lama had been advised that there had never before been a number of reincarnations of the Karmapa at the same time. Furthermore, in the interests of peace within the lineage, the Kagyu representatives had pleaded with the Dalai Lama not to meet with or ordain Thaye Dorje. 'Therefore,' the letter stated, 'for the sake of preventing further problems and for the sake of reconciliation, H.H. The Dalai Lama cannot give an audience or monastic vows to the young reincarnate for the time being.' The letter then addressed Shamar's evidence about the authenticity of Thaye Dorje. Shamar, it said, had repeatedly informed the Dalai Lama in the past about the existence of a person with whom the late Karmapa had left his instructions, without ever naming him. From their conversation at the meeting in early January, it had seemed to the Dalai Lama that Shamar was inferring this person must be Chobgye Tri Rinpoche. The Dalai Lama had contacted Chobgye Tri Rinpoche who had replied that he had not made the recognition at all. 'This letter made it clear that you don't have an authentic source for your claim. Thus, there is no possibility of a second Karmapa reincarnation.'

On 7 February, Shamar wrote his reply. The Dalai Lama, he suggested, had misunderstood, leaping to the assumption that his recognition of Thaye Dorje as Karmapa was dependent on Chobgye Tri Rinpoche. In fact, Shamar wrote, Chobgye Tri's 'indication' was but one source among others which he, the Shamar, had investigated. 'Fundamentally, it is on the basis of my own efforts that I have arrived at my decision.' It was, he went on, merely 'for the sake of showing respect', and in a spirit of reconciliation, that he had requested the Dalai Lama to give monastic vows to Thaye Dorje. He had not requested the Dalai Lama to acknowledge Thaye Dorje as a body, speech or mind incarnation. 'I have no need at all for such an acknowledgement.' The office of the Dalai Lama, he went on, had stated 'that it might consider to allow a body, speech or mind reincarnation of the late Karmapa on the basis of a reliable letter of instruction by the late Karmapa. This amounts to a medieval dictatorial command and I understand that this is the approach that you desire. But it is completely unacceptable to me.'

One thing, at least, was clear from this correspondence; whomever the mysterious man that Shamar claimed held the 'true instructions' of the 16th Karmapa might be, Shamar had no intention of naming him.

In the lounge in the Hyatt Regency Hotel, I asked him directly: who is it?

Shamar smiled at the question. He had met him in Varanasi, he said, at a meeting of lamas convened by the Dalai Lama. 'He said he has some instruction, but he will only tell when time ripens. He also told that to Jamgon Kongtrul. I know that . . .' He paused. 'He is quite an old lama. He was a very close friend to Karmapa. He's about seventy now, a Karma Kagyu lama. He's a yogi . . .' I felt I was being played along. 'And then we held a conference in Delhi [at KIBI in 1996], and I said, if you all want then I will reveal his name. Because he does not want me to say. But if you people want then I will disclose it. But nobody wanted it.'

He shrugged, as if to say the decision was out of his hands.

I asked him, will you tell me?

Again, Shamar smiled. 'No . . . Well, I'm thinking of disclosing his name now. But then two procedures should go ahead for that. There are big rumours here about the age of Ogyen Trinley, people saying he was replaced by his elder brother.'

I had heard them, I said.

'So for me to disclose his name, two things: first Situ Rinpoche's letter should go into forensic science test, number one. Number two, Ogyen Trinley should have bone marrow test. And then I can disclose this man's name.' The message was clear. He would not be naming the man.

CHAPTER THIRTEEN

An Audience with the Dalai Lama

Dharamsala: March 2001.

At the gate of the Dalai Lama's residence in Dharamsala, I presented my passport. At the gatehouse, I was frisked by a security guard, instructed to step through a metal detector, then led up a steep hill, through lushly cultivated gardens, to the house itself. I was ushered into a waiting room, lined with the innumerable awards, medals and honorary doctorates that the Dalai Lama has been given over the years. After a few minutes the assistant to his personal secretary appeared and led the way into the audience room itself. It was large and airy, light flooding into the rooms from the French windows that led on to a patio outside. In one corner stood a shrine, surmounted by an exquisite golden statue of the Buddha. In another, comfortable armchairs were arranged around a low coffee table. The Dalai Lama, the assistant secretary explained, would be with us shortly. He spelled out the seating arrangement. 'You will sit there,' he said. 'His Holiness always sits here.'

The Dalai Lama had been giving an audience in the gardens to a large group of Western meditation teachers. Now the meeting was apparently over. Through the windows, the teachers could be seen walking back towards the gate, draped in *khatas*, many of them wearing the slightly dazed smiles and beatific expressions common to anyone who comes into close proximity with the Dalai Lama. Behind them, his private secretary came running down the hill at a clip and, a minute or two later, the Dalai Lama himself came into view, walking briskly, two monks at his side, puffing to keep up. He came into the audience room, proffered a vigorous handshake, took my *khata* and passed it perfunctorily to his attendant. He was not a man who stood on ceremony. He waved me to my chair, sat down himself and turned to me expectantly. First question?

What, I asked him, could he tell me of the 16th Karmapa?

He sat back in his chair and thought for a moment or two. His predecessor, the 13th Dalai Lama, he began, had been very kind to the 16th Karmapa when the Karmapa was a young man. 'When the Karmapa first came from Kham to Lhasa, when he was very young, he met the 13th Dalai Lama and then, when he reached Tsurphu monastery, the Dalai Lama would occasionally send him some packages – fruit and so on. The 16th Karmapa related this to other people; that whenever he heard a bell on a horse he would immediately rush to look out of the window, hoping it was a messenger from the Dalai Lama . . . oh, more food!'

The Dalai Lama laughed. When he met Karmapa himself for the first time, he, the Dalai Lama, was still young. He had given the Karmapa some teachings in Lhasa, and in 1954 the Karmapa accompanied him to China for his fateful meeting with Chairman Mao. In 1956 he had visited the Karmapa at Tsurphu, and spent a few days there. 'One thing I remember quite clearly. He had a film projector and a generator, but the generator had broken down. So my driver, who also repaired my generator in the Norbulingka Palace, had some experience of this and within one day he was able to repair the Karmapa's generator. The Karmapa was very pleased! That night we were able to watch a film – a Hindi picture. Lots of fighting scenes!' The Dalai Lama laughed and clapped his hands delightedly. 'So through these things we became very close friends. And, of course, he was a very nice person, a very good human being.'

After the flight of both into exile, he went on, their relations had remained cordial. The Karmapa had visited him once or twice in Dharamsala, and had stayed at the residence of the Dalai Lama's mother, 'so very close like that'.

He paused. 'But we are recounting past history, so we have to be truthful . . .'

It was at that time that the disputes had arisen between his government-in-exile and the refugees from Kham and Amdo who made up the Thirteen Settlements group. These arguments were partly regional and partly sectarian, stretching back to the earliest days of the Gelugpa school, when the yellow hat Gelug had suppressed the old red hat schools. But they gave rise to suspicions that permeated the Tibetan community in exile. The head of the religious department in Dharamsala at that time was a man named Shasur Shankar – 'A very sincere person,' said the Dalai Lama, 'one of the Cabinet members, from Lhasa, very religious minded, but he considered yellow hat sect the best, and others not so good. One of his deputies was a Nyingma lama. Later, this Nyingma lama described Dharamsala as being like a yellow umbrella but with the point slightly crooked.' He laughed. 'So he was saying that the Dalai Lama too is a little bit sectarian! In fact, my basic attitude is, of course, non-sectarian. But at the same time my contact with Buddhist traditions other than the yellow hat sect was very limited at that time. So perhaps there was some ground for suspicion.'

In 1962, lamas from all the four schools gathered together in Dharamsala for the first major convocation since coming into exile. Among them was Dujom Rinpoche, the head of the Nyingma school. 'Later Dujom Rinpoche told me that after that conference he returned to Kalimpong, and one of his followers came to him showing shock and great disappointment. [The follower] said he had heard that a conference had taken place and the decision was that all non-yellow-hat sects should be banned! Dujom Rinpoche asked him, "Who told you this?" He said, "Actually, I participated in that meeting and such a resolution never took place." On the contrary, it was agreed that all religious traditions must be preserved. But these were the rumours, very strong rumours at that time.'

In this atmosphere of suspicion, he went on, his relationship with the Karmapa had suffered. 'On a personal level, still old friends; no problem. But as to the Tibetan community and the politics, a little bit of doubt, a little distance . . .' The Karmapa, he went on, had refused to contribute to the booklet for independence. 'And later, I heard that in talking to some of his centres in Europe and America he said the Tibetan freedom struggle is politics, and that as spiritual practitioners they should not be involved.' The Dalai Lama shook his head. 'Some people get the wrong impression, that this struggle is something political, a struggle for a few officials' benefit: the Tibetan government's benefit. But this struggle is necessary. It is Buddha-dharma! I remember once, in France, a monk telling me they did not want to participate in political activities. So I asked him, do you pray for the flourishing of the Buddha-dharma? He said, "Yes." And I said, "In that case Tibetan freedom is a very important factor for Buddhism to flourish. Without Tibetan freedom, Tibetan Buddhism has no future." And eventually he realized that.'

The Dalai Lama was growing more animated. This was clearly a subject that exercised him greatly. 'Then also, one Chinese friend, a Buddhist, he has a very good centre in Taiwan, he once told me that one of his close friends, a Chinese businessman, had told him, "The Dalai Lama is a politician; genuine lama is Karmapa." ' The Dalai Lama sighed. 'This man actually didn't want to see me because he believed this! But then he came to listen to one of my lectures, and he saw that the Dalai Lama is not just a politician. After listening to the teaching he got the impression that the Dalai Lama is also very spiritual! So this is how wrong impressions are created. So Karmapa Rinpoche, I think perhaps he misled people a little bit, and that made me a little sad . . .' The Dalai Lama shrugged, as if to say, but all that was in the past.

And now the relationship had been renewed . . . Pondering this I was struck by the curious nature of the continuity proposed by the theory of reincarnation: how these relationships spanned not only lifetimes, but centuries, the characters like actors in an endless drama, merely donning different masks and costumes to play their parts. What similarities, I wondered, could the Dalai Lama see in the young Karmapa to his predecessor?

The 16th Karmapa, he said, was not a scholar 'but by nature and his deep insights, his experience, there was some kind of special blessing, some kind of spiritual dignity there. This young boy is very similar in that respect. But right from the beginning, I have told him study is very important. The time has gone when we can be high lama on a high throne without much study. We must learn! And Karmapa Rinpoche really puts a lot of energy into his studies. And by nature, he is very good at composing poems. Very remarkable. As far as poems are concerned, he is much better than me! A sixty-six-year-old monk, and then a fifteen-year-young monk – his gift for that is much better! He has great potential. And as a person he seems to be very tough; steadfast, and strong-willed. Actually, I think Tai Situ Rinpoche and some others are afraid of him! I think for Situ Rinpoche it's much easier to tell me something than to tell Karmapa!' The Dalai Lama burst out laughing.

'Actually I told Indian officials – some of the officials have the suspicion that Situ Rinpoche is something unreliable and that his influence on Karmapa must be avoided. I told them, firstly that Situ Rinpoche is not at all unreliable or some sort of suspicious person. No, I have 100 per cent trust in him. There is nothing wrong with Situ Rinpoche's influence on Karmapa. But even if he was unreliable, I doubt whether Situ Rinpoche could influence Karmapa because he's very much afraid of Karmapa Rinpoche! I told this to the officials!' Once again the Dalai Lama let out a peal of laughter.

Our conversation turned to the recognition of the Karmapa. It was quite straightforward, said the Dalai Lama. Situ and Gyaltsab had come to Dharamsala when he was in Rio; they had sent him the documents and he was satisfied the choice was the right one. 'And then before that I had one dream. One valley facing the south, some stream and a lot of rocks and also a little grass. In the dream, no tent, or buildings; just that kind of land. Then in this dream, some sound telling me, here is the Karmapa's reincarnation. This is what I told Situ Rinpoche. And then he found that place, the same. So when Situ Rinpoche came here and telephoned me in Brazil, then I was almost certain. But then, after the boy came to Lhasa, I think his own attitude showed and demonstrated that he was the real Karmapa; and a very good one. He showed that he was a very strong-willed person, and he showed quite a tough attitude towards the Chinese. And I think that's the real indication.'

Situ Rinpoche had done well, he went on. He had found the Karmapa, and secured Chinese approval, but not before the Dalai Lama himself had recognized the boy. 'My divination was also there, and then afterwards the Chinese recognized him. So, here is good collaboration between the Dalai Lama and the Chinese – without the Chinese knowing about it!' He laughed.

But, I wondered, wasn't it a high-risk strategy to decide to leave the Karmapa in Tibet rather than to smuggle him out?

He pondered the question for a moment. 'I don't think so . . .'
Following Ogyen Trinley's discovery, he said, he had met with Tai
Situ and Gyaltsab to discuss how best to proceed. 'The original
idea was to leave him there, then ask the Chinese government for
recognition, then bring the Karmapa Rinpoche to Tsurphu and
then eventually, bring [him] to India, to receive teaching, oral
transmissions; all these things. That was the original scheme.
We'd already discussed how to ask Indian government. Theoretically, as a Chinese citizen there may have been some complica-
tions about how he was to live in Rumtek and own Rumtek; how
to settle that. All these points, we raised them and discussed. So
that was our original idea. We also hoped the Chinese may accept
that . . .'

That, at least, had been the plan. But then China had reneged on
their agreement to give the Karmapa permission to leave. And
India showed no inclination to let him come. 'And then also the
whole Chinese attitude towards me becoming harder; this is also a
complication.' The Dalai Lama shrugged.

'But there is positive and negative. Positive . . . because after all,
Tibet is our land, so some spiritual leaders must be there. I often
used to tell some of these lamas coming from Tibet, of course it's
entirely up to them, but when some express to me that they want
to return to Tibet, I always give them encouragement. It's a great
thing, to remain there and work for the preservation of Tibetan
spirituality. Quite a number of lamas are actually doing that, and
it's wonderful. The risk is they have to handle things very carefully
without provoking the Chinese; but at the same time trying to
preserve our Buddhist culture and religion, [which] is very important – very important.'

Our talk turned to the subject of the Shamar Rinpoche and
Thaye Dorje. In June 1992, the Dalai Lama said, following the
discovery of Ogyen Trinley, Shamar had come to see him. It was
the same day that he met Tai Situ and Gyaltsab; they came in the
morning; Shamar came in the afternoon. 'I don't think Shamar
Rinpoche wanted to come with them!' He laughed. At that
meeting the Shamarpa had told him for the first time of the
'trustworthy person' who, he claimed, had the true instructions
of the 16th Karmapa. 'He told me he did not want to divulge the
name of that monk until the appropriate time.' The Dalai Lama

shrugged, as if to say, what to do? 'I said to him, "If the stories are reliable and convincing then it makes it much easier for me to recognize another emanation." But still he wouldn't tell me the name.'

Eventually, he said, Shamar had written to him and mentioned the name of Chobgye Tri Rinpoche – the lama whom Shamar had claimed had first told him about the remarkable boy in Lhasa. The Dalai Lama wrote to Chobgye Tri Rinpoche, asking whether he was the lama who had recognized Tenzin Khyentse as the re-incarnation of the 16th Karmapa. 'And Chobgye Rinpoche wrote back to me and said he'd never done that! He said he had told Shamar Rinpoche only that he heard that this son of the Mipham Rinpoche could be a consideration as one of the candidates of the Karmapa. In fact, Chobgye Rinpoche told Shamar Rinpoche that the recognition of the Karmapa, who is a very high lama, can only be decided by someone like the Dalai Lama; that he could not do that. . . . So my thinking that this boy could be another emanation of Karmapa was on the basis of Shamar Rinpoche's statement; then Shamar Rinpoche's statement becomes weak, so there is no ground to recognize [Thaye Dorje] as another emanation . . .' The Dalai Lama shrugged, as if to say, that's that. (It should be remembered that Shamar claimed he had told the Dalai Lama that he was not relying solely on Chobgye Rinpoche's testimony as evidence in his choice of candidate.)

The Dalai Lama had made his point clear to Shamar at a meeting in the very room where we were now sitting. He pointed to my seat. 'He was sitting right there! I told Shamar Rinpoche that Ogyen Trinley has been officially recognized as the 17th Karmapa. There can be no argument about this. It has been decided so there's nothing more to be said about it. At that time also, Shamar Rinpoche told me that since his own candidate was so convincing to him, he had no other choice but to take care of him. But he said he had no desire to demand the throne of the Karmapa.'

That, he said, was the last time he had seen the Shamar until June 2000. The Dalai Lama was on a visit to Washington; Shamar was also in America and had requested a meeting. 'There he gave a little different interpretation. He said, when he mentioned there was no desire to argue about the throne, he meant Tsurphu, in Tibet!' The Dalai Lama laughed. 'And that Rumtek must belong to his candidate. I told him clearly, this is impossible. The late 16th Karmapa's main centre in Tibet was Tsurphu monastery. After 1959 he became a refugee; then outside Tibet his main place is Rumtek. So logically, Rumtek belongs to the 17th Karmapa! And I told him, still I hope within their lifetime there will be reconciliation. I told him, this is my hope.'

The Dalai Lama gave a deep sigh, as if despairing of the follies of mankind. Our meeting had been scheduled to last forty-five minutes; we had been talking for almost an hour and a half, yet he showed no sign of having exhausted the subject. His secretary was agitating to bring the conversation to a close. At length the Dalai Lama slapped his hands on his knees and rose from his seat. His attendant produced a *khata*, which the Dalai Lama put around my neck.

Before leaving for India, I had been asked by a Western nun to bring a photograph of her dying mother, to give to the Dalai Lama for his blessing. I gave him the envelope, expecting him to pass it to his secretary to deal with. Time was pressing. Instead, he opened it. Carefully, he read my friend's letter. His secretary hovered, almost willing the Dalai Lama, it seemed, to finally bring the meeting to an end. But now he turned his attention to the photograph. He held it cupped in his hand for what seemed like an eternity, regarding the image of the dying woman with an expression of the utmost compassion on his face, as if there was nothing more important in the world that he could be doing at that moment. At length, he placed the letter and the photograph back in the envelope and tucked it inside his robe, beside his heart. Throughout our conversation I had been aware of a nagging doubt growing in my mind; the talk of politics, of disputation had somehow made me momentarily forget the essence of the Buddhist practice. It had dented my faith. In this one small gesture, the Dalai Lama had restored it.

A few days later, I received an e-mail from my nun friend. The day after my meeting with the Dalai Lama she had received an e-mail from his private secretary. His Holiness wished her to know, it said, that I had given him her letter and that she and her mother were in his thoughts.

CHAPTER FOURTEEN

Love the Big Family

For his first three years at Tsurphu, the Karmapa had been allowed to live relatively unhindered by the Chinese. His value as a propaganda tool was exploited by stage-managed visits to major Chinese cities and Tibetan monasteries, a carefully orchestrated meeting with Premier Jiang Zemin and a succession of statements in which he had reportedly sworn loyalty to the motherland and the socialist cause. But his Buddhist education and activities continued without any interference; he had been able to fulfil his traditional role of making recognitions of other *tulkus* and he could receive visitors for public and private audiences.

But by 1996, conditions in Tsurphu were becoming more problematic. The Chinese honeymoon with Tibetan Buddhism was over, one of the principal catalysts being the thorny question of the reincarnation of the Panchen Lama. From the moment of the Panchen's death in January 1989, the Dalai Lama had made overtures to the Chinese about fulfilling his traditional role in the search for the next incarnation, offering to send a delegation to Tibet to make prayers and conduct divinations at the sacred Lake Lhamalatso. The Chinese rejected his request, and in August of that year announced their own five-point plan for the search, selection and recognition of the Panchen Lama. The first three steps acknowledged the traditional methods of using divinations to find the likely candidates and a choice of objects to test them. The fourth step was, for the Chinese, the most critical, invoking once again the use of the lottery system – the Golden Urn. The fifth step was approval of the final decision by the Beijing government.

While attempting to establish their sovereignty over the process, at this stage the Chinese still apparently wished to exploit the authority of the Dalai Lama in ratifying whichever candidate they chose. In July 1993, Chadrel Rinpoche, the abbot of Tashilhunpo monastery, and the head of the search party constituted by the Chinese government, wrote to the Dalai Lama with full government compliance, informing him that traditional divinations had confirmed that the Panchen Lama had reincarnated. The search for the new incarnation began. Within a few months, however, the mood of the Chinese government had changed, and it became apparent they had no intention of involving the Dalai Lama in the recognition procedure. Chadrel Rinpoche had no alternative but to continue the search under Chinese jurisdiction, while following the highly dangerous course of keeping the Dalai Lama secretly informed of developments, and supplying him with a shortlist of possible candidates.

On 14 May 1995, the Dalai Lama announced that following the appropriate divinations and consultations with the oracles he was formally recognizing a six-year-old boy, Gendun Choekyi Nyima, as the 11th Panchen Lama. The Chinese moved swiftly to express their displeasure. Two days after the Dalai Lama's announcement, Chadrel Rinpoche and his secretary Jampa were arrested. In Lhasa, Shigatse and Nakchu, meetings were called to announce a ban of any gathering of three or more people and to prohibit public discussion of the Panchen reincarnation. At Tashilhunpo, Party cadres moved in to conduct 're-education' sessions in which the monks were ordered to criticise Chadrel Rinpoche and denounce the Dalai Lama's statement. Forty-eight monks refused and were arrested. The unfortunate Gendun Choekyi Nyima and his family were detained and removed to Beijing.

On 8 December, following a carefully contrived ceremony of drawing lots from the Golden Urn, China enthroned its own Panchen Lama, a six-year-old boy named Gyaltsen Norbu, whose parents were loyal Party members. The fate and whereabouts of Gendun Choekyi Nyima remain unknown.

The outbreak of popular sympathy for the Dalai Lama's choice of the Panchen Lama confirmed the growing belief among the Chinese leadership that the liberal reforms of the 1980s had gone too far. From 1989, with the ascendancy of Jiang Zemin to the position of Party Secretary and President of China, the central plank of Beijing's policy towards Tibet had been to accelerate economic development within the region as a counter to the ever-present spectre of Tibetan nationalism. The policies nurtured in the 1980s by Hu Yaobang had also stressed development, but with an understanding that it should be led by Tibetans themselves, or at least directed towards advancing the interests of the Tibetan community. Under the new policy of Jiang Zemin the notion that there were any 'special characteristics' about the Tibetan people or their situation was abandoned. Inherent in this was the assumption that encouraging the development of Tibetan cultural identity was itself a dangerous thing. From now on, it was decreed, Tibetans should instead be encouraged to see themselves as part of, and to love, the 'big family' of China. Tibetan Buddhism would be tolerated, but more rigorously controlled.

This approach was spelt out in Jiang Zemin's so-called 'three sentences' on religion. These were:

1) To implement the party's religious policy fully and correctly.
2) To strengthen the management of religious affairs according to the law, and
3) To actively guide religion so that it can be adapted to socialist society

Central to this policy was a renewed attempt to eradicate the influence of the Dalai Lama. In the spirit of tolerance inherent in the 'freedom to believe' policies of the 1980s, the Chinese had made a subtle distinction in their attitude towards the Dalai Lama, continuing to attack him as a political figure, while at the same time tolerating the popular devotion towards him as the spiritual leader of Tibetan Buddhism. Now that distinction evaporated, and vilification of the Dalai Lama intensified. In 1994, as part of a policy to 'eradicate the Dalai's image', Party members in Tibet were reminded of the Party's commitment to atheism and ordered to remove any altars, rosaries or pictures of the Dalai Lama from their homes, and the first proscriptions on selling or displaying

pictures of the Dalai Lama among ordinary Tibetans were introduced. Newspaper articles stepped up the attack on the Dalai as
the leader of a 'splittist political clique' determined to gain Tibet's
independence from the motherland. 'The Dalai is no longer a
religious leader,' wrote the Tibet Daily in December 1995. 'He has
degenerated from being the leader of a rebellion against the
motherland into a naked anti-China tool who has bartered away
his honour for Western hostile forces' patronage.'

The following year, attention turned to the monasteries, which
were targeted as the 'strongholds where the Dalai clique promotes
its sabotage and splittist activities'. In June 1996 're-education'
teams were despatched to Tibet's three major monasteries, Sera,
Drepung and Ganden, in the first stage of what the authorities
referred to as the 'Loving the Motherland and Loving Religion'
campaign. Compulsory Maoist study sessions were introduced
with the specific intention to 'cleanse the feudal, foolish and
backward atmosphere poisoned by the Dalai clique'. Monks were
forced to sign statements denouncing the Dalai Lama, and swear
allegiance to the government. At Ganden monastery, angry demonstrations against the new measures led to one monk being
shot dead and the monastery being closed for several months. By
January 1997 a State broadcast of Chinese regional radio in Tibet
was confidently claiming that monks in all three monasteries had
welcomed the campaign to 'strengthen education, patriotism and
establish normal order. Having come to realize how the Dalai has
deceived them, the great majority of monks are now bold and
assured in their opposition to splittism and their criticism of the
Dalai. As the inscription on the banner presented to the autonomous regional task force by the monks of Drepung monastery
read: "Patriotic education has warmed the hearts of the monks;
the beneficence of saving the monastery and monks will last for
one thousand years." '

As the seat of the most important – Chinese-approved – incarnate
in Tibet, Tsurphu enjoyed special exemption from the most
extreme effects of the new policies. But, nonetheless, the screw
began to tighten. Vigilance on monks increased, enforced by an
extensive network of spies and informers within the monastery
itself. According to one close observer, monks would be required

to report every aspect of their neighbours' activities and threatened with reprisals if they refused:

'Even the smallest thing would be noted – "Tashi Karma always goes to the toilet at three in the morning and he spends two or three minutes there before he comes back." All the monks had to do that, which meant that in a sense they all had to be spies, or they wouldn't have been allowed to stay there. So they had to strike a fine balance between serving Karmapa and doing what was necessary for their survival. And this meant that it became more difficult for Karmapa to speak privately because there was always the risk that there might be someone around who would report that conversation back – "Oh, I was with Karmapa at three o'clock this afternoon and he was telling some foreigners that he'd like to go to America." '

The Karmapa's movements too were increasingly circumscribed. Security guards were posted outside his rooms. His mail was monitored; visitors checked and double-checked. Any movement outside Tsurphu had to be approved by the local government, and any movement beyond Lhasa by the central government in Beijing. Even to make an excursion within the monastery grounds to the summer palace required permission from a government official. His daily public audiences now took place under restricted conditions. Under orders from the government officials he was kept separate from visitors, behind a rope of *khatas*. No physical contact between the Karmapa and devotees was allowed; instead, visitors would be blessed by a contraption in which he could dip a tassel on their head by means of pulling on a rope. 'People would be hurried forward, take the blessing, then be hurried away,' recalls one visitor. 'There was no pausing to look into his eyes. That wasn't allowed.'

Still, even within the tightening cordon around him, the Karmapa was able to lead a semblance of normal life. He acquired a pet deer, which roamed the grounds of the summer palace, but which became so domesticated that it would occasionally follow him into his rooms. An Italian devotee, a musician, taped the young boy reciting prayers, which were then dubbed on to a music track and subsequently released as a CD. His education had now been broadened beyond the traditional Buddhist syllabus to include 'patriotic education' in Chinese language and Chinese culture – lessons in which the necessity to play the role of the loyal and dutiful lama would be emphasized. At the same time, he was coming under increasing pressure to denounce the Dalai Lama, and to shore up the largely futile campaign by the authorities to win popular support for the newly installed, puppet Panchen Lama. In 1996 he was taken to the Panchen's monastery at Tashilhunpo for his first meeting with the Chinese candidate. Crowds who had assembled for the occasion pointedly made their own distinction between the two boys by bowing at the appearance of the Karmapa and ignoring the unfortunate young pretender to the Panchen throne.

In that same year, he survived what appeared to be an attempt on his life. A Tibetan who regularly met the Karmapa at Tsurphu told me the story. One day, he told me, the Karmapa had suddenly announced that he wanted to visit the summer palace in the grounds of the monastery. The head official had refused him permission, but the Karmapa had ignored the order and run to the palace. While he was gone, a monk discovered two men, hiding in the library next to the Karmapa's private rooms. The men were not armed. They were seized and questioned. They said that they were Chinese farmers from Szechuan; in Lhasa, they had met some Tibetans who told them they would be paid if they killed the Karmapa. They were on a reconnoitring mission. One of the Karmapa's inner circle, Tomo-la offered them money if they would tell him who had contracted them to do the killing, but they claimed not to know the names of the men. They were handed over to the police in Lhasa, but, curiously, subsequently vanished. The incident was never explained, but it was becoming clear that there were dangerous currents eddying around the Karmapa, and that his position was becoming ever more precarious.

In 1998, one of Tibet's most senior religious figures, the Agya Rinpoche embarrassed Chinese authorities by defecting to the United States whilst on a visit to South America. The forty-nine-year-old Agya Rinpoche was the abbot of Kumbum monastery in Qinghai (formerly Amdo) province. Regarded by the authorities as a 'loyal' lama, he had been rewarded with a number of important posts, including vice-chairman of the Political Consultative Committee. But he had come under mounting pressure to

make public statements denouncing the Dalai Lama, and incurred
official disapproval by resisting attempts to move the puppet 11th
Panchen Lama to Kumbum from his traditional seat in Tashilhunpo monastery in the Tibetan Autonomous Region. With his
defection, vigilance on the Karmapa and his activities in Tsurphu
was stepped up. The Karmapa's endeavours were now being
curbed in other, crucial ways.

Since his recognition of the Pawo Rinpoche in 1995, the Karmapa
had recognized a number of other new incarnates, most impor-
tantly – in 1996 – the 4th Jamgon Kongtrul Rinpoche, whose
predecessor had died in the car crash four years earlier. These
recognitions had proceeded under the terms of Beijing's five-point
ruling on the recognition procedure, under which lamas would
identify and discover a candidate by traditional means, and the
government would confer their final, official approval. It was a
system by which both sides could claim some satisfaction: the
lamas could be assured that the chosen child was the right one,
while the government could demonstrate their sovereignty over
the process. But the debacle over the recognition of the Panchen
Lama had changed all that. To the Chinese, the Tibetan lamas
could no longer be trusted to produce 'acceptable' candidates by
the traditional means. The five points of recognition were now
increased to fourteen. No longer were the clergy entrusted with
the initial discovery and recognition of a candidate. The new
strictures demanded that the government should be consulted
from the very start of the process, effectively claiming the authority to decide not only which boy, or boys, should be the candidate
for a new incarnation, but whether or not that incarnation could
be reborn and recognized at all. In short, from now on no
recognition could carry any sort of credibility at all.

The Karmapa's activities were also being undermined in yet
another critical way. His historical role – one might say his entire
raison d'être – was to act as the crucial link in the Golden Rosary
of the Karma Kagyu teachings. To fulfil this role it was necessary
for him to receive the most important teachings and transmissions
of the lineage from the lineage holders, Tai Situ and Gyaltsab
Rinpoche. Without these teachings and empowerments, the Karmapa told his closest attendants, he would be unable to fulfil his

spiritual destiny, and would be no more than 'an ordinary monk who happens to be called Karmapa'. Not only was the Karmapa forbidden to travel to India to meet his teachers, his teachers were now forbidden to enter Tibet to see him. Both Tai Situ and Gyaltsab's applications for visas were refused by the Chinese. Persistent requests from the Karmapa for his teachers to be allowed to come were met with a stony refusal. 'I don't think the Chinese fully understood what it meant for the Karmapa to be Karmapa,' Akong Rinpoche told me. 'The high political people don't understand the system of educating *tulkus*, what is involved in that. They think once the *tulku* is chosen, that's the end of the process; but that's just the beginning of the process.' Without the necessary teachings and empowerments from his lineage holders, the Karmapa could not fulfil his spiritual potential. In the summer of 1999, he gave his first teachings from scripture to other monks on the activities of the bodhisattva. He was now fourteen. The pupil had outstripped his teachers.

At the same time his relationship with his government overseers reached crisis point. When a local party official asked him to read a prepared speech denouncing the Dalai Lama, the Karmapa refused. 'Do you wish me to say,' he asked, 'that I am giving this speech on your behalf?' No, the official explained; the speech was to be given as if it were the Karmapa's own. 'In that case,' the Karmapa replied, 'I have no need of this text.' The speech was not given.

In the autumn of 1999 the Karmapa presided over a fifteen-day practice for the deity Sero Ngadra. Each day he gave two long talks to the assembled company of monks, emphasizing the importance of the community of the *sangha*, the need for study and the importance of the teacher. In one talk he stressed the nature of impermanence. 'Everything compounded is imperma- nent. You may be looking at me now and thinking, he is young and we will often meet, but given that all is impermanent, maybe I won't be around for so long. Even if impermanence gives you problems, you should always study and maintain your discipline. In the future we will have the chance to meet again.'

In September 1999, his American devotee Ward Holmes visited the Karmapa in Tsurphu. 'The last thing he told me was, don't come back here. I'll meet you outside Tibet,' Holmes remembered.

'I was sad. I thought maybe I'd done something wrong or he didn't need my help any more.'

At the beginning of October, the Karmapa summoned his most trusted teacher and attendant, Lama Nyima. He was thinking, he told Lama Nyima, of leaving Tibet.

CHAPTER FIFTEEN

The Escape

Gyuto: November 2000.

Lama Tsewang told me we could talk in his room. He sat on his bed in his vest, and poured tea from his thermos flask. The afternoon sunlight flooded in through the windows. It was October, he said, when his friend Lama Nyima first approached him, and told him that the Karmapa was considering escape. As the head of Nyenang monastery, and the man who had organized the search party for the Pawo Rinpoche, Tsewang had come to know the Karmapa well.

'Lama Nyima and I are very close friends, and trusting our friendship, he told me this. So I went to Tsurphu to see the Karmapa. I told His Holiness, "I hear you are planning to leave, please consider this well – think carefully." The Karmapa said, "Yes." Then he said, "I think you should be connected with Lama Nyima, talk with him about this." For generations my family have had great faith in the Karmapas, and the 17th Karmapa has been very kind to Nyenang. So I have a lot of faith and trust in him. Whatever he told me to do, I would do it without question. So Lama Nyima and I arranged to meet in Lhasa. Lama Nyima told them at the monastery that he was sick, and that he had to go to Lhasa for a check-up; that's how he got out of Tsurphu to meet me. I have a business in Lhasa, and because I'm doing a lot of work with the monastery and so on, I can come and go and nobody pays me much attention. So Lama Nyima came to my house. We talked for a long time but we couldn't decide on anything. Lama Nyima said to me, "We're having trouble finding people who are stable and reliable to help with the escape. We hesitate to ask you because you have the responsibility of Pawo Rinpoche's monastery, his upbringing, the school and so on – you have lots of work." But my thinking was, the Karmapa is going to India for the benefit of the teachings and the benefit of all sentient beings; I'm a follower of the Karmapa and his disciple. So I told Lama Nyima, "If you want me to go, I will. My work in Nyenang is small compared to the vast activity which the Karmapa will engage in." '

Still, said Lama Tsewang, two people was not enough. They needed more help. Together, they approached another monk at Tsurphu, Lama Tsultrim Gyaltsen, a close friend of Lama Tse-wang, who also agreed to join them. 'So now there were the three of us. And we said we will work with all our hearts to help the Karmapa. We will not tell anyone, even if we lose our lives. We made this commitment to do this.'

They worked out the plan between them. It was Lama Nyima's responsibility to devise a way to get the Karmapa past his security guards and out of the monastery itself. Once he was clear of the monastery grounds, it was the job of Tsewang and Tsultrim Gyalt-sen to get him to the border and across into India. 'When we were talking in Lhasa, I said to Lama Nyima, this is not a movie; this is going to be very difficult. And if we fall into Chinese hands, we're small – it's not a big thing for us; but for the Karmapa they could make it very difficult. This could be a big problem. Then Lama Nyima said, "Karmapa has precognition, he knows what's going to happen – he sees – and he has said, 'If I don't go this year, I'll never be able to leave. Now is the time I have to go.' And the Karmapa said, 'We will definitely make it. There is no doubt we will get there.' " So I said, "OK, I am a follower of the Karmapa. If he says this, I will go." Then Lama Nyima was very happy I was coming along.'

Some 3,000 Tibetans each year are believed to attempt the perilous crossing of the border. Winter is regarded as the best time to make an escape bid. While the weather is at its most inclement, with temperatures plunging below zero, and the ever-present risk of avalanches, the border security tends to be at its most lax. Those who survive the journey often lose fingers or toes from frostbite. But suffering the ravages of the elements is feared less than the possible risk of capture.

The closest border crossing to Tsurphu was some 200 miles distant. But leaving Tibet at that point, Tsewang realized, would require the escape party to cross a glacier-covered pass near Mount Everest. The most direct route out of Tibet, and thus one favoured by many attempting to escape, it is also the most dangerous. Another option was to drive west, and cross the border into Mustang 400 miles away, and then to traverse the Annapurna mountain range at its north-western edge. The road from Lhasa to the Mustang border, while not good, would be navigable in the right vehicle. And the border crossing itself was often unmanned. Some four hours from the border is the old royal Mustang capital of Lo Manthang, located at the top of the Kali Gandaki river valley. Since 1992 this area has been opened by special permit to trekkers, and at the southern end of the valley is the western leg of Nepal's Annapurna trekking circuit, where it would be possible to find shelter and transport. It was this route that the conspirators would finally settle on.

While Lama Nyima stayed in Tsurphu, said Tsewang, he and Lama Tsultrim Gyaltsen planned an expedition to scout the proposed route. Tsultrim Gyaltsen told the monastic authorities that he had to make a trip to visit his sponsors in western Tibet, to make long-life prayers for them. At the same time, he suggested that the monastery needed a new vehicle, to replace the old, battered truck normally used. Lama Tsewang quietly gave him the money to buy a Toyota jeep. Lama Tsewang had to make up his own excuse for leaving Lhasa. 'I said that Bokar Rinpoche, who is from western Tibet, was putting up some buildings there, and that I'd been asked to look after things and make sure it was going well. Furthermore, I said, "I have no car, but Lama Tsultrim Gyaltsen has one, so we are going together." '

With permissions granted, the two monks set out for western Tibet, driving the planned escape route, carefully taking note of any potential problems such as roadblocks and army encampments along the way. Nearing the border with Mustang, they came to Kuyug Gompa, an outpost of Tsurphu under the administration of one Lama Pema. Tsewang explained to Lama Pema that they were making pujas at different monasteries, to remove obstacles in advance of the forthcoming enthronement of the Pawo Rinpoche. 'Then I told him, I have relatives in Mustang.

I would like to go and visit them, but I need a special pass to do that. Could he help me with that so I could see my family? And Lama Pema said he would help me. We had to go to this military encampment to get this particular pass. It was for four people: a driver and the three of us. Lama Pema was going to show us the way.' With the Chinese permit secured, the party made their way across the border into Mustang. In Lo Manthang, Lama Tsewang located his relatives. He told them that at some time in the future he might want to cross into Nepal, but he didn't have a Chinese passport. Would they help him? The relatives said they would. 'I kept the pass that Lama Pema had given me, and we made our way back to Tibet. Lama Pema returned to his monastery, and Lama Tsultrim and I returned to Tsurphu. All the time that I was going back and forth I was looking out for checkpoints, seeing how many soldiers there were, when they go to sleep, where they walk from their posts and so on. I was noting all this mentally.'

Back in Lhasa, Tsewang met with Lama Nyima to tell him about the trip. At the same time, in Tsurphu, Tsultrim Gyaltsen was giving a detailed account of their findings to the Karmapa. 'At that time the Karmapa didn't say anything; he just listened, but he didn't make a decision. We waited a day or two; we didn't know what was going to happen. And then I had a telephone call, summoning me to Tsurphu. I met with Karmapa, and he asked me, "How is it? What's the road like?" So I told him. I said to His Holiness, "Whether we go or not, it's your decision. We will give our lives to you whatever you decide." And then the Karmapa said, "I'll go. You must get ready." So I returned immediately to Lhasa.'

With Lama Nyima, he began to finalize the details of the escape. The telephones between Lhasa and Tsurphu were tapped, he said, and they had devised a code for their conversations, using the language of commerce. 'We were saying, if we don't do this deal quickly, then we're not going to get the goods. That kind of thing.' Tsewang made his own preparations for departure. Despite having his own business, he said, he was not a wealthy man. He had used his money to build a house in Lhasa, and houses near Nyenang monastery for the monks. Now he began borrowing what he could, to leave to the monastery and the school. 'I told them I was going on a business trip, and I gave them enough

money for food for six months, and something for the teachers to
live on.' He stocked up on provisions for the journey, bought
clothes and blankets, while Lama Tsultrim Gyaltsen made the
final checks to the car, then drove it back to Tsurphu, in readiness
for the escape.

A few days earlier, the Karmapa had announced to the monastery authorities that from 27 December he would be going into
solitary meditative retreat for twenty-one days. Such a retreat
was not unusual. During this time, his security guards and the
monastery spies would not be watching his movements. With
luck, this would give him the time to make good his escape
without his absence arousing suspicion. According to the plan,
his cook Thubten would continue to go in and out of the
Karmapa's rooms with food and drink, as if he were still there.
Lama Nyima often stayed in the Karmapa's rooms. He would play
the bell and *damaru*, or small hand drum, at certain times, and
receive *thankas* and protection cords for the Karmapa's blessing
as if the Karmapa himself were present.

On 27 December 1999, Lama Tsewang telephoned the Karmapa
in Tsurphu. 'I said, "You were going to lend money to a friend, is it
ready?" And the Karmapa said, "Yes, it's all packed and ready to
be delivered." ' The following morning, the Karmapa went into
retreat. From Tsurphu, Lama Nyima telephoned Tsewang. 'He told
me, "This evening at ten-thirty the Chinese are showing a special
programme on TV; why don't you watch it?" What he was saying
was that the Karmapa would make his move then.'

Lama Tsewang paused. Now there was a knock at the door
and another monk came into the room. It was Drupngak, the
Karmapa's chamberlain. He too had made the journey from Tibet,
although seeing him again, as small, skeletal and apparently fragile
as he was, it seemed impossible to believe that he could have
struggled 900 miles across some of the world's most inhospitable
terrain and survived. But Tibetans are extraordinarily hardy people,
and you could see a thread of steel in Drupngak's bony frame. A
badge of Karmapa was pinned on his robe. Lama Tsewang acknowledged him with a brief nod, and gestured to him to find a seat on the
bed. The old monk settled himself in the corner and began working
the beads of his *mala* between his fingers, his head cocked like a bird
to listen to Lama Tsewang's account.

At nine o'clock on the evening of the 28th, Tsewang went on, he left Lhasa in a taxi, carrying the provisions for the journey. With him was his driver. 'I'd told him, I have to go and do some work and I need you with me.' From Lhasa, the taxi took the road towards Shigatse. At the junction where the road branches off to Tsurphu, they parked and waited. Shortly after ten-thirty, Tsewang's mobile phone rang. 'It was Lama Nyima, saying our purpose had been accomplished.'

Half an hour earlier, in his private quarters the Karmapa and Drupngak had changed out of their monks' robes. The Karmapa donned a thick down jacket and brown trousers. A woollen scarf was wrapped around his mouth, a hat pulled down tightly over his ears. A pair of spectacles completed the disguise. On the table in his room the Karmapa placed a letter that he had written earlier, giving the reasons for his flight. This he explained had nothing to do with dislike for the Chinese; he was leaving so that he could receive the dharma. He had made many applications in the past to meet his teachers and all had been refused. Alongside his letter, the Karmapa left another, which he had received from the Dalai Lama several years earlier, in which the Dalai Lama had impressed upon him the importance of studying well and serving the Buddhist teachings in Tibet. Opening the door, the Karmapa and Drupngak slipped quietly out of the room, and down a flight of steps to the next floor. Moving past the audience room where the Karmapa would receive visitors, they stepped quickly into a storage room. A window opened on to the roof of a neighbouring building, the shrine halls for the protector deities. Clambering through the window, they dropped on to the roof, and paused.

I looked at Drupngak. He was listening carefully and nodding, verifying the account.

It was a bitterly cold night, said Tsewang. Most of the monks were occupied with their evening studies. Those that weren't had taken Lama Nyima's advice, that on a night like this there was nowhere better to be than gathered around the television with a bowl of hot soup, watching the television with the Chinese guards. From the roof of the shrine rooms there was another drop, of some ten feet, into an alleyway adjoining the main courtyard. As the Karmapa and Drupngak prepared to jump, they heard a voice. Keeping watch in the courtyard below, Lama Tsultrim Gyaltsen had been alarmed to see another monk suddenly appear. Thinking quickly, Lama Tsultrim called out to him, 'Have you seen my driver?' On the roof, the Karmapa and Drupngak froze. Below, they could hear the brief exchange of conversation and then the monk went back inside. The Karmapa and Drupngak dropped silently into the alleyway and made their way to the car.

'Lama Tsultrim Gyaltsen was waiting behind the monastery with the car,' said Tsewang. 'He had told everybody he was going to western Tibet to do prayers for his sponsors. It must have been the blessing of the Karmapa, because the head of the police at Tsurphu had gone on his vacation.' He laughed. 'Without their boss there the others were taking it easy. I was waiting at the junction with my driver. I'd sent the taxi away. And then the car arrived. There was Karmapa, Lama Tsultrim Gyaltsen, Drupngak and the driver. Just before they arrived I told my driver, "Actually, I'm going to India!" He was stunned. I said, "It's up to you whether or not you come with me." And he said, "OK, I'll come." It was only that morning that Lama Nyima had told the other driver what we were doing. So nobody knew until the last minute.'

With the escape party now complete, the car sped off towards Shigatse. The Karmapa sat in the back seat, with Drupngak and Tsewang. In the front was Lama Tsultrim and the two drivers, Tashi and Dargye. By day, Shigatse is a busy town, with a large police presence. But in the depths of a freezing night the streets were all but deserted, and the car passed through untroubled. 'On the other side of Shigatse, the road forks,' said Lama Tsewang. 'One road goes to Dram, which is the route most people take when they go to Nepal. The other goes on to western Tibet, which is the route we were taking. Usually at this fork there are police and there are two barriers. These barriers are usually down, and they check whether you have a pass and whether your car has a pass. We were very lucky, because the barrier was down on the road going to Nepal, but on the road we were taking to western Tibet it was up. And there was nobody there.' He paused. 'It was the blessing of His Holiness.'

Drupngak had been listening intently through Tsewang's account, working the beads of his *mala* between his fingers, saying nothing. But at this he nodded and smiled his agreement. 'The blessing of His Holiness.'

All the next day, Tsewang went on, they drove on towards the border, stopping only to change drivers. At dusk they came to the Brahmaputra, the great river that traverses almost the entire length of southern Tibet. It took more than an hour to find a local person who could direct them to a point where the ice was solid enough to carry the weight of the jeep, and to navigate the slippery route. And another hour to find their way back on to the road on the other side. It was late in the evening of the 29th as they neared the border, and reached what Lama Tsewang had anticipated would be the most dangerous part of the route, passing through the Dranggo army camp.

'Usually the guards in the camp did not go to sleep until around one-thirty in the morning. So we waited some distance away,' said Lama Tsewang. 'Usually the guards stand out by the road, but it was so cold that they were sitting in their hut beside the road. We started driving towards it, but then I had a feeling it was not going to go well, so we waited. We'd broken the back lights of the car, so we wouldn't be seen from behind. I took the Karmapa, Drupngak and the driver Dargye and we set off up this small mountain. I said to Lama Tsultrim Gyaltsen and the other driver Tashi, drive very slowly and we'll walk around the mountain and meet you on the other side.' There was no moon, said Lama Tsewang, and it was pitch black. As the car vanished into the darkness, the Karmapa and his companions set off to skirt round the army camp. They picked their way up the hillside, pushing through thorny scrub, which tore at their hands and clothing, frequently tripping and stumbling over rocks in the darkness. It was four hours before they finally managed to clamber back down the other side and reached the road, bruised and exhausted.

The road was completely deserted. Where were the others? 'My first thought was that the Chinese must have suspected something and arrested them,' said Lama Tsewang. They had three choices: to walk back along the road and risk capture themselves; to wait; or to walk on, in the hope that the others had overshot the rendezvous point. They decided to walk on towards the border, dreading the arrival of Chinese soldiers at any moment. After an hour, they could see the faint glimmer of lights on a vehicle parked on the road ahead. It was the Toyota. 'We were very relieved,' said Lama Tsewang. 'We'd been thinking the Chinese must have captured them. And Lama Tsultrim Gyaltsen and the driver were waiting there and thinking the Chinese had caught us! So we were both worried about each other.'

After driving for a further two hours they came to Chongya, and another fork in the road. One road led due west, towards the sacred Mount Kailash; the other forked south, towards Mustang. Here, they passed by another, smaller army encampment, but the road was deserted and they drove past unchallenged. They crossed the border, marked by a single stone, without incident. But coming down an icy pass on the other side, a wheel of the jeep became lodged in a hole. It was impossible to move, and they had no choice but to take what provisions they could, and continue on foot. At length they came to the tiny hamlet of Nechung, where a relative of Lama Tsewang lived. 'It was early morning. I had to shake him awake. I said to him, we're going to Nepal on pilgrimage, we need horses. So he arranged that.' The two drivers and Tsewang's relative went back to retrieve the car, before leaving it with some local people. Tsewang gave instructions that it should be looked after safely until his return. 'I said, look after this car well, because when I come back from Nepal I'm going to need it, and I gave him some money. If I'd said I didn't need it any more they would have suspected something.'

The Karmapa, Drupngak, Tsultrim and Tsewang proceeded towards Lo Manthang, and the house of the other relative whom Lama Tsewang had visited on his earlier trip. There they enjoyed their first night's rest since leaving Tsurphu. 'My relatives asked, who are these people with you?' said Lama Tsewang. 'It was easy with Lama Tsultrim Gyaltsen – he's a Tsurphu monk and they'd met him before. As for Drupngak, we explained that he was the *nyerpa*, the man who looks after the goods in the monastery. The drivers were drivers, no problem. The Karmapa, I said that he was one of my young monks from Nyenang. We were all wearing lay clothes. I had to play the big lama, and all of them were supposed to be lower than me. So the Karmapa was carrying my clothes and serving me tea. He was playing the role very well! When I needed to communicate with the Karmapa in secret, we both know Chinese so we would speak like that. Lots of people came from the village to see us. They knew I was a big lama, and they were saying, "We have this great desire to meet the Karmapa and perhaps one day in the future we can come to Tsurphu and you could help us to meet him and make a connection." I said, "Don't have any doubt, you'll meet the Karmapa – no problem!" '

The next morning, having acquired a guide in the village, the party set off on horseback. 'We walked for a day, down the valley,' said Lama Tsewang. 'The path was very difficult, extremely winding. Sometimes we could ride the horses and sometimes we had to lead them.' At around ten-thirty that night they came to a small village. Here, the path forked. One way led south, to Mustang's principal town of Jomsom. The other led east, across the daunting Thorong La pass towards Manang. In recent years, this route has been opened up to experienced Western trekkers. Guidebooks make ominous warnings about the dangers of the Thorong La pass, the risk of avalanches, altitude sickness and even death. The trekking season is over by November, and few would risk the pass in midwinter. But this was the path the Karmapa's party took.

'Our guide said it's too dangerous to go through the capital,' said Tsewang. 'He said, you need to go over the pass to Menang, and then you can rent a little helicopter there. But there were too many people for the helicopter. So the two drivers, whom we no longer needed, took the path to Jomsom, and the Karmapa, Drupngak, Tsultrim Gyaltsen, and I took the path to Manang. We had some food, and then we walked all night long, and all day long, and then we came to this mountain, 6,000 metres high, that we had to cross. Again the road was very difficult; sometimes we could ride and sometimes we had to walk. Once we got over the high pass, it was a very difficult path coming down the other side. It was very dangerous; if you were on your horse and got too comfortable and fell asleep there was a danger of falling off the cliff. There was no sleep. We had to be alert the whole time. His Holiness' stomach was upset and he was very sick. It was everything together – the altitude, the fact of having had no sleep, the path being so difficult. He hadn't had good food.'

Tsewang paused and reached for his glass of water. Dusk had settled, and Drupngak rose from the bed to switch on the light, then resumed his place and his methodical attentions to his *mala*. Lama Tsewang had been talking for almost an hour, brooking no interruption, silencing my attempts to ask questions with a raised finger. But now I asked him, how had they managed to keep up their spirits during their ordeal?

He smiled. 'If we were Westerners in this situation, our spirits would have been down and we'd have been trying to cheer ourselves up. But if you talk about being discouraged it would mean we were thinking, oh we shouldn't have come; it's all a mistake. But we had no doubts. Our minds were not at all affected in that way. What we did have was worry. We were concerned about His Holiness being sick, what would happen if his condition got worse and what we could do for him. And we were concerned about the Chinese and what would happen if they found out and tried to catch us. Looking at the Karmapa, to know this was the Buddha who had taken human form, and to see him at such a young age going through such huge difficulties for the sake of sentient beings, my mind was in torment. Seeing His Holiness struggle in this way, I cried. At one point, His Holiness was going on ahead, and he looked back at us and he said, "We're escaping now!" He was encouraging us. He said, "You have to go crawling on all fours. Escape is not a comfortable time. It's a time when you really have to go through hardship." '

Now Drupngak spoke for the first time. 'His Holiness saved my life,' he said. 'It was at night, we were going along a narrow path, crossing that very high pass. It was very difficult and I slipped. I yelled out and the Karmapa grabbed me by the arm and saved me.'

Tsewang nodded at this, and then continued with his account. On the far side of the mountain, he said, they finally came to Manang, where they stayed the night in a trekkers' lodge. From there, their guide telephoned to Jomsom and ordered a helicopter. In this region, where there are no roads, helicopters – often decommissioned Russian military craft – are a favoured form of transport. From the lodge, Lama Tsewang telephoned Tai Situ Rinpoche's closest attendant, Lama Tenam, to give news of the escape, and make plans to liaise in India. He also risked a telephone call to the Karmapa's room at Tsurphu, to check on Lama Nyima's well-being. An unknown voice answered the telephone. Tsewang immediately hung up. They could now as- sume that the escape had been discovered.

The helicopter arrived at nine o'clock the next morning. It took two flights to ferry the party to another tourist lodge at Nagarkot, close to the Nepalese capital of Kathmandu. After saying farewell to their guide, they took a taxi, crossing over the border into India at Rauxal on the night of 3 January, paying off the border guards with a bribe. From here they travelled to the nearby railway junction at Gorakhpur, where they boarded a train to Lucknow. Here, in a hotel, Lama Tenam was waiting to greet them. Barely pausing to rest, the party rented two taxis that drove them through the night to Delhi. From there, another taxi carried them on the last leg of their extraordinary journey, twelve hours north to Dharamsala. Ironically, having travelled for some 900 miles without mishap, tragedy almost overtook them just a few hours from their destination, when their car skidded off the road into a ditch. Miraculously, no one was hurt, and they were delayed only for as long as it took to summon another taxi. Finally, at around seven-thirty on the morning of 5 January the taxi bumped up the last stretch of rutted road to the Bhagsu Hotel in Dharamsala. Their epic journey was over.

'Having been with His Holiness in Tibet, I saw him as omniscient and the Buddha,' said Lama Tsewang. 'But my faith and devotion in him has grown even more through this. Usually, when people don't know a lot about Buddhism, they hear stories about great lamas who can fly or leave handprints in rock or do some miraculous activity, and they think, "Oh, yeah . . .?" ' He laughed. 'But I've been with the Karmapa, I've seen him and know these things to be true. For example, the pass we crossed in Mustang, the year before they had huge snowfalls and tremendous winds, so strong they had to tie the children down so they wouldn't get blown away. The snow was so deep you couldn't move. But when we crossed the pass, there was no wind, and no snow! Usually there would be barriers and people checking passes; but the barriers were up, the guards weren't there. All of this was a sign of Karmapa's activity. I was the one that planned the escape, and accompanied His Holiness. But His Holiness was the one who made all the decisions along the road. It was because of him that we got through.

'If you talk about ordinary human beings, usually they have to train and study and then they know something. In order to do that you need diligence, you need to make efforts and you need a clear intelligence. Some people have diligence, but their intelligence isn't so clear; and some people have clear intelligence but they lack diligence. It's hard to find those two together. The Gyalwa Karmapa, even though he's such a young age, has a very unusual diligence – very special and strong. And the reason it's so great is that he is working for the benefit of the teachings and for the benefit of all sentient beings, and with that goal in mind his diligence just blazes. And as far as his intelligence goes, he has a very clear mind. When you speak of the Karmapa, he is considered to be the embodiment of the body, speech, mind quality and activities of the Buddhas of the three times and the ten directions. Or you could say that he is the heart-mind of all the Buddhas and the bodhisattvas – his heart-mind and theirs are inseparable. So he has tremendous diligence and this tremendous mind and they are inseparable.'

Lama Tsewang fell silent. Night had fallen now, and it was time to eat. Tsewang and Drupngak rose to leave.

Did I know, asked Drupngak, that the Karmapa had said nothing to his parents about the escape? 'He said, "Don't tell them that I'm leaving because they will be worried." He was concerned about them being worried, and thought it better not to say. Showing these kinds of qualities, which pertain to a great mind that's taken rebirth, is the natural sign of a noble being.'

And what of Drupngak himself, I asked. Was he worried too?

'I had great concerns because I was leaving my country and coming to India and I'd never been here before. But wherever the Karmapa goes, that is where I must go too.'

During your escape, I asked the Karmapa, were you afraid?

He thought for a moment. 'Generally, I'm not a person who is afraid of dying . . .'

But there must have been moments when you thought you might not arrive in India.

'Yes, that's true. Escaping makes lots of anxiety in the mind. You have to cross borders, and each time you have to think carefully because you might be caught by the guards; not only inside Tibet, but also when reaching Nepal. You have to know how to deal correctly, whether by money or person or whatever. There are many things that bring fear in your mind. And the fear of the elements is also there.'

But it was necessary to leave Tibet when you did?

He paused. 'Yes, it was necessary. I thought, when I get older then maybe the Chinese will take me to Beijing. Right now I am quite young, so I could not be used too much. But when I became an adult, then I think it would have been different. I would have been given responsibilities related to politics, to make more trouble between the Chinese and the Dalai Lama. And I did not want that.' There was more that he could say about his life in Tsurphu, he said, but not now. It would be dangerous for others who had been left behind. He glanced towards the security guard at the back of the room.

And what, I asked, of his parents? Following his escape, the Chinese had announced that his parents had left Lhasa and returned to their home in Kham, but nothing had been heard of them.

A flicker of sorrow passed across his face. 'My parents are very kind, and now they are quite old. I hope that I can one day see them again; this depends on karma, but I pray and I believe that I will see them again.'

It was now almost a year since his epic journey across the mountains, but little had changed. He had escaped from imprisonment in Tibet into a hall of mirrors in India. The Indian government had still made no pronouncement on his status. Subject to India's Foreigners' Act, neither citizen nor officially a refugee, he remained stateless. He was still forbidden from travelling to Rumtek, although the Indian government had given no official explanation why. Despite having been questioned on several occasions by Indian intelligence officials about his escape, despite the pleas and reassurances of the Dalai Lama, and despite the pleas from the State government in Sikkim, the Indian government, it seemed, still harboured suspicions about the Karmapa's escape and his motives, and still feared the consequences of what might happen were he to assume his throne in the highly sensitive area of Sikkim.

In a personal letter to the Indian Prime Minister, Bihari Vajpayee, the Karmapa had attempted to assuage the fears of the Indian government, reiterating that he had escaped from Tibet 'by my own choice', and stating that he wished to go to Sikkim, 'in

India', to fulfil the wishes of his followers – the careful wording suggesting that he was alive to the political ramifications of such a move. But still the ban on his movements remained.

The years of rumour and conspiracy that had swirled around him and Tai Situ, invoking the spectre of a Chinese plot, had left their mark. And there was another reason for the Indian government's prevarication. The legal case brought by Shamar against Gyaltsab Rinpoche and the state of Sikkim, disputing the ownership of Rumtek, rumbled on with no end in sight. Shamar was continuing to do everything in his power to obstruct the Karmapa entering the monastery of his predecessor and claiming ownership of the Black Hat.

To this was added yet another layer of intrigue: the speculation that it was not only the government of India who wished to keep the Karmapa under close supervision in Gyuto, but that it was in the interests of the government-in-exile too. With his explicit accusations of a 'plot' to take over the Kagyu school, the Shamar Rinpoche and his followers had set themselves at loggerheads with the Dalai Lama and the government-in-exile. But even among some followers of Ogyen Trinley, who venerated the Dalai Lama as Tibet's supreme spiritual leader, and who welcomed his blessing as confirmation of Ogyen Trinley's status as Karmapa, there remained the residual suspicions about the intentions of the Gelugpa and the government-in-exile. It was a line of speculation I heard constantly in the restaurants and tea houses of Dharamsala. The theory went like this: rather than allowing the Karmapa the freedom to develop on his own terms as a spiritual leader, it was useful to the government-in-exile to keep him under close supervision, and to groom him as a future successor to the Dalai Lama, as the figurehead not only for Tibetan Buddhism around the world, but also for the cause of Tibetan independence. In this scenario, the Karmapa had jumped from one political problem into another, from being manipulated by the Chinese in Tibet to being manipulated by the government-in-exile in Dharamsala.

The death of the Dalai Lama is the great imponderable among Tibetans. For more than forty years he is the man who has both carried the fight for Tibetan freedom and kept the plight of the Tibetan people in the focus of the world's eye, by the sheer force of his perseverance and charisma. He is surrounded by faceless bureaucrats of mixed abilities and motives, the cause of 'Tibetan nationalism' a disparate rag-bag of conflicting positions and agendas, held together only by the universal respect which he, the Dalai Lama, commands. Painfully aware of his own mortality, and of the turbulence and confusion that will follow his death, the Dalai Lama, in recent years, has attempted to reduce his role in Tibetan political life, moving his government-in-exile slowly along the road to democracy, introducing a system of direct elections, designed to ensure a smooth succession of leadership at the time of his death. He has made clear that with his death, the position of the Dalai Lama as the temporal ruler of the Tibetan people will be gone for ever, and that the role of any future Dalai Lama will be purely spiritual. In order to thwart any Chinese attempts to co-opt his spiritual position, he has declared publicly that he will not be reborn in an occupied Tibet.

Who, then, is left to step into the vacuum? Even if the Dalai Lama's planned transition to democracy is successful, so riven is Tibetan political life with the old regional antagonisms, that there is no politician who will be able to command the universal respect and affection of all Tibetans in the way the Dalai Lama has done, and effectively emerge as a figurehead for the Tibetan cause.

Sitting in a cafe in Dharamsala, a young political activist – a Kagyu – spelled it out. 'Forget the illusion of unity among the Tibetans in exile. Let us say, the Dalai Lama dies, and someone from Ur – central Tibet – who is very charismatic, good politician, good leader, takes over; still I don't think people from Kham or Amdo would accept him. And the same thing if the leader is from Kham or Amdo.' In this scenario, my friend went on, only a strong religious figure could command universal respect as the *de facto* leader of the Tibetan people and their cause. And that figure was the Karmapa. 'The Karmapa is very charismatic and has been accepted by everyone. The Dalai Lama and the government-in-exile know this. They see the Karmapa as being ripe for the cause. He's young, he's intelligent. The Dalai Lama can put him on the right track, train him up, and then die peacefully. He wants Karmapa close to him to secure a political successor. But this is completely somebody else's agenda; it's not the Karmapa's agenda. Karmapas have never been political rulers of Tibet; they are spiritual teachers. They have never wanted power.'

This line of speculation, the suggestion that the Karmapa was being deliberately kept close to the Dalai Lama to groom him for future leadership, went further. For not only was the Karmapa forbidden from travelling to Rumtek; he was forbidden even from visiting Sherab Ling, the monastery of his senior regent, Tai Situ. The most likely explanation for this was the Indian government's lingering suspicions over Tai Situ – a legacy of the campaign of whispers against him which had resulted in him being, at one point, banned from India. But, one heard it said, the prohibition also fitted nicely with the wishes of the government-in-exile. The row between Tai Situ and the Shamarpa had not been good for Tibetan Buddhism. And whoever was to blame for the row, for the Karmapa to be seen to be closely associated with such a controversial figure as Tai Situ was bad public relations, threatening to bring Buddhism into disrepute. It was for this reason, it was said, that Tai Situ had become far less visible in the Karmapa's life. He continued to visit Gyuto for teachings, but was seldom seen at the Karmapa's side at his public appearances and functions.

So how much credence could be put in this web of interlocking theories? Over dinner one evening, a senior official in the Tibetan government-in-exile contemplated the charges with a pained expression on his face, and sighed deeply. The idea that the Karmapa was being groomed as a future political leader, that the government-in-exile had a game plan to bring the Kagyu lamas under Dharamsala's control – it was all 'total rubbish', he said. 'As far as our position is concerned, we've publicly stated many times that there is only one Karmapa and that Rumtek is his legitimate seat, so it is proper and right for him to go there as soon as he can. This is our stated position and this is the truth. And the second thing is that Situ Rinpoche has a special connection with Karmapa, and Sherab Ling is the monastery belonging to the tradition, so it is right and proper for Karmapa to go to Sherab Ling and stay there for the time being. We believe that, and we continue to say that. But the Indian government has certain difficulties in agreeing to this at the moment . . .'

He paused, choosing his words carefully. 'This is just a personal view. But there is seen to be this controversy between Shamar and Situ Rinpoche. In fact, because Karmapa has been recognized by the Dalai Lama this perception should not be there. But on another level there seems to be this kind of . . . struggle. So quite probably the government of India would like the Karmapa to be closer to the Dalai Lama, and slightly out of all this. Maybe they feel more comfortable with that. If he went to Sherab Ling he would be seen as aligning himself with Tai Situ. We are guided by the government of India, and the government of India say they feel more comfortable if he stays in Gyuto until things become clearer.'

Once again, he sighed. The Tibetan government-in-exile had sustained a working relationship with the government of India for the last forty years. 'We have an understanding. So if they say we would like something to be done, we can't say we don't want to do that. But the moment the government of India say that Karmapa can travel then he will immediately go to Sherab Ling or Rumtek. And whatever they want him to do is up to them.'

As for grooming the Karmapa as a political successor to the Dalai Lama, he went on, there was no such plan. 'As far as the Dalai Lama is concerned, in terms of political leadership our constitution has very clear provisions that in the absence of His Holiness there will be a collective, elected leadership. Then there will be his reincarnation after a year or so, so in terms of the spiritual connection the whole focus will be on the new reincarnation. In the meantime there will be a political leadership. So there will be no gap. Obviously the 14th Dalai Lama would be missed greatly. But in terms of Tibetan unity, mental focus, emotional focus, that will remain. His Holiness has been so important, his influence so strong, but I think people would come together again.'

He paused. As for the role which the Karmapa played in Tibetan politics, that was up to him. 'Politically he is very concerned and very committed and has a very strong view on issues. But there is no question of our grooming him in that way. It is our duty, our responsibility to look after him well. And after that he has to assume his own religious role as Karmapa. It will never be us holding on to him.'

Whatever the rumours, the Karmapa himself had made clear his devotion to the Dalai Lama, and his commitment to the cause of Tibetan independence. He had made it clear that his escape was partly prompted by his desire to be close to the Dalai Lama. In the course of his journey across the Himalayas he had composed a poem, 'A Joyful Aspiration', which was published shortly after his arrival, and which had included a moving stanza praising the Dalai Lama.

> Inspiring festivals of merit in the Land of the Snow
> You are the Supreme One holding a pure white lotus
> With the beauty of all good qualities,
> a treasure for eyes to behold,
> May your life be long, steadfast as a diamond vajra.

He would not, he had announced, return to Tibet until the Dalai Lama too had returned. A free Tibet was necessary for the free practice of Buddhism. Nobody knew this better than him.

In the sitting room of his home, the Dalai Lama contemplated the question of the Karmapa's present and future circumstances with characteristic equanimity and good humour. It was his express desire, he said, that the Karmapa should be able to go to Rumtek as soon as possible and, failing that, to Sherab Ling. 'I've said this to Indian officials many times – what is the point in him being so close and not being allowed to go?' His shrug eloquently described his exasperation at the complicated labyrinth of secular and theological politics which kept the Karmapa marooned in Gyuto. 'Actually, I'm always teasing Karmapa and his attendants about this. His own monastery, Rumtek, is very good and he should be there; and also, near here, there is a very good Kagyu monastery, Sherab Ling. But he can't go to these places. So he has to hire one Gelugpa monastery, Gyuto! I told them, they should send a big invoice to the Tibetan government!' He laughed.

And what place, I asked, did he envisage for the Karmapa in Tibetan spiritual and political life?

It was, he replied, too soon to say. 'I have told Karmapa – and also Situ Rinpoche, Gyaltsab Rinpoche, Thrangu Rinpoche, Tenga Rinpoche and Ponlop Ronpoche – that I am getting older, sixty-six already, so in twenty years' time a new situation will definitely be coming. Then will be a very important time for Karmapa; but not only Karmapa, for all the young lamas coming up. The reincarnation of my old tutor, Ling Rinpoche is a very good one. The sons of the Sakya Rinpoche, they are great scholars, very promising. So in Gelug, Sakya, Nyingma, Kagyu – in all the four major traditions – the younger generation of lamas, that's to say fifteen to twenty years old, there are some very good ones. This is the generation who – when I say my final goodbye – will carry the Tibetan spirituality. But the preparation for that needs at least fifteen to twenty years. So not easy, is it? As soon as Karmapa came here to India I told him, now you need a tutor and you must study Buddhism, philosophy, from all sides. Nowadays, it's not enough for anybody to be just a great lama in name; they must be a great lama in practice. So that is his future, I think.'

And what, I asked, of Thaye Dorje?

The Dalai Lama gave the matter some thought. 'My thinking is, first let the 17th Karmapa, the real Karmapa, the officially recognized Karmapa, let him settle properly in Rumtek monastery, mentally and psychologically; let his position become well established. But Shamar Rinpoche is also there. His candidate is also there. That's the reality. So eventually I think these two boys, through their connections, will work it out. So the real Karmapa remains in Rumtek and carries on his spiritual work. Thaye Dorje remains in Delhi and works with Karmapa Rinpoche and carries on with his service to Buddhism and the Tibetan nation.' He paused. 'That is what is important. When it comes to qualified teachers, even a hundred is not sufficient.'

CHAPTER SIXTEEN

Emptiness Is Fullness

Bodh Gaya: March 2001.

In February 2001, after a year deliberating on his status, the Indian government finally granted the Karmapa refugee status, and gave their formal permission for him to remain in India. They also indicated that restrictions on his travel, to everywhere but Rumtek and Sherab Ling, would be lifted. The announcement was made that his first trip would be on pilgrimage to Bodh Gaya, to walk for the first time in the footsteps of the Buddha.

I took the night bus from Dharamsala to Delhi, carefully tipping the driver's mate. I had heard that Tai Situ was in Delhi. It was some months since I had last seen him. I contacted him and he suggested we should meet for dinner at the Ambassador Hotel. He had visited a friend there recently, he said, and eaten an excellent *tali* on room service; the restaurant should be good.

I presented myself in the lobby at the appointed time and waited. Businessmen lounged at tables, jabbering into mobile phones and making deals. A wedding party came and went. At length, a white minibus pulled up outside, and Tai Situ swept into the lobby. He was accompanied by a young attendant, an elderly lama, heavily built and with a wispy Fu-Manchu beard, and his driver. I had not expected a party, but Tibetan lamas, it seemed, never travelled alone. We made our way to the restaurant. The expectations engendered by Tai Situ's room service meal dissolved in an instant. This was not a traditional Indian establishment. Instead we had walked into a bizarre Indian notion of a New York diner, decorated in lurid Americana. A disco song, 'Rock the

Boat', was playing at ear-piercing volume. Tai Situ looked momentarily disconcerted, then shrugged and purposefully led the way to a table. A waiter brought menus which were jazzed up to look like a newspaper, each dish a different story. The other members of Tai Situ's party examined them gingerly, unsure perhaps of burger-joint protocol. 'You order for yourself,' Tai Situ instructed me, 'I'll order for them.' The waiter brought mutton stew for the elderly lama and the young attendant, chicken for the driver. I had noticed that Tibetans shared none of the qualms that tended to afflict Western Buddhists about eating meat when it was on offer. Tai Situ joined me in the vegetarian platter, I think out of politeness. We sat for a few moments in silence. 'Rock the Boat' had now given way to 'Crazy Little Thing Called Love'. The elderly lama slowly chewed his food, looking nonplussed.

I asked, what opinion did Tai Situ have of Western culture?

He liked opera, he said, and symphony music, but his favourite was ballet. The first time he visited the West he had been taken to see Rudolf Nureyev dance. 'I forget the name of the ballerina, but she was very beautiful. But the amazing thing was watching Nureyev, the way he seemed to hang in the air for such a long time.' He had also seen opera. 'It was Italian. I can't remember the title . . . One with a king, some people are thrown into prison, and some wonderful costumes. But some of it is very neurotic, I think.' He laughed and toyed with his food.

What about Western novels, I wondered.

He had read one once, he said, *The Far Pavilions*; his expression suggested he didn't think much of it. But he was an avid reader of periodicals – *Newsweek*, *Time* and *National Geographic*. 'And *Mad* magazine. I used to love that! Alfred E. Neuman!' He laughed and pulled a comical, buck-toothed Alfred E. Neuman face. 'I love *Mad* magazine!'

And what did he think the West had gained from Tibetan Buddhism?

The virtue of lineage, he said. The relationship between teacher and student, 'the fact that knowledge is a gift given with compassion and received with respect. That idea seems to have been lost in the West, but it is absolutely central to Vajrayana Buddhism.'

He paused. 'You know, the thing that really surprised me when I first went to the West was to hear people saying, "I hate myself",

I could never understand that. But now I think I understand; when people say, "I hate myself" what they really mean is, "I love myself too much", and they are always disappointed for not fulfilling the expectations they have of themselves! I think what they mean is, "I am always disappointed in myself".'

We talked on, his companions eating their food in deferential silence. I could not tell which of them, if any, could understand our conversation. None of them had said a word since we sat down. I was unsure how to steer the conversation. Tai Situ did not initiate any topic. I found myself cast, once again, in the role of interlocutor, struggling to make sense of the more abstruse aspects of Buddhist philosophy – a particularly surrealistic role, given the disco music that was now pounding out of the speakers around us. Tai Situ seemed not to notice it.

A Karmapa, he said, could have a million manifestations, in whatever form he chose – as a man, an animal, a bird, a bridge, even a drop of rain – whatever was useful. But that was not to say there could ever be more than one person called Karmapa.

But how, I asked, would we recognize that a bird, a bridge or a drop of rain was a manifestation of the Karmapa?

'It would not be for us to say.'

But would the Karmapa know that he was manifesting in these forms?

'He would know.'

And would you ever ask him?

'No, because I have faith.'

So even asking the question means that I have doubt?

'Of course.'

But the Buddha, I went on, taught that you must test his ideas, like a goldsmith testing gold.

'Only if you don't believe them!' Tai Situ laughed.

And now with the 17th Karmapa, I said, you have gone from being the son of the father, to the father of the son.

'Well . . .' He paused. 'I don't know about that. I'm just doing my best to serve and do whatever I can. As to being the father . . . that's not my intention. I'm just doing my best, and then if he considers in the future that he received the transmission of our lineage from me, that's fine. But that's for him to decide; it's not for me to pursue. I just do my best. And that's the case with everybody. Thrangu Rinpoche, myself, His Eminence Gyaltsab Rinpoche; we will do our best to offer him whatever we have, and whatever he wants. That is how our lineage continues. And in our thinking, our principle, if the lineage is gone then everything is gone. But Karmapa is very remarkable. What he knows, his standard, is unbelievable. His poetry, his ritual, his philosophy and the knowledge of the texts; unbelievable. If I say ten times better than me I'm not exaggerating; maybe not in everything, but in certain ways. I saw him composing this text of ritual, involved with deities and prayers and protectors and all of that – he has composed almost 200 pages already, just in the last month. Karmapa was just saying and the monk was just typing into his computer. He goes on like that for ten pages, spontaneous and very perfect. It's unbelievable.'

And what of Shamar Rinpoche and Thaye Dorje?

Tai Situ gave a deep sigh. He did not want to enter into arguments, he said, otherwise these things go backwards and forwards without end. Shamar's accusations of a plot between he and the Dalai Lama were not true. 'The identification of Karmapa is very simple. I found the letter in the amulet. His Eminence Jamgon, Gyaltsab and Shamarpa, we all sat down and I offered them the letter. Then after that Jamgon was supposed to go and search for it. He died. We were supposed to discuss, but Shamarpa went away. Gyaltsab Rinpoche and I discussed, and then we announced to everybody there in Rumtek and sent people to Tibet. Tsurphu searched and found. The message came back. I went to deliver this to the Dalai Lama. Dalai Lama confirmed. This is 100 per cent the true story of how it happened.'

It was unthinkable that the 16th Karmapa's letter should be forensically tested, said Tai Situ. Unthinkable. 'If Shamar Rinpoche is saying I faked Karmapa's letter, then for what? What do I get from faking such a thing? What does he think I want? And since this is Karmapa's letter, it is a sacred relic of our lineage. It's like wanting to go to Bodh Gaya and forensic test whether the Buddha was really enlightened there or not.' He paused, shaking his head. 'It's just crazy.'

The dispute with Shamar had been a cause of deep sadness and regret to him, he said. 'I really consider him my best friend. And he considers me his best friend – that's what I thought anyway. But the problem is we have *samaya*, which we have to acknowledge, and from my point of view – from all the Karma Kagyu's point of view – he has broken the *samaya* with our guru and our lineage, and therefore we can't have anything to do with him. We can only pray for him and wish him well. Beyond that there is nothing we can do, unless he purifies. But for me personally there have been beneficial things in all this. Shamar Rinpoche has taught me so many things. He brings my ego down; he gives me more incentive to be more careful. Lots of things. I know this is unfair to say, because the situation is very bad and very confusing for lots of people, and also maybe very bad for him. But it's definitely made a new man out of me! How can I regard him as my enemy?' 'Hotel California' was playing at full volume. Tai Situ gave a slight smile. 'He is my friend', he said, 'who thinks I'm his enemy.'

Bodh Gaya is the centre of the Buddhist world, the holiest of all pilgrimage sites. It was here, 2,500 years ago, that the young Nepali prince Gautama attained enlightenment after meditating under the Bodhi tree, and became the Buddha, or awakened one. The path to the Mahabodhi temple in Bodh Gaya reminds you of the harsh truth of existence seen by the Buddha – you grow old, you suffer, you die – and the possibility of liberation. The most wretched and benighted of humanity assail you at every step; beggars proffering stunted, leprous hands, or dragging their crippled bodies through the dust and rubbish to plead for alms. To pause is to be lost, submerged in a tumultuous sea of imprecations and outstretched hands. Monks and nuns walk calmly through this tempest, apparently immune to assault, dropping handfuls of coins into each tin cup they pass.

Entering the grounds of the Mahabodhi temple, you look down into a natural bowl in which stands the main stupa itself, one of the great structures of the ancient world; a tower of honey-coloured stone soaring 180 feet into the air, encrusted with niches and turrets, tapering at its peak to a point. On every side stands a multitude of lesser shrines and bell-shaped reliquaries. The sound of chanting fills the air, and the whisper-like scuffle of bare and stockinged feet as hundreds upon hundreds of pilgrims slowly circumambulate the temple. Inside, a monumental gilded statue of the Buddha sits in the *bhumisparsha mudra*, or 'touching ground' pose, right hand extended to the earth, to bear witness to his enlightenment. The statue is said to be 1,700 years old, the face modelled from memory by an artisan who in an earlier incarnation had been one of the Buddha's disciples. Behind the temple stands the Bodhi tree itself.

It was here that Guatama sat in the cross-legged posture of meditation, faced to the East, and vowed not to leave until he had attained enlightenment, remaining 'through the three watches of the night', resisting the temptations of the demon Mara, until finally realizing supreme enlightenment with the coming of the dawn. At this moment, it is said, the air was filled with flowers and light, and the earth trembled seven times. The tree is a wondrous thing; its branches spreading thirty or forty feet either side of its broad, gnarled trunk, strung with hundreds of prayer flags, faded in the sun and rain. At its base is a shrine – the Vajra seat – where the Buddha is said to have sat, now laid with a huge golden cushion on which pilgrims leave offerings of flowers and incense. Behind a low stone wall abutting the shrine, and under the huge spreading canopy of the tree, a phalanx of Tibetan monks sat in serried ranks, chanting and praying, their voices like water bubbling over rocks, rising and falling in harmony with the clamour of birdsong. At its base, pilgrims lowered themselves to the ground in full prostration, and pressed paper transfers of gold on to the tree's rough bark – rituals that seemed as ancient as the tree itself. Beside the Vajra seat a Thai monk sat in serene meditation, his ochre robe draped with perfect, artless symmetry across his shoulder, hands folded in his lap and eyes downturned, a mirror image – across 2,500 years – of the Buddha himself.

The Karmapa's procession came towards the shrine. It was three months since I had last seen him. The heavy, preoccupied figure I remembered had gone. Freed at last from his fourteen months' confinement, he looked lighter, more animated, like a spring uncoiled. He walked into the main temple, followed by a dozen monks, guards blocking the entrance to the crowd that trailed in his wake, and remained there for half an hour, making prayers, before emerging to begin his circumambulations around the temple and the Bodhi tree. In front of the tree, he paused, his hands folded in front of him. He closed his eyes for a moment, and then opened them again. It was as if something had happened; as if he was seeing not the tree and the monks and the crowd gathered around him, but somehow beyond that – as if his gaze were encompassing all of the pilgrims who had ever come to this seat in search of enlightenment, back to the Buddha himself, and all who ever would come in the future. I thought of the name of the first Karmapa, and by implication of all the Karmapas since then: Dusum Khyenpa, the knower of the three times – past, present and future. He blinked, and walked on.

The Karmapa was staying at the Mahayana guesthouse, which had been built and was run by the nearby Namgyal monastery. It was a spacious, modern, two-storey building. Armed police stood at the gates, and security men were posted at the door. In the foyer was a shrine, surmounted by a large picture of the Dalai Lama, to which someone had added a photograph of the Karmapa. The foyer had become a meeting-place for devotees who had made their way from around the world to join the Karmapa on his pilgrimage: students from Malaysia and Taiwan; seasoned dharma bums in their forties and fifties from America and Europe who had been disciples of the 16th Karmapa; a party from Brazil. Indian security men lounged on plastic chairs, looking alternately bored and hostile. Monks came and went, or paused to rest, their arms draped casually over each other's shoulders, or resting on each other's knees. (This easy, unselfconscious intimacy was characteristic. Talking with one lama I had been surprised when he had taken my hand, continuing to hold it as we walked across the foyer together, almost as if leading me to a dance floor.) At odd times of the day, Lama Phuntsok, the Karmapa's secretary, would appear, to be immediately engulfed in a hail of pleas and supplications. He looked more beleaguered than ever. There was, he told me, no possibility of private conversations with His Holiness. His programme did not allow it.

The Karmapa was sequestered on the first floor of the hotel, the stairs guarded by security men and police. The security was, if anything, even tighter than at Gyuto. A metal detector had been erected at the foot of the stairs, where each day a queue of devotees would form, awaiting a blessing. The numbers were so great that it was necessary to book with Phuntsok first. Passing through the metal detector, you would be frisked, and then frisked

twice more before reaching the top of the stairs. Devotees complained quietly among themselves at how security was getting in
the way of the devotion. A man had come from Taiwan seeking
the Karmapa's blessing for a school project, but had been hurried
out by the security men before he had even had the chance to make
his request.

It was the time of Holi, the Hindu festival of colours, which
symbolizes the vanquishing of selfishness, greed and hatred,
the triumph of righteous over demonic forces. The shops and
restaurants were hung with tinsel and bunting and young men,
glassy-eyed with alcohol and *charas*, roamed the town, armed
with pots of coloured powder to fling with delirious abandon over
anybody foolish enough to stray across their path. Only the brave
took to the streets. The Karmapa remained confined in his room.
The foyer filled with the monks, the pilgrims and the dharma
bums, huddled together on the sofas, swapping stories, waiting
out the storm of colour that rained on the streets outside.

My number had come up, and that afternoon I passed through
the metal detector and climbed the stairs to join the queue of
people waiting outside the audience room. One by one they were
called in to receive their blessing, to emerge a few seconds later
clutching a red protection cord. At length I was waved into the
room. It was dimly lit and stiflingly hot. A large shrine stood at the
end of the room. I was aware of a line of people standing on
the left – plain-clothes security guards, monks. But I couldn't see
the Karmapa anywhere. I set off for the far end of the room,
looking around for him. Too late, I realised that I'd walked right
past him without even noticing. Feeling foolish and disorientated,
I retraced my steps, bowed in front of him and presented a *khata*.
He looked as disconcerted by all this as I felt, but managed a
sympathetic smile. Afterwards, Lama Phuntsok teased me, 'I think
you were high on Holi . . .'

The next day, the Karmapa gave a long-life empowerment at
the nearby Namgyal monastery. The usual protocol for such
occasions had been observed. Rows of monks and nuns occupied
the spaces closest to the shrine, coughing and murmuring among
themselves while they waited for the rituals to begin; Tibetans sat
behind them, clutching children, plastic bags, blankets – all the
trappings of a day out. One woman held a *khata* in one hand and

a bottle of ketchup in the other. Westerners were squeezed in at the back, spilling out of the temple into the small courtyard, craning and pushing to secure a view of the proceedings. The Karmapa arrived to the drone of *gyalings*, and after being led through the throng took his place on the throne in front of the shrine and donned an ornately embroidered ceremonial head-dress. He recited the prayers, elaborating a series of carefully orchestrated gestures using a bell, a drum and a peacock feather. Then he addressed the congregation.

He invoked the tradition of the great *mahasiddhas*, all of them Indian, who had attained enlightenment, and paid tribute to India as the birthplace of Buddhism. He praised the lineage of the Dalai Lamas, singling out the 5th Dalai Lama who had inaugurated the Namgyal monasteries, and with whom, he said, he felt a particular connection. He asked for special prayers for the Tibetan people who were suffering oppression. It was a speech, in short, that skilfully played on all the themes of gratitude to his Indian hosts, Buddhist non-sectarianism and Tibetan nationalism. We divide people into three groups, he said: our friends and those who are close to us; our enemies; and 'those who are in between, neither friend nor enemy. We should have the same wish for all of them, to lead long and happy lives.'

Slowly, the congregation came forward to receive the empow-erment, the Karmapa touching each person on the head with a small reliquary as they passed in front of him. The ceremony at an end, the crowd flooded out of the temple into the brilliant midday sunshine. The mood was celebratory, exultant. The Tibetan woman, I noticed, had given her *khata*, but was still clutching her bottle of ketchup.

After attaining enlightenment at Bodh Gaya, we are told, the Buddha made his way to Sarnath. It was there, to his first disciples, that he taught what became known as the First Turning of the Wheel, embodied in the Four Noble Truths. The first two, the Truths to be Known, state that life is *dukha*, fraught with difficulty, struggle and pain; the cause of *dukha* is craving or attachment, which grows from our ignorance of the true nature of existence. The third and fourth truths are the Truths to be Practised. The third truth is that the cessation of *dukha* is possible, and that this end is nirvana or enlightenment; the fourth is the path of the cessation of *dukha*, which the Buddha elaborated in the Noble Eightfold Path: right action, right speech, right livelihood, right view, right mindfulness, right meditation, right intention and right effort. Having made the First Turning of the Wheel, we are told, the Buddha began his mission of teaching, gathering more disciples along the way. After sixteen years, he came to the town of Rajgir, where he taught what is known as the Second Turning of the Wheel, the Prajna Paramita Sutra, which contains the very essence of his teachings on the nature of emptiness – the illusory nature of all phenomena.

There is no record of how the Buddha travelled to Rajgir. The Karmapa made the journey from Bodh Gaya in a gleaming white Ambassador; a pennant fluttering on its bonnet, a small garland of marigolds dangling from the rear-view mirror, at the head of a straggling convoy of jeeps, buses and cars, crammed with police, officials, monks and a ragtag army of devotees and followers. Juddering over the rutted, potholed roads, the convoy rolled through the Bihar countryside, past neat, rectangular fields of wheat, fringed with palm trees and conical haystacks, barely slowing to pass through villages in a cloud of dust and cacophony of horns.

We came first to the ancient University of Nalanda. The world's first Buddhist university, which flourished between the fifth and twelfth centuries, Nalanda at its height housed 10,000 students and 2,000 teachers. It is now an archaeological heritage site. It was here that the Indian monk Naropa, one of the great patriarchs of the Kagyu lineage, studied in the eleventh century, becoming the University's greatest scholar, before setting out on his quest to find his teacher Tilopa, thereby setting in train the lineage of teachings that would lead to the founding of the Kagyu school.

A sign at the gate read: 'Our VIP of the Day: Venerable Ogyen Trinley Karmapa'. Swallowed in a crowd of dignitaries, the Karmapa made his way around the ruins, his progress visible by the bobbing canopy of the umbrella shielding him from the sun, a straggling line of police, rifles over their shoulders, bringing up the rear. He paused at a podium to make a speech of thanks, and then stepped down for a souvenir photograph with the monks. A woman had been agitating to get closer to him throughout his tour

of the University. She was a Westerner, with short, cropped hair
and dressed in red robes. Now she pushed her way through to be
included in the group photo. A guard blocked her way.

'Lamas only, no foreigners.'

'I'm not with the foreigners,' she said, trying to push past. 'I'm a
tulku rinpoche.' *Tulku* rinpoche? I had never heard anybody use
the term before, let alone to describe him or herself. The woman
was growing increasingly agitated.

The guard stood his ground. 'Not coming here. Lamas only!'

I stepped forward to intercede on her behalf. 'She's a nun,' I
said.

She turned on me with a baleful look. 'I'm a *tulku* rinpoche,
idiot!' she hissed.

The sun was growing hotter as the caravan moved on, to Rajgir.
In the time of the Buddha, Rajgir was one of the most important
cities of the Gangetic plain. Today, as if bearing witness to the
Buddhist teaching of impermanence, it is a little more than a
village. The mountain where the Buddha gave his teachings rose
from the plain like an exclamation mark. The caravan of vehicles
parked at its base. Led by monks clutching batches of incense to
perfume his path, the Karmapa and his entourage set off on a slow
march up the mountain path. Vulture's Peak, where the Buddha is
said to have given his teachings, is a rocky promontory set like a
shelf on the mountainside. Immediately below it is a series of
caves, historically places of meditation for pilgrims, where monks
now prostrated themselves and lay white *khatas*. An advance
guard of attendants had arrived at the Peak. The site was marked
by what appeared to be the ruins of a small temple, with a
courtyard of flagstones. A large embroidered carpet had been
laid on the stones; a Western devotee in a white fedora stepped
forward and fastidiously tugged at the tassels of the carpet,
ensuring they were perfectly straight. Now an elaborately embroidered cushion was, in turn, laid on the carpet, in readiness for
the Karmapa's arrival. The small area was already crowded with
devotees, seated cross-legged around the flagstones, or scrambling
over nearby rocks to secure a better position. A sweet, keening
chant began to go up, Karmapa Chenno – Karmapa, heed me.

From here, the procession could be seen, painstakingly winding
its way up the side of the mountain, the ceremonial umbrella

golden in the sunlight, vanishing momentarily from view behind an outcrop of rocks, to finally arrive at the shrine – a plain-clothes security man with a walkie-talkie; a soldier with a rifle; then the Karmapa himself. He was smiling broadly, the beads of his rosary clicking between his fingers. He walked across a carpet of flowers, thrown by his disciples, and settled himself on the cushion, flanked by his monks. There was a moment's silence, and then the gentle murmur of prayers.

According to the Mahayana teachings, it was at this spot that the Buddha taught the Prajna Paramita Sutra. Prajna Paramita means the Profound Perfection of Transcendent Wisdom – the wisdom that goes beyond our relative, dualistic view of the world and recognizes the essential nature of all things. The Buddha's audience, we are told, numbered 5,000 people, including monks, nuns, laity and innumerable bodhisattvas, including the bodhisattva of compassion, Avalokiteshvara. And now, Avalokiteshvara had returned, manifest in the form of the Karmapa, to turn the wheel once more. The essence of the Prajna Paramita is contained in what became known as the Heart Sutra, which has come down to us as a dialogue between Avalokiteshvara and his disciple Sariputra. Having practised the Profound Perfection of Transcendent Wisdom, the Sutra states, Avalokiteshvara saw that the five aggregates of experience – form, feeling, perception, formation and consciousness – were 'empty', and thus he overcame all suffering. 'Emptiness' in the Buddhist sense does not mean the void. Rather, it is the primordial state from which all things arise. It is, in fact, fullness. Avalokiteshvara addressed his disciple, Sariputra:

Form does not differ from emptiness, what is empty does not differ from form. Form is emptiness, emptiness is form. Feeling, perception, discernment and consciousness is also the same.

The monks chanted in unison.

All things having the nature of emptiness have no beginning and no ending, they are not defiled and pure, increased or decreased. Thus in emptiness there is no form, no feeling, no perception, no intention, no consciousness. There is no eye, no ear, no nose, no tongue, no body, no mind. Therefore, there is no sight, sound, odour, taste, object and knowledge. There is nothing from the visual element to the conscious element.

At the ultimate level of wisdom, there are no distinctions between the perceiver and the object of perception.

There is no ignorance, no end of ignorance and so on up to no old age and death, and also no end of old age and death. There is no suffering, no cause of suffering, no cessation of suffering, no path, no wisdom, no attainment and no non-attainment.

Since the Bodhisattvas have no attainment, they abide by means of the Perfection of Transcendent Wisdom, and so their minds are unhindered. Since there is no obscuration of mind, there is no fear. They transcend falsity and attain complete Nirvana.

The sublime, and the mundane, the sacred and the profane – ultimately all are inseparable. Everyone has Buddha nature.

The Karmapa sat cross-legged, his eyes closed, his head swaying slightly from side to side, caught on the rhythm of the recitation. I thought of all that had brought him to this moment. The drama that had played out over the last twenty years, and the centuries before that, through countless reincarnations, countless aeons of time; the sanctity and the greed, the humility and the hunger for power, the truth and the falsehood. The strength of human aspiration and the frailty of human nature.

Since there is no obscuration of mind, there is no fear. They transcend falsity and attain complete Nirvana

The voices of the monks rose in unison and were carried on the wind.

Therefore the Profound Perfection of Transcendent Wisdom is known as the great divine mantra, the great enlightenment mantra, the supreme mantra, the incomparable mantra, and the destroyer of all suffering. This is all true and not a lie. The mantra of the Profound Perfection of Transcendent Wisdom is said like this:

Gate, gate, paragate, para-samgate, bodhi svaha – gone, gone, gone beyond, completely gone beyond. Awake! So be it!

The chanting had stopped, and for a moment there was silence.
   Another recitation about the illusory nature of phenomena came to my mind.

> Our revels now are ended . . . These our actors,
> As I foretold you, were all spirits and
> Are melted into air, into thin air;
> And, like the baseless fabric of this vision,
> The cloud-capped tow'rs, the gorgeous palaces,
> The solemn temples, the great globe itself,
> Yea, all which it inherit, shall dissolve,
> And, like this insubstantial pageant faded,
> Leave not a rack behind. We are such stuff
> As dreams are made on, and our little life
> Is rounded with a sleep . . .
>
>   (William Shakespeare, *The Tempest*)

Slowly the Karmapa rose to his feet, and gathered his robes about him. The spell had been broken. With his monks beside him he walked back through the crowd. Beyond the ruins of the shrine, his monks and devotees gathered round him for a souvenir photograph, laughing and jostling each other like children. I set off back down the mountain. The sun had moved from its highest point, but the heat rose in waves from the path where I was walking. I stopped and looked back. I could see the Karmapa. The rituals at an end, he had sought refuge in the shadow of an outcrop of rock, and was gulping from a bottle of water, a vulnerable teenage boy, pausing before making his own journey back down the mountain to the waiting world.

Postscript

In April 2001, sixteen months after his escape from Tibet, the Karmapa was finally given permission to talk to the media, and conducted his first formal press conference in the shrine hall at Gyuto. Described in subsequent reports variously as 'a Buddhist boy god' and 'the most powerful teenager in the world', the Karmapa impressed journalists, who had gathered from all over the world, with his maturity, authority and sense of humour.

He offered his first account of his escape, emphasizing that fleeing from Tibet had been his own idea, and commenting wryly on the Chinese statement that he had left merely to retrieve some musical instruments and the Black Hat. 'Why would I want to retrieve that from India and bring it back to China? The only thing that would be served or accomplished by doing that would be to place the Hat on Jiang Zemin's head.' Asked whether he intended to work with the Dalai Lama 'in the cause of Tibetan independence or autonomy', he replied that it was his 'duty and responsibility' to support 'Tibetan religion and culture . . . as much and as vigorously as I can . . . In that sense, I will assist His Holiness the Dalai Lama as much as I can.'

In a subsequent interview with *Time* magazine, the Karmapa made his first public comment on the schism within the Karma Kagyu school, and the 'rival Karmapa' Thaye Dorje, expressing his concern at the effect the divisions could have on Buddhist teachings. 'But I constantly pray for the welfare of everyone, without thinking or making a distinction between those who are on my side and the rest.' Asked whether he was the 'real Karmapa', he replied, 'The identity of the Karmapa is not decided by popular vote or debate. It is decided only by the prediction of the previous Karmapa.'

Shortly after the Karmapa's escape from Tibet, the six-year-old Pawo Rinpoche was taken from his monastery at Nyenang by Chinese soldiers. He is now living in Lhasa as a layperson, forbidden from wearing robes, and attending a secular school.

In September 2001, in accordance with the Dalai Lama's policy of democratizing Tibetan-exile politics, sixty-one-year-old Samdhong Lobsang Tenzin Rinpoche was sworn in as the first democratically elected Prime Minister, or Kalon Tripa, of the Tibetan government-in-exile. He had polled eighty-four per cent of the vote in elections held in July 2000 among Tibetan exile communities around the world. Samdhong Rinpoche's mandate was to bring greater power to the Prime Minister's office, but his first statement was to acknowledge that the Tibetan people would still be likely to look for inspiration to a charismatic religious leader once the Dalai Lama was gone. He did not rule out such a role for the Karmapa.

'He's young, he's dynamic and every sort of potential is there,' he said. 'But it is very early to say that he alone would be the future candidate to fill the gap when His Holiness is not around with us. We can hope, but we cannot pronounce it now . . .'

In January 2002, the Karmapa returned to Bodh Gaya for the annual Monlam Chenmo ceremonies – the major Karma Kagyu prayer festival. Once again, he sat under the Bodhi tree, where he addressed a large congregation on the Jewel Ornament of Gampopa. He spoke of his pride at being the first person from his village of Bakor ever to have had the chance to visit Bodh Gaya, and displayed a light, almost surrealistic, sense of humour when talking of his predecessor. 'A lot of you were fortunate enough to meet the 16th Karmapa,' he said with a smile. 'Unfortunately, I didn't meet him . . .'

In January 2003, the Karmapa returned once more to Bodh Gaya and Sarnath, again to take part in the Monlam Chenmo ceremonies. Along with tens of thousands of devotees from around the world, he joined the Dalai Lama who was performing a Kalachakra initiation. In a public statement, the Dalai Lama repeated his position that the Karmapa 'has full rights to his native place' of Rumtek, and said that he had once again personally requested the Indian government to allow the Karmapa to go to Sikkim and assume his ancestral seat.

In June 2003 the Karmapa celebrated his eighteenth birthday, and the following month he toured Tibetan settlements in the Shimla area, and made a further plea himself to be allowed to go to Rumtek, expressing his sadness that 'present circumstances and political trappings' prevented him from the fulfilment of his spiritual duties.

Tai Situ Rinpoche now spends six months of each year in closed retreat. For the rest of the time, he continues to give initiations and teachings at his monastery in Sherab Ling, and frequently travels to Delhi to teach at the request of a growing number of Indian devotees. In March 2003, Tai Situ marked his fiftieth birthday with a week-long round of instruction and celebrations at Sherab Ling attended by more than 1,000 students from around the world.

Ole Nydahl continues to travel the world at a frenetic pace, promulgating his message that 'experiencing the true nature of mind is more exciting than the best moments of making love or the free fall before the parachute opens.' Nydahl is an experienced parachutist. On 31 July 2003, making his eightieth jump, Nydahl's parachute failed to open in time and he was badly injured, necessitating his hospitalization for some months. He has now resumed teaching.

Shamar Rinpoche also continues to travel, teaching and promoting his candidate Thaye Dorje as Karmapa. In June 2003, he accompanied Thaye Dorje to America to conduct initiations at a Buddhist centre in Menlo Park, California. In Sikkim, the court case over the ownership of Rumtek monastery – Shamar Rinpoche and the KCT versus Gyaltsab Rinpoche, the State of Sikkim and the Secretary of the Department of Ecclesiastical Affairs of the government of Sikkim – continues to rumble on.

In January 2004, the Karmapa again attended the Monlam Chenmo ceremonies in Bodh Gaya. At the time of writing, he was still resident at Gyuto monastery, the armed police and security guards still in place.

Chronology

Sixth century BC	The Buddha attains enlightenment under the Bodhi tree
Eighth century AD	Guru Rinpoche establishes the first Buddhist monastery, Samye, in Tibet
1110	Birth of the 1st Karmapa, Dusum Khyenpa
1923	Birth of Ranjung Rigpe Dorje, the 16th Karmapa
1949–50	Invasion of Tibet by Mao Zedong's People's Liberation Army of China
1951	Ngabo Ngawang Jigme signs the Seventeen Point Agreement on the Peaceful Liberation of Tibet
1954	12th Tai Situ Rinpoche recognized at the age of one
1956	14th Shamar Rinpoche recognized at the age of four
1959	Dalai Lama and the 16th Karmapa flee Tibet for exile in India, followed by tens of thousands of Tibetans

| 1974 | 16th Karmapa visits Europe and America for the first time |

1974   16th Karmapa visits Europe and
                       America for the first time

5 November 1981   16th Karmapa dies aged fifty-eight

December 1981   Agreement that under a 'rotating
                   regency' each of the four heart sons will
                   hold the office of Regent for three years

February 1986   Following a meeting of the four heart
                   sons at Rumtek it is announced that
                   two letters have been found – an 'outer'
                   one and an 'inner' one – which, it was
                   said, would reveal the identity of the
                   17th Karmapa

26 June 1985   Birth of Apo Gaga, who will later be
                   recognized as the 17th Karmapa and
                   given the name Ogyen Trinley Dorje

28 January 1989   Death of the 10th Panchen Lama

September 1989   Tai Situ discovers what he believes is
                   the 16th Karmapa's prediction letter
                   during a retreat at his monastery
                   Sherab Ling

19 March 1992   At a meeting of the four heart sons in
                   Rumtek, Tai Situ presents the
                   prediction letter. Shamar Rinpoche
                   accuses him of forging the letter.

26 April 1992   Jamgon Kongtrul Rinpoche dies in a
                   car crash

12 May 1992   Search party leaves Tsurphu to follow
                   the instructions of the prediction letter

9 June 1992   Dalai Lama unofficially confirms the
                   recognition of Ogyen Trinley as the
                   17th Karmapa

15 June 1992   17th Karmapa arrives at Tsurphu

30 June 1992   Dalai Lama issues the Buktham
                        Rinpoche, his official Seal of Approval

27 September 1992 Ogyen Trinley is enthroned as the 17th
                        Karmapa at Tsurphu monastery

March 1993   Jiang Zemin becomes President of the
                        PRC

26 January 1994   Shamarpa announces his rival claimant
                        to the Karmapa's throne, Thaye Dorje

17 March 1994   Thaye Dorje is enthroned at KIBI in
                        Delhi

28 December 1999 Karmapa leaves Tsurphu monastery
                        under cover of darkness, beginning his
                        flight from Tibet

5 January 2001   Karmapa and his party arrive in
                        Dharamsala

February 2001   The government of India grants the
                        Karmapa refugee status and lifts the
                        limitations on his travel; the Karmapa
                        makes his first pilgrimage to Bodh
                        Gaya and other holy sites

Bibliography

Avedon, John F., *In Exile from the Land of the Snows* (New York, Alfred Knopf, 1984)

Batchelor, Stephen, *The Awakening of the West: The Encounter of Buddhism and Western Culture* (Berkeley, California, Parallax Press, 1994)

Butterfield, Stephen T., *The Double Mirror: A Skeptical Journey into Buddhist Tantra* (Berkeley, California, North Atlantic Books, 1994)

Chögyam Trungpa, *Born in Tibet* (London, George Allen & Unwin, 1966)

Craig, Mary, *Kundun* (London, HarperCollins, 1997)

H.H. Dalai Lama, *Freedom in Exile* (London, Hodder & Stoughton, 1990)

Douglas, Nik and Meryl White, *Karmapa, The Black Hat Lama of Tibet* (London, Luzac, 1976)

Dowman, Keith, *The Sacred Life of Tibet* (London, Thorsons, 1997)

Fields, Rick, *How the Swans Came to the Lake: A Narrative History of Buddhism in America* (Boston, Shambhala Publications, 1992)

Foster, Barbara & Michael, *The Secret Lives of Alexandra David-Neel* (Woodstock, New York, The Overlook Press, 1998)

French, Patrick, *Tibet, Tibet: A Personal History of a Lost Land* (London, HarperCollins, 2003)

Goldstein, Melvyn C., *A History of Modern Tibet, 1913–1951* (Berkeley, California, University of California Press, 1989)

Hilton, Isabel, *The Search for the Panchen Lama* (London, Viking, 1999)

Hollingshead, Michael, *The Man Who Turned on the World* (London, Blond & Briggs, 1973)

Holmes, Ken, *His Holiness the 17th Gyalwa Karmapa Urgyen Trinley Dorje* (Forres, Scotland, Altea Publishing, 1995)

Jamgon Kongtrul Labrang, *EMA HO! The Reincarnation of the Third Jamgon Kongtrul* (Pullahari Monastery, Nepal, 1998)

Jamgon Kongtrul Lodro Thaye, tr. and with a foreword by Ngawang Zangpo, *Enthronement: The Recognition of the Reincarnate Masters of Tibet and the Himalayas* (Ithaca, New York, Snow Lion Publications, 1997)

Kagyu Thubten Choling, *Karmapa: The Sacred Prophecy* (Wappingers Falls, New York, Kagyu Thubeten Choling Publications, 1999)

Kalu Rinpoche, *The Dharma that Illuminates all Beings Impartially Like the Light of the Sun and the Moon* (Albany, New York, State University of New York Press, 1996)

Karma Thinley, *The History of the Sixteen Karmapas of Tibet* (Boulder, Colorado, Prajna Press, 1980)

H.H. the 16th Gyalwa Karmapa, *Dzalendara and Sakarchupa: Stories from the former lives of the Gyalwa Karmapa* (Langholm, Scotland, Kagyu Samye, 1981)

Lehnert, Tomek, *Rogues in Robes* (Nevada City, California, Blue Dolphin Publishing, 1998)

Levine, Norma, *Blessing Power of the Buddhas* (Shaftesbury, Dorset, Element, 1993)

Lopez, Donald S. Jr., *Prisoners of Shangri-La: Tibetan Buddhism and the West* (Chicago, University of Chicago Press, 1998)

Lopez, Donald S. Jr., *Buddhism: An Introduction and Guide* (London, Allen Lane, 2001)

Maheshwari, Anil, *The Buddha Cries! Karmapa Conundrum* (New Delhi, UBSPD, 2000)

Maraini, Fosco, *Secret Tibet* (London, The Harvill Press, 2000)

Martin, Michele, *Music in the Sky: The Life, Art & Teachings of the 17th Karmapa, Ogyen Trinley Dorje* (Ithaca, New York, Snow Lion Publications, 2003)

Nydahl, Lama Ole, *Riding the Tiger* (Nevada City, California, Blue Dolphin Publishing, 1992)

Nydahl, Lama Ole, *Entering the Diamond Way* (Nevada City, California, Blue Dolphin Publishing, 1999)

Ray, Reginald A., *Indestructible Truth: The Living Spirituality of Tibetan Buddhism* (Boston, Shambhala Publications, 2000)

Ray, Reginald A., *Secret of the Vajra World* (Boston, Shambhala Publications, 2001)

Richardson, Hugh, *Tibet and its History* (Oxford, Oxford University Press, 1962)

Richardson, Hugh, *High Peaks, Pure Earth: Collected Writings on Tibetan History and Culture* (London, Serindia Publications, 1998)

Rinchen Palsang, *Tsurphu Gon Gyi Karchag Kunsai Melong* (Beijing, Nationality Press, 1995)

Rumtek Sangha Duche, *Document of the International Karma Kagyu Conference* (New Delhi, March 1996)

Rumtek Sangha Duche, *The Siege of Karmapa* (New Delhi, 1999)

Santideva, tr. Vesna A. Wallace and B. Allen Wallace, *A Guide to the Bodhisattva Way of Life* (Ithaca, New York, Snow Lion Publications, 1997)

Schuhmacher, Stephan & Ger Woerner (eds.) *The Rider Encyclopaedia of Eastern Philosophy and Religion* (London, Rider, 1989)

Shakabpa, W.D., *Tibet, A Political History* (New York, Potala Publications, 1984)

Shakya, Tsering, *The Dragon in the Land of the Snows* (London, Pimlico, 1999)

The 12th Tai Situpa, *Relative World, Ultimate Mind* (Boston, Shambhala Publications, 1992)

The 12th Tai Situpa, *Awakening the Sleeping Buddha* (Boston, Shambhala Publications, 1999)

Tibet Information Network/Human Rights Watch, *Cutting off the Serpent's Head: Tightening Control in Tibet 1994–95* (Jackson, Wyoming, 1996)

Tibet Information Network, *Relative Freedom* (London, 1999)

Various, *Karmapa Khenno* (Rumtek, 1992)

Various, *The Karmapa Papers* (Paris, 1992)

Readers might also be interested in a selection of videos about the life of the 17th Karmapa.

1) *Karmapa: The Lion Begins to Roar* (2000)
Film of the Karmapa at Tsurphu monastery in 1999, shortly before his escape to freedom. The film contains footage of the Karmapa engaging in various activities such as debating, performing the sacred lama dancing, performing the Mahakala Offerings, bestowing blessings and empowerments and giving teachings.
Produced by Ward Holmes
(80 minutes)

2) *The 17th Karmapa's Return to Tsurphu (1993)*
Film of the Karmapa's first arrival at Tsurphu monastery, the hair-cutting ceremony in the Jokhang temple in Lhasa, and his enthronement in September 1992.
Produced by Ward Holmes
(90 minutes)

3) *Karmapa: In the Footsteps of the Buddha* (2001)
Film of the Karmapa's first pilgrimage to the sacred Buddhist sites of India

in 2001, including Sarnath, Bodh Gaya, the ancient Buddhist University of Nalanda and Vulture's Peak in Rajgir.
Produced by Ward Holmes
(75 minutes)

4) *Tsurphu: Home of the Karmapas* (1988)
Film about Tsurphu monastery and its reconstruction.
Produced by Ward Holmes
(60 minutes)

5) *Karmapa: The Thanka Ceremony*
Film of the unveiling at Tsurphu monastery in 1994 of the famous silk appliqué *thanka*, reconstructed in the style of a *thanka* originally designed by the 9th Karmapa, and destroyed during the Cultural Revolution.
Measuring 60' by 100', it is one of the largest *thankas* in the world.
(25 minutes)

To obtain these video documentaries or for further information about them, contact the following distributors:

Pacific Foundation
1135 Makawao Ave, Suite 129
Makawao, HI 96768
Tel: +1 866 966 6999, or +1 808 573 8145
E-mail: pacarts@yahoo.com

Mystic Fire Video
PO Box 422
New York, NY 10012
Tel: +1 800 292 9001
Web site: http://www.mysticfire.com
E-mail: mysticfire@ordering.com

Karmapa Trust Holland
Tel/fax +31(0)519 293 883, or Tel +31(0)251 653 112
Email: karmapa_videos@yahoo.com

The Meridian Trust
5 Torrens Street
London, EC1V 1NQ
Tel: +44 (0)207 278 2576
Fax: +44 (0)207 837 2800
Web site: http://www.meridian-trust.org
E-mail: meridiantrust@compuserve.com

7) *Living Buddha* (1996)
A documentary on the search for, and discovery of, the Karmapa, shot on location at his birthplace and home in Lhatok, and in Tsurphu.
Director: Clemens Kuby
(114 minutes)

8) *The Making of Living Buddha* (1996)
A documentary about the making of *Living Buddha*, with additional footage of the 17th Karmapa.
Director: Clemens Kuby
(60 mins)

Both available from
Mind films GmbH,
Kreuzeckweg 16,
D-85748 Garching
Germany
Tel: +49 (0)89 326 79811
E-mail: mindfilms@t-online.de

Glossary

Avalokiteshvara: (Sanskrit, lit., 'the lord who looks down') The bodhisattva of compassion. In Tibetan, Chenresig. Both the Dalai Lama and the Karmapa are held to be manifestations of Avalokiteshvara.

bardo: (Tib., lit., 'the in-between state') The state between death and rebirth, when the practitioner has the opportunity to recognize the nature of mind and so attain liberation.

bodhisattva: (Sanskrit) A person who has vowed not simply to attain enlightenment for himself or herself but to help all sentient beings through his or her compassion.

Buddha: (Sanskrit, lit., the 'awakened' or 'enlightened' one) According to Buddhist teachings there have been four 'historical Buddhas' over the aeons of past history. The last was the Indian prince Gautama (*circa* sixth century BC), known in Tibetan as Shakyamuni, or 'sage of the Sakyas'. The next, who will appear at some unspecified time in the future, is Maitreya, the 'Buddha to come'.

Buktham Rinpoche: The document formally ratifying the Dalai Lama's recognition of a new incarnate, or *tulku*.

Chenresig: (Tib.) See Avalokiteshvara.

chuba: (Tib.) The traditional robe worn by both men and women in Tibet.

dakini: (Sanskrit) A female celestial being or deity.

dharma: (Sanskrit, lit., 'carrying', or 'holding') An all-embracing term used to refer to that which determines our true essence, the ethical foundation of the universe, and the law of karmically determined rebirth. More particularly, the teaching of the Buddha, who recognized this eternal law. The path, the way.

dorje: (Tib.) A small sceptre used in Buddhist rituals in conjunction with a bell. The bell is the symbol of the female principle, or wisdom; the *dorje* (or in Sanskrit *vajra*, meaning 'diamond' or 'thunderbolt') represents that which is indestructible, and is a symbol of the male principle, or method. Together, the union of wisdom and method symbolizes the attainment of enlightenment. Dorje is also a common given name for Tibetan men.

dukha: (Pali) Suffering, not simply in the sense of unpleasant sensations, but as the fundamental condition of existence. The First Noble Truth holds that everything both material and mental that is conditioned, and is subject to arising and passing away, is *dukha*. The Second Noble Truth holds that the cause of *dukha* is craving, or attachment.

Golden Rosary: The lineage of the Mahamudra teachings.

gompa: (Tib.) A small monastery or place of meditation.

guru: (Sanskrit) A teacher, particularly a spiritual master.

gyaling: (Tib.) A reed instrument with a distinctive droning sound, used to greet important lamas and in religious ceremonies.

Gyalwa: (Tib., lit., the 'Victorious One') The Karmapa is referred to as the Gyalwa Karmapa, or the Gyalwang Karmapa, meaning 'Victorious and Powerful'.

KCT: The Karmapa Charitable Trust. The trust established by the 16th Karmapa before his death.

khata: (Tib.) A billowing ceremonial scarf, usually in white silk, which it is customary to present to a lama when meeting him, as a mark of respect.

khenpo: (Tib.) An esteemed teacher, the equivalent of a doctor of divinity, or head of monastic studies in Tibetan Buddhism.

KIBI: The Karmapa International Buddhist Institute, New Delhi. Founded by the 16th Karmapa, and presently under the administration of Shamar Rinpoche.

KTD: Karma Triyana Dharmachakra. The Karmapa's main monastic seat in North America, located in Woodstock, upstate New York.

labrang: (Tib.) The administrative body of a *tulku*, or high lama.

lama: (Tib., lit., 'non-above') A religious master, or guru, in Tibetan Buddhism.

Living Buddha: A term used by the Chinese government to describe a *tulku*, or reincarnate.

Mahakala: (Sanskrit, lit., 'great time', or 'great black one') The wrathful manifestation of Avalokiteshvara, the bodhisattva of compassion, and the primary Dharmapala, or protector deity, in Tibetan Buddhism. Mahakala is usually represented as black or dark blue in colour, with a fearsome countenance, and wearing a crown of human skulls. Despite his formidable appearance, Mahakala is held to be inseparable from compassion and loving-kindness. In one hand he holds a chopper, to cut away hatred and ignorance, and he is usually depicted standing on two dead human bodies – symbolizing the complete annihilation of all negative emotions and patterns.

Mahamudra: (Sanskrit, lit., 'Great Seal') The supreme spiritual practice in the Kagyu school, leading to a recognition of the true nature of mind, often defined as the union of bliss and emptiness.

Mahayana: (Sanskrit) The Great Vehicle, and the second of the three 'vehicles', or bodies of teaching, that comprise Tibetan Buddhism – the Hinayana, the Mahayana and the Vajrayana. The Hinayana, or 'Small Vehicle' emphasizes individual enlightenment. Mahayana practice focuses on compassion and emptiness, emphasizing the bodhisattva ideal of liberation for all beings. Vajrayana, or the 'Diamond Vehicle', concentrates on tantric practices which are believed to cut swiftly through all delusions to realize the true nature of mind.

mala: A rosary, or prayer-beads.

mantra: (Sanskrit) Sacred syllables which are repeated during spiritual practice to invoke protection or focus the mind. Each bodhisattva has a particular mantra. *Om mani padme hung* is the mantra for Chenresig, the bodhisattva of compassion.

Nalanda Institute: The monastic college at Rumtek. Named after the world's first Buddhist university in northern India, which flourished between the fifth and twelfth centuries.

namaste: (Sanskrit, lit., 'I bow to you') A form of greeting, in which the two hands are pressed together and held near the heart, and the head is gently bowed, as one says 'namaste'.

Norbulingka: The summer palace of the Dalai Lamas in Lhasa. The Norbulingka Institute is a body founded by the Tibetan government-in-exile to preserve Tibetan arts and culture and is located near Dharamsala.

-pa: Suffix attached to the names of religious schools, meaning the people of that school, for example Gelugpa or Kagyupa.

Padmasambhava: The Indian *siddha* attributed with introducing the Buddha dharma into Tibet, and founder of the first Buddhist monastery at Samye in the eighth century. He is universally revered throughout Tibet, where he is also known as Guru Rinpoche.

PLA: The People's Liberation Army of the Republic of China.

puja: (Sanskrit) A religious ceremony or ritual.

Rinpoche: (Tib., lit., 'precious one') An honorific given to all reincarnate lamas, and also sometimes to other esteemed and respected teachers who may not necessarily be *tulkus*.

Rumtek: The monastery in Sikkim founded by the 16th Gyalwa Karmapa following his escape from Tibet in 1959, and his principal monastic seat until his death in 1981.

sadhu: (from Sanskrit *sadh*, meaning 'to lead to fulfilment') A holy person who has renounced all worldly possessions.

samadhi: (Sanskrit, lit., to 'establish' or 'make firm') A state of meditative consciousness beyond waking or deep sleep in which the mind is exceptionally clear.

samaya: (Tib.) The bond of loyalty and devotion which ties a disciple to his guru, or to the body of teachings. To break *samaya* is believed to jeopardize not only the integrity of the lineage, but also one's future rebirths.

samsara: (Sanskrit, lit., 'journeying') The cycle of birth, death and rebirth to which every human being is subject. In Mahayana Buddhism, *samsara* refers to the world of phenomena, and is considered to be essentially the same as nirvana, in that both are nothing other than labels without real substance.

sangha: (Sanskrit, lit., 'group') The Buddhist community, comprised of monks, nuns and laypeople. The *sangha* is one of the Three Jewels of Buddhism, the other two being the Buddha as teacher, and the dharma, his teachings.

siddha: (Sanskrit, lit., 'perfect, complete') A realized being who has attained the goal of liberation.

siddhis: (Sanskrit, roughly meaning 'perfect abilities') The supernatural powers which arise as a result of spiritual practice and development. There are two types of *siddhis*: mundane *siddhis*, such as clairvoyance, and supramundane *siddhis*, which is the realization of the true nature of mind.

tantra: (Sanskrit, lit., 'continuum') In Tibetan Buddhism, a term used to describe a collection of texts and esoteric teachings often ascribed to the Buddha. These teachings are the basis of the Vajrayana (see 'Mahayana').

TAR: Tibetan Autonomous Region. This was set up by the Chinese government in 1965 and covers the area of Tibet, west of the Yangtze River, that was previously under the jurisdiction of the Dalai Lama's government and is often referred to as central Tibet in English. The old Tibetan provinces of Kham and Amdo were absorbed into the Chinese provinces of Qinghai, Sichuan, Yunnan and Gansu.

thanka: (Tib.) A scroll painting depicting a mandala or deities, usually framed in silk.

Tsurphu: (Tib.) The ancestral seat of the Karmapas, located in the Tölung valley, near Lhasa in Tibet.

tulku: (Tib., lit., 'transformation body') A term for a person who is identified as the reincarnation of a previously deceased person.

Vajra Crown, or Black Hat: The ceremonial crown traditionally worn by the Karmapas. When the Karmapa dons the hat during the Vajra Crown ceremony he is believed to become the living embodiment of Avalokiteshvara. The Karmapa also wears a smaller black 'activity' hat as a symbol of his lineage on ceremonial occasions.

Acknowledgements

Innumerable people have provided help in the research and preparation of this book. Some have preferred to remain anonymous. I am indebted to them all for their time, patience and kindness.

I would particularly like to thank Norma Levine, who from the outset acted as my guide through the labyrinthine intricacies of Tibetan Buddhism, who helped to open doors that would otherwise have remained closed, and who shared unstintingly in her knowledge and her wisdom. This book could not have been written without her help. I am indebted to Ani Chudrun, whose belief was an inspiration in launching this project, and whose unflagging support and encouragement have been critical in seeing it through to the end. I would also like to thank Ani Ea, for all her help and advice, and the endless flow of e-mails. Thanks too to Rinchen Kandro and Lama Zangmo. I am particularly grateful to Michele Martin, who gave so generously of her time with translations, corrections and suggestions. Michele's own book on the Karmapa, *Music in the Sky*, is invaluable for anyone who wishes further to explore the Karmapa's life and teachings. I am also indebted to Edward Henning, who generously shared the fruits of his long experience as a scholar of Tibetan Buddhism and offered invaluable guidance on Tibetan terminology and teachings. I am, too, very grateful to Robbie Barnett for sharing his unparalleled expertise on Sino-Tibetan affairs.

I would also like to thank all of the following for giving so generously of their time, knowledge and help: Kabir Bedi, Rahul

Bedi, Robert Chalmers, Thierry Dodin, Keith Dowman, Martina Draszczyk, Mary Finnigan, Louise Fournier, Chloe Fox, Patrick French, Claire Galez, Professor Erlendur Haraldsson, Ken Holmes, Ward Holmes, Yeshey Jungney, Franklin Kiermeyer, Clemens Kuby, Mitchell Levy, Martin Marvet, Jock Miller, Birgitte and Jurgen van den Muyzenberg, David Nutt, Richard Oppenheimer, Erma Pounds, Lama Phuntsok, John Reacroft, Ringu Tulku, Thubten Samphel, Kate Saunders, Claire Scobie, Tsering Shakya, E. Gene Smith, Emma Soames, Andrew Stalbow, Terry Sullivan, Tenzin Taklha, Lodro Tarchin, Lama Tenam, Deepak Thakur, Dalha Tsering, Tenzin Geyche Tethong, Deepak Thakur, Ven Thrangu Rinpoche, Lama Tsewang, Tashi Wangdi, Naomi West, Alex Wilding, Catherine Wilson and Lama Yeshe.

I would like to thank Will Ellsworth-Jones, Richard Branson and Hamish Dewar for their friendship and support – and a large, cold beer to Hamish for travelling the road.

I am particularly grateful to Caroline Dawnay for all her help and understanding. I owe special thanks to Liz Calder and Ruth Logan at Bloomsbury for believing in this project from the outset, and for all their faith and encouragement, and to Katherine Greenwood for her meticulous editing and infinite patience.

Above all, I owe everything to my wife Patricia and my children Celeste, Dominic and Clementine for their endless support, forebearance and their love.

Finally, I am deeply indebted to H.H. the 17th Karmapa, whose words on my first meeting with him were to serve as my template throughout the writing of this book, and which I hope I have honoured.

A NOTE ON THE AUTHOR

Mick Brown is the author of four previous books: *Richard Branson: The Inside Story, American Heartbeat: Travels from Woodstock to San Jose by Song Title, The Spiritual Tourist: A Personal Odyssey Through the Outer Reaches of Belief* and *Performance*. He is currently writing a biography of Phil Spector for Bloomsbury. Born in London, he is a journalist and broadcaster.

A NOTE ON THE TYPE

The text of this book is set in Linotype Sabon, named after the type founder, Jacques Sabon. It was designed by Jan Tschichold and jointly developed by Linotype, Monotype and Stempel, in response to a need for a typeface to be available in identical form for mechanical hot metal composition and hand composition using foundry type.

Tschichold based his design for Sabon roman on a fount engraved by Garamond, and Sabon italic on a fount by Granjon. It was first used in 1966 and has proved an enduring modern classic.